THE NOSTALGIC IMAGINATION

This unusual book explores the historical assumptions at work in the style of literary criticism that came to dominate English studies in the twentieth century. Stefan Collini shows how the work of critics renowned for their close attention to 'the words on the page' was in practice bound up with claims about the nature and direction of historical change, the interpretation of the national past, and the scholarship of earlier historians. Among the major figures examined in detail are T.S. Eliot, F.R. Leavis, William Empson, and Raymond Williams, while there are also original discussions of such figures as Basil Willey, L.C. Knights, Q.D. Leavis, and Richard Hoggart. *The Nostalgic Imagination* argues that in the period between Eliot's *The Sacred Wood* and Williams's *The Long Revolution*, the writings of such critics came to occupy the cultural space left by academic history's retreat into specialized, archive-bound monographs. Their work challenged the assumptions of the Whig interpretation of English history, and entailed a revision of the traditional relations between 'literary history' and 'general history'. Combining close textual analysis with wide-ranging intellectual history, this volume both revises the standard story of the history of literary criticism and illuminates a central feature of the cultural history of twentieth-century Britain.

Stefan Collini studied at Cambridge and Yale. He taught at the University of Sussex from 1974 to 1986, and thereafter at Cambridge where he became Professor of Intellectual History and English Literature in 2000. He is a frequent contributor to the *London Review of Books, Times Literary Supplement, The Guardian,* and *The Nation,* and an occasional broadcaster. He is a Fellow of the British Academy and of the Royal Historical Society.

T0346706

ALSO BY STEFAN COLLINI

As author:

Liberalism and Sociology: L. T. Hobhouse and Political Argument in England 1880–1914

(with Donald Winch and John Burrow) *That Noble Science of Politics: A Study in Nineteenth-Century Intellectual History*

Public Moralists: Political Thought and Intellectual Life in Britain 1850–1930

Matthew Arnold: A Critical Portrait

English Pasts: Essays in History and Culture

Absent Minds: Intellectuals in Britain

Common Reading: Critics, Historians, Publics

That's Offensive: Criticism, Identity, Respect

What Are Universities For?

Common Writing: Essays on Literary Culture and Public Debate

Speaking of Universities

As editor:

John Stuart Mill, *On Liberty and Other Writings*

Umberto Eco, *Interpretation and Overinterpretation*

Matthew Arnold, *Culture and Anarchy and Other Writings*

C. P. Snow, *The Two Cultures*

(with Richard Whatmore and Brian Young)
History, Religion, and Culture: British Intellectual History since 1750

Economy, Polity, and Society: British Intellectual History since 1750

F. R. Leavis, *Two Cultures?*

THE
NOSTALGIC IMAGINATION

History in English Criticism

THE FORD LECTURES 2017

STEFAN COLLINI

OXFORD
UNIVERSITY PRESS

OXFORD
UNIVERSITY PRESS

Great Clarendon Street, Oxford, OX2 6DP,
United Kingdom

Oxford University Press is a department of the University of Oxford.
It furthers the University's objective of excellence in research, scholarship,
and education by publishing worldwide. Oxford is a registered trade mark of
Oxford University Press in the UK and in certain other countries

Published in the United States of America by Oxford University Press
198 Madison Avenue, New York, NY 10016, United States of America

British Library Cataloguing in Publication Data
Data available

Library of Congress Cataloging in Publication Data
Data available

ISBN 978–0–19–880017–0 (Hbk.)
ISBN 978–0–19–886033–4 (Pbk.)

To the memory of John Burrow and Frank Kermode

Preface

One comfort I have taken from having Leslie Stephen as a predecessor in the Ford Lectureship is confirmation, in the earliest years of the series, that a topic connected to literary criticism may not be wholly scandalous. The Ford Lectures are devoted to 'British history' (only in 1994 was the remit thus broadened from 'English history'), but Stephen was not deterred by any restrictive understanding of that field, confidently titling his lectures 'English Literature and Society in the Eighteenth Century'. Discouragingly for me, the published version of his lectures, which appeared under the same title the following year (1904), was not quite up to the standard of his best earlier work, and, more discouraging still, I note, first, that when he was due to deliver them he was exactly the same age as I was at the comparable point; and, second, that a little over a year later he was dead. I say 'due to deliver them', because his illness meant that they had to be read in his absence by his nephew, the celebrated liberal historian H. A. L. Fisher, and when facing for the first time the intimidating vastness of the South School in Oxford's Examination Schools I found myself regretting that this seductive precedent had not become established custom. Nonetheless, it is helpful for my purposes to recall Stephen, and indeed his nephew, since my own topic concerns aspects of the relationships among literary criticism, intellectual history, and what Fisher and others of his generation were used to calling 'general history'.

While this book had its origins in a set of lectures, the process of revision and amplification has been so extensive that my acknowledgement of those beginnings may risk misrepresenting its character. However, it is right that I should begin by expressing my gratitude to the electors to the Ford Lectureship, both for the initial stimulus and for their warm hospitality. I owe particular thanks to Roy Foster and Steven Gunn for advice and encouragement at crucial moments. For Hilary Term 2017, when the lectures were delivered, I was fortunate to be made a Visiting Fellow of All Souls College, which provided an ideal base and congenial company: I particularly thank the Warden, John Vickers, the Dean of Visiting Fellows, Cecilia Heyes, and those Examination and Postdoctoral Fellows who ensured that the term was as memorable for its parties as for its soberer activities.

For support, advice, correction, and distraction I owe thanks to the usual suspects: in addition, the whole script was read (and significantly improved) by Chris Hilliard, Angela Leighton, Ruth Morse, Helen Small, John Thompson, and Ross Wilson. Several colleagues and former students have provided me with information or references; they are thanked at the relevant points below. For practical assistance in checking references, I am indebted to Abi Glen and Jo Shortt-Butler. At Oxford University Press I am grateful to Robert Faber for encouragement at an early stage, and to Cathryn Steele, Lisa Eaton, Hilary Walford, and Andrew Hawkey for their care and professionalism during the process of production.

For access to unpublished material (and, where relevant, permission to quote from it), I am grateful to the following: Cambridge University archives (with special thanks to the archivist, Jacqueline Cox) for records of the Board of Graduate Studies, Cambridge University Library; Random House for the archives of Chatto and Windus, Reading University Special Collections Service; the National Library of Scotland for the papers of H. J. C. Grierson, National Library of Scotland, Edinburgh; the late Richard Hoggart for the Hoggart Papers, now held at Sheffield University; Ben Knights for material by L. C. Knights, Cambridge University Library; Downing College (with special thanks to the archivist, Jenny Ulph) for the F. R. Leavis Papers, Downing College, Cambridge; Penguin Books for the Penguin Archives, University of Bristol; Bill Noblett for the J. H. Plumb Papers, Cambridge University Library; the Harry Ransom Humanities Research Center, Austin, Texas, for the C. P. Snow Papers; Merryn Williams and the University of Swansea for the Raymond Williams Papers, University of Swansea Library.

Perhaps I should explain, since so much contemporary scholarly practice tends in the opposite direction, that I have for the most part restricted my endnote references to primary sources, citing secondary works only when I have quoted from them or otherwise made direct use of them. This book draws on reading and research carried out over many years, and extensive compilations of scholarly authorities could be assembled in a showy attempt to buttress its claims. But, in my view, such formulaic recitations serve little purpose in most cases, and I have abstained from them here. Finally, I should make clear that, although my engagement with this topic and its central characters is of long standing, the contents of this book are here appearing in print for the first time. The only exceptions are parts of the second half of Chapter 3 (about L. C. Knights) and of the last third of Chapter 5 (about Richard Hoggart); full details of the earlier versions of those two sections are given at the relevant points.

Contents

The historian of literature must count with as shifting and as massive forces as the historian of politics.

T. S. Eliot, The Athenaeum (1919)

Every Englishman born since 1800 has...been born into a view of English history.

R. G. Usher, The Historical Method of S. R. Gardiner (1919)

Introduction

I

Situating oneself in relation to selected versions of the past may be an inescapable activity, perhaps part of the human condition. At its most modest, the past in question may be purely autobiographical: we are all driven, from time to time, to be historians of our own characters, even if our source materials amount to little more than patchy and unreliable memories. When such situating takes place on a collective scale, where the reference has to be to narratives that are more extensive and more public, the range of possibilities is hugely increased. Attempting to subjugate the multiformity, we easily fall into talking about 'identity' and 'inheritance', the quasi-determinist vocabularies of genetics and the law mingling uneasily with the more voluntarist language of recognition and affiliation. In reality, the pasts that are invoked in such narratives are always chosen and constructed as well as given and encountered. Above all, they are, of necessity, imagined, even when what is imagined into existence takes on the appearance of necessity.

The attempt to create some systematic form of intelligible or usable order out of the residues of the past is a task that falls, most naturally as well as most enduringly, to historians. But at various moments figures who are not primarily or professionally defined as historians may, for local and contingent reasons, play a major part in shaping a society's self-understanding in time. This book focuses on one such instance: the role filled in Britain between about 1920 and about 1960 by a number of prominent literary critics. Literature—or, more precisely, the sequence of writers who were conventionally held to constitute the core of 'English Literature'—had long been central to national self-definition in Britain (the slippage between

'England' and 'Britain' has an extended and revealing history of its own). But in the early decades of the twentieth century the intimate, even fond, relationship between appreciation of the monuments of the national literature and understandings of the character and trajectory of the national polity was disrupted in various ways. A stronger emphasis came to be placed on the notion of literary *criticism*, understood as a strenuous, probing, even discomfiting activity, removed both from the forms of gushing belletristic 'appreciation' that had been the dominant mode in so much nineteenth-century literary discussion, and from the descriptive taxonomies, arranged in chronological sequence, that constituted the main forms of literary scholarship in the same period. This newer type of criticism was taken by its adepts and their admirers to have a unique access to existential truths about the character and quality of lived experience. For several reasons, criticism carried on in this vein enjoyed a particular standing or prominence in British culture in the middle decades of the century, exercising a wide influence over attitudes extending well beyond the confines of literary history and literary judgement.

Insofar as the history of literary criticism may be said to exist as a distinct scholarly subdiscipline, it is usually written in terms of a series of isms—that is, of theoretical or methodological 'approaches'—rather than as a congeries of more or less disorderly practices. In those programmatic terms, the figures whom this book focuses on are frequently grouped under one or more overlapping labels, such as 'Modernism' or 'Practical Criticism' (or, in the related American version, 'New Criticism'). Common to these imputed 'schools' or 'approaches' was, according to the received view, a rejection or denial of historicity. In the course of the three or four decades after 1920, it became common to think of the dominant style of literary criticism in both Britain and the United States as an activity defined by its repudiation of historical approaches in favour of concentration on matters of form—on, as the slogan of the time had it, 'the words on the page'. It will be a central contention of this book that, despite appearances to the contrary, this critical discourse additionally functioned as an influential way of communicating understandings of the past, especially the national past. For this reason among others, the subject matter of this book also forms a part—in some respects a small and somewhat specialized part, but in others a ramifying and significant part—of the intellectual history of Britain in the mid-twentieth century.

II

If we ask how educated English readers in the first half of the *nineteenth* century tended to understand their and their society's place in history, the answer would in the first instance have to be given in constitutional or religious terms. A story that connected, however loosely, Magna Carta, the Glorious Revolution, and the Great Reform Act still had considerable power to relate the present to the past in an animating way and to distinguish the English people's heritage from that of their less fortunate neighbours in other countries. At a different level, a story that focused on the Reformation, the role played by the defeat of the Spanish Armada in securing England from continental Catholic tyranny, the Act of Settlement, and the subsequent growth of limited religious toleration within a solidly Anglican setting—all this provided another usable form of self-definition, one that was given weekly reinforcement. For the more sophisticated and well informed, the legacy of eighteenth-century Scottish thinking about the progress of polite and commercial societies could provide another illuminating framework, one that Macaulay partly domesticated within the more familiar Whig narrative. In his celebration of progress and prosperity, especially in his famous third chapter, Macaulay 'made a bid to incorporate the Industrial Revolution into the Whig interpretation of English history'.[1] (Reversing this observation, one might say that Alfred Marshall, in his celebration of economic progress and prosperity as the outcome of national traits of thrift and character, made a late bid to incorporate the Whig interpretation of English history into the principles of economics.[2])

Such an act of incorporation was necessary if the Whig interpretation was to maintain its relevance, especially since there grew up in the mid-nineteenth century a rather different story, chiefly articulated by such 'sages' as Carlyle and Ruskin and amplified by the Tractarian tradition of social criticism. 'The Tory–Radical critique of English society, as it had developed from the 1820s onwards, was essentially based on a primitive social history of England.'[3] That is to say, by shifting the focus from constitutional or religious matters to 'the condition of the people', a far less rosy picture could be painted, taking in the destruction of the monasteries, the dispossession of the small farmer, and the degraded living and working conditions of the machine age. J. A. Froude was an interestingly hybrid figure here: his *History of England from the Fall of Wolsey to the Defeat of the Spanish Armada* (1856–70)

celebrated the energy and creativity of the Elizabethan era and the successful emergence of the national spirit from its trials, but he denied that he was
positing any kind of Golden Age with which, in more familiar Ruskinian or
Tractarian fashion, to criticize 'the conclusions of political economy',
though in his occasional writings he evinced a good deal of nostalgia for the
small farmer displaced by commercial prosperity.[4]

The Victorian Whig historians could write with confidence about the
onward march of liberty—or the constitution, or the spirit of the English
people, or however else they identified the underlying protagonist of their
histories—because they were essentially at ease with their present. History
had not taken a wrong turning; their society had not fallen into a state of
terminal decadence. Such history encouraged a pride in ancestry and a confident fortitude in the present. As we shall see, one of the things that is most
striking about so much of the *literary* history produced in Victorian Britain
is the way it replicated and confirmed the Whig story as narrated by the
'general' historians. In these terms, literary history, too, could be told very
largely in celebratory mode. We need, for example, to recognize what a
'Whiggish' (in this sense) document Palgrave's famous *Golden Treasury* was,
as it charted the growing maturity of English poetry from the sixteenth
century to his own time. In some ways, Palgrave's 'Preface and Notes' to
what he hoped would be 'a true national Anthology' functioned as the literary equivalent of Macaulay's famous third chapter, glorying in a story of
progress that was distinctively English. The story culminated in the achievements of the poets of the early decades of the nineteenth century: 'In a
word, the Nation which, after the Greeks in their glory, may fairly claim that
during six centuries it has proved itself the most richly gifted of all nations
for Poetry, expressed in these men the highest strength and prodigality of its
nature.' (The book had gone into twenty-eight printings by the time of
Palgrave's death in 1897; it was still selling on average 10,000 per year up to
1939, by which date over 650,000 copies had been printed.)[5] More generally, this form of literary appreciation also involved a sense of the immediate
accessibility of past writing, as part of the shared expression of the national
character. It was not the function of Victorian and Edwardian literary history
to estrange the present from the past or to propose a story of irretrievable
loss. The classics of English literature were presented as a common possession, all equally and actively available.

In the second half of the nineteenth century, several of these familiar tropes
came to be reworked in the fashionable language of social evolutionism.

This tended to give such historical stories a more impersonal and less parochial character. For example, the project of 'comparative literature' did not signify, as that term has come to be used, merely the study of literature in more than one language. It was part of the wider intellectual programme of applying the 'comparative method'—as in 'comparative law' or 'comparative politics'—the method of placing types or species on an evolutionary scale. It was taxonomic and transnational in the way that comparative philology was, identifying roots and stems and tracing the spread of variations.[6] Social evolutionism turned on a temporal axis yet it was not genuinely historical: descent, sequence, affiliation were all categories that simultaneously presupposed and ignored actual time. And the focus was not literary-critical but theoretical, tracing units or memes across generations, seeing them as pieces of evidence on a par with legal and political forms rather than as unique expressions of the distinctive faculty of artistic imagination. The fashion for this particular application of social evolutionary method passed in the early decades of the twentieth century, though as late as the 1950s René Wellek and others in the United States still felt the need to eradicate any lingering theoretical ambitions of this kind and to make 'comp lit' a properly literary-critical study of literature in more than one language.[7]

In practice, most histories of English Literature written between, say, 1850 and 1920 were content to combine mere sequence with occasional forays into social and political history. Such surveys did not display any anxiety that this approach made literature secondary, an expression of 'deeper' social forces, though towards the end of the century, Aestheticism, which was duty-bound to be acutely sensitive to such anxieties, tended to favour strongly internalist or immanentist narratives, in which the focus was on literary form, as, for example, in George Saintsbury's numerous compilations. After 1870, the needs of the expanding educational system, and above all the rapid growth of the 'black-coated' clerical lower middle class, created new markets for serviceable surveys that could introduce newly literate readers to their cultural inheritance, a situation favouring histories that were both superficial and celebratory. For this purpose, there was a substantial repository of Victorian criticism to draw upon. The leading periodical critics of the day, though obviously well aware of the historical remoteness of literature from much earlier eras and in some cases genuinely learned about such writing, nonetheless tended to treat the monuments of English literature as a common possession, not as an object of anthropological inspection.

The melancholy could find company in Burton just as the playful could
in Sterne; an educated reader appreciated the wit of Pope no less than
that of Wilde, and so on. Popular literary history incorporated this easy
familiarity: it emphasized community across time, not estrangement. This
was the heyday of what I have elsewhere called 'the Whig interpretation of
English literature'.[8]

It was scarcely surprising that the outbreak of the First World War should
provoke various attempts to mobilize these cultural resources to bolster the
national cause. A representative example of attempts to put literary history
to work in this way, and one that reveals the longevity and continuing
vitality of this mode of relating to earlier literature, was Ernest de Sélincourt's
English Poets and the National Ideal, published in 1915. The author, the
Professor of English at the University of Birmingham, justified turning four
public lectures into a slim volume on the grounds that, at this great crisis of
the nation's affairs, 'we' needed 'to draw upon the immense spiritual
resources of our poetry, which are not the least glorious nor the least precious part of our heritage as Englishmen'. Following affectionate appreci-
ations of the work of Shakespeare, Milton, and Wordsworth, a concluding
chapter on 'Poetry since 1815' unembarrassedly drew the political moral.
Tennyson was magnificent, but perhaps a little lacking in the required
democratic and internationalist sentiments. Swinburne was better in these
respects, since to him, 'as to most of our poets, love of England is bound up
with that love of freedom on which her claim to greatness is based'. This
entailed having a cultivated enthusiasm for freedom everywhere, not just at
home. On this score, Meredith was commended even more highly, and 'thus
during the last century did our poets pass on the torch which they received
at the hands of Shakespeare, Milton, and Wordsworth'.[9] The discussion is
animated by the conviction, too widely shared to be identified as 'Arnoldian'
though Arnold gave it particularly memorable expression, that poetry is
what most powerfully stirs our noblest aspirations. At the same time, de
Sélincourt sustains a recognizably Whiggish relation to the past: continuity
and celebration are the key notes, there is no great caesura or impassable
barrier between present and past, and all that is best continues as part of a
living national heritage. De Sélincourt's lectures are a good example of the
ease with which literary and historical modes could be combined: the great
writers of the past speak to us directly and at the same time we are nourished by understanding the national tradition of which we are a part.

The flexible historicism illustrated in this instance assumed a firmer form
in the robust understanding of the stature and distinctiveness of History as

a form of scholarly enquiry that was establishing itself at the beginning of the twentieth century. There is now a well-documented story of how the partial and uneven professionalization of history in the second half of the nineteenth century, largely but not entirely within the universities, brought together elements of German historicism, ideals of scientific accuracy and disinterestedness, and an inherited focus on the political, administrative, diplomatic, and legal machinery of the state. This amalgam had an enduring power in shaping academic historians' conception of their role. The contemporary political resonances of such scholarship may have become more muted or indirect by the early decades of the twentieth century, but the marriage of 'scientific' method and largely political subject matter continued to define what counted as 'serious' history.

In the second half of the nineteenth century, attempts to legitimate the academic study of English literature had reflected some of the same ideals: the enterprise had to be historical, factual, 'objective', and hence—this was a crucial requirement in the celebrated debate at Oxford over introducing English as a subject—examinable. Not that historians had always recognized the credentials of what aspired to be a cognate discipline. After Modern History had been separated from Jurisprudence in Oxford in 1873, it was proposed that a Chair of English Literature (which at that point Oxford did not possess) should be founded and assigned to the historians. William Stubbs, as Regius Professor of Modern History, opposed the proposal, declaring to the 1877 Commission: 'I think that to have the History School hampered with dilettante teaching, such as the teaching of English Literature, must necessarily do great harm to the School.' Generalizing his case, he maintained that 'there is no special connection between English Literature and Modern History'.[10] The spirit of Stubbs survived in English historiography, notably among Oxford-trained historians, for many decades after this gruff rebuff, and not the least part of that legacy was the conviction, more a matter of professional habit than intellectual contention, that 'there is no special connection between English Literature and Modern History'. (Writing to H. J. C. Grierson as late as 1931, Firth lamented the consequences of this for students of English at Oxford: 'The weak point of our students of English lit is that they have no adequate knowledge of English history, or European literature and history.'[11]) But elsewhere institutional arrangements often presumed just such a connection. In the early days of the civic universities founded in the second half of the nineteenth century in cities such as Manchester, Birmingham, Liverpool, Leeds, and Sheffield, resources were exiguous and the teaching staff tiny. Professors often had responsibility for more than one subject, and the pairing of History and English was not uncommon. The emblematic figure here was Adolphus William Ward. Appointed 'Professor of History, and English Language and Literature' at the fledgling Owens College, Manchester, in 1866 (at the age of 29), he worked hard to raise the institution's status, eventually becoming Vice-Chancellor of the new Victoria University. During the greater part of his career he published scholarly work in both fields: set alongside detailed studies of nineteenth-century British foreign policy were such monographs as *A History of English Dramatic Literature to the Death of Queen Anne*. Fittingly, he became the editor-in-chief of both the *Cambridge Modern History* (1901–12) and the *Cambridge History of English Literature* (1907–16), the twin monuments to this positivist form of historicism.

Thus, at the beginning of the period covered in this book, a strong and largely shared conception of what counted as serious scholarship was well established in both disciplines. Those who found their sense of their professional and disciplinary identities adequately represented by, on the one side, the *English Historical Review* or the *Transactions of the Royal Historical Society*, and, on the other, *Notes and Queries* or (from 1925) the *Review of English Studies*, could equally give their allegiance to a similar notion of respectable academic work, where 'respectable' suggests both the prevailing canons of propriety and an anxiety about falling into some derogated lower or more popular category. But in the course of the first half of the twentieth century, as academic specialization developed and hardened, Literature (or, in practice in Anglophone countries, simply 'English') came to be seen as a distinct mode of understanding, grounded in close attention to the formal properties of a canonical body of writing, principally poetry, drama, and, eventually, the novel, while History, centred on political history but with economic and social history increasingly prominent, strengthened its established position as another mode or discipline. Periodically, attempts were made at some kind of rapprochement or interdisciplinary cooperation, but indirectly such efforts confirmed the largely separate and autonomous existence of the two activities: Literary Criticism was one thing, History was another.

Indeed, the period between about 1920 and 1960 may even have witnessed an intensification of the historians' self-conception and a still firmer exclusion of those approaches and subject matters that did not belong in 'serious' history. At a time when the tone had been set by such austerely technical historians as Pollard and Tout, detailed archival-based research in public records provided the gold standard of guild qualification. A generation ago, one survey concluded that 'the divide between academic and popular history was stronger in England in the middle decades of the twentieth century than at an earlier period'.[12] In similar vein, more recent scholars have detected something of a 'retreat' into specialized scholarly works in these years, consigning the production of more readable and wide-ranging forms of history to the several categories of non-academic historians.[13] A further expression of this development has been noted with reference to the middle decades of the century: 'As male historians became firmly established in the academic community, a vacuum or space was created in the public sphere for the role of public historian which could be filled by women,' instancing the successful careers of C. V. Wedgwood and Cecil Woodham-Smith.[14] Whether or not the metaphor of a 'vacuum' quite catches the dynamic of the forces at work in this development may be debatable, but I shall suggest that literary critics, too, were among those who came forward to fill the space, however characterized.

A contraction in the public presence of works of academic history can also be identified in other terms. Peter Mandler's figures suggest that the number of titles published per year that could be classified as 'History' fell from a peak of c.800 in the decade before the First World War to c.400 just before the Second. 'The number of history titles published in the 1950s reached its lowest point since records began. From a peak in 1900 representing 10 per cent of all titles, history had shrunk to barely 1 per cent by the late 1950s', before starting to rise quite sharply from the mid-1960s.[15] Narrowness of another kind may be indicated by Michael Bentley's suggestion that, unlike in France, Germany, and the USA, 'the claims of sister disciplines made comparatively little impact on English historians in the first half of the twentieth century'.[16] Christopher Parker additionally emphasizes the longevity of the late Whig form of constitutional history:

> The strength of continuous English constitutional history, exemplifying undeniably Whig characteristics, was such that, by the end of the period of reaction against it, its pedagogical role had not only survived but had expanded until it dominated the history degrees of very nearly all British universities, old and new, in the 1930s, and it mostly retained and extended this position for thirty years thereafter.[17]

This continuity was not the whole story, of course. Economic and social history developed notably in the 1920s and 1930s (very few academic historians cultivated any form of cultural or intellectual history), while beyond the university walls a small number of popular historians commanded large sales, whether offering interpretations of world history on the grandest scale, as in H. G. Wells's *Outline of History* (1919), A. J. Toynbee's *A Study of History* (1934–61), and, somewhat more modestly, H. A. L. Fisher's *History of Europe* (1935), or in celebrating features of the national story, as in the numerous works by G. M. Trevelyan, Winston Churchill, and Arthur Bryant. Trevelyan is a complicating case, since he returned to academia as Regius Professor at Cambridge in 1927, but he had made his reputation as a free-lance historian before that and continued to write for a wide popular audience thereafter.[18] As Parker observes of Fisher's *History of Europe*, it 'was not a specialist work, nor was it based on up-to-date scholarship and, though vastly influential in schools and amongst the general public, for which it was much reprinted, the day when such a survey, however elegantly written and superficially wise, could have academic influence, was gone'.[19] For the most part, university-based historians in the decades from 1920 to 1960 stayed close to what they understood to be the Rankean commandments, bestowing professional commendation on, above all, detailed, impersonal, archive-based studies in political and diplomatic history.

Wide-ranging judgements about 'the quality of living' were not part of 'serious scholarship'; insofar as scholars might ponder any questions about 'correlating' the disciplines of History and English, they would do so in more limited, technical, or pedagogic terms. But, as we shall see, that was not always the view taken by a new generation of literary critics after 1920, with the result that a striking one-sidedness developed in their subsequent relationship with their historical colleagues. While these critics oscillated between mannerly seduction and annexationist ambition, the great majority of academic historians in the first half of the twentieth century maintained their defences and protected their virtue.

III

Disciplines, like nations, cultivate foundation myths—quasi-historical stories that underwrite identity and confer legitimacy. One of the main such narratives informing the self-understanding of contemporary literary studies involves, in some form or another, a three-stage development. In the first stage, as the earliest version of the academic study of English began to emerge from the primeval slime (this Jurassic Age is generally placed in the late nineteenth century), philological, historical, and biographical approaches predominated. Knowledge *about* literature and language was the prized currency; attention was focused on origins, development, and context. This may be called the Age of Scholarship. The second stage, corresponding perhaps to the wars of liberation in national narratives, redirected attention from context to text, from philology to meaning, from biography to 'the words on the page'. This stage, whose beginnings are commonly dated to the 1920s and 1930s and in which Cambridge is judged to have played the leading part, insisted that the distinctive mode of English studies was literary-critical; that the chief capacity students needed to develop was that for close verbal analysis; and that the standing and legitimacy of the discipline depended upon its emancipating itself from both the belletristic and the *Wissenschaftlich* modes inherited from the nineteenth century. This may be called the Age of Criticism. The third stage, and the beginning of the era in which we still live, is usually thought to date from the 1970s and 1980s. Among the tales of heroism and nation-building gathered about this stage, the following tend to be celebrated at moments of ritualistic self-consciousness: a relativizing of the categories and starting points of previous forms of liter-ary study; a challenge to the standing and scope of the inherited literary canon; an acknowledgement of the part played by power and ideology in all discursive formations, including the critic's own; and a thorough-going historicization which has seemed to some commentators to risk turning all literary study into a form of cultural history. This may be called the Age of Theory. Whether we might now be at the beginning of a fourth stage, which will be marked by the so-called return of the aesthetic or revival of formalism, it is perhaps too early to judge.

These textbook periodizations are, needless to say, misleadingly simple: we can all plume ourselves on our greater sophistication in understanding about overlap, coexistence, and the reality of intellectual untidiness in gen-eral. Nonetheless, the outlines of this three-stage story are repeatedly visible not just in the condensed histories of recent criticism that occupy the first chapter in the more conscientious of the innumerable handbooks, guides, and companions that now bulk so large in academic publishing, but also in those revealing moments of self-situating when literary scholars, speaking on behalf of their favoured methodological approach or ism, try to lay claim to a particular genealogy. And at the heart of these schematic narratives is the oft-repeated contention that the critical style dominant in the second age—for which 'practical criticism' is usually the favoured, if misleading, metonymic label (at least in Britain)—was ahistorical.

It is something of a commonplace to observe that those changes in literature and culture from the 1910s and 1920s onwards that we refer to as 'Modernism' involved a fundamental hostility to or denial of history. Joseph Frank gave this view a particularly influential formulation many years ago when he argued that Modernist literature 'resisted and erased the concept of history by adopting a "spatial" method instead of a temporal one'.[20] The styles of criticism that developed in the 1920s and 1930s were seen as enactments of this new denial or dislocation of temporality in literature. Edmund Wilson was one of the first to have proclaimed that the new approaches in criticism were, as he put it, 'fundamentally non-historical', and many years later Frank Lentricchia summarized the by now well-established view that the legacy of the New Criticism was a 'denial of history'.[21] Emblematic of this percep-tion of the character of the new style of criticism was the frank declaration by I. A. Richards, the founder of so-called 'Practical Criticism', that he 'didn't think History ought to have happened'.[22]

Of course, it is acknowledged that the close analysis of verbal texture favoured in this style of criticism was sometimes accompanied by various meta-historical generalizations, often of a markedly declinist kind. But nonetheless, the critical method itself, the attention to the formal and semantic properties of 'the words on the page', has been widely understood as inherently—and, according to the critiques of later theorists, damagingly—ahistorical, divorcing text from context and treating past works of 'literature' (another subsequently contested category) as all equally and unproblemat-ically available for analysis and judgement by the modern reader.

Slaying predecessors is an essential part of the cycle of intellectual fertility. It was important to the polemical energy of 'Theory' to represent what had gone before as formalist and as all the more the prisoner of history because unaware of its own historical presuppositions. In reality, of course, all criticism has historical presuppositions (as does all theory), just as any discussion that is to be both fruitful and manageable depends upon leaving some things implicit. But the critique, and, very often, dismissal, of what was lumped together as 'formalism' or 'New Criticism' was too indiscriminate and itself too historically incurious. Each of the three 'ages' of the discipline constantly threatens to congeal into a stereotype, and the stereotype of 'the age of criticism' as ahistorical or even anti-historical—a stereotype sustained by the needs of 'Theory's' self-image—is particularly deep-rooted. In considering the ways in which the work of some of the most prominent representatives of that 'age' continued to involve forms of both literary his-tory and 'general history', this book tries to offer a partial corrective.

IV

One helpful preliminary step may be to take a more probing look at the familiar category of 'literary history' itself. This has a venerable pedigree, even if in the course of the twentieth century literary history in its scholarly forms has come to seem like the eternal poor relation, an inescapably boring, subordinate activity. It lacks the allure of literary criticism, with criticism's (at its best) dazzling display of insight and interpretation, but it also lacks the reach and power of what in the first half of the twentieth century was usually referred to as 'general history'—what its advocates are sometimes prone to think of as 'real history'—or what in disciplinary terms is just classed as 'History'. While the lowly status and dowdy image of literary history may be understandable, this may mask the fact that it is not only a genre with a long lineage of its own, but one that has continued to be an essential part of, or concomitant to, all other forms of literary study. At the same time, the peculiarity of this form of history—insofar as it is a form of history—tends to be overlooked, so it may be worth pausing to consider the nature of that peculiarity.

In its everyday forms, literary history is bound up with 'general history', but selectively and inconsistently. This is even true for such basic categories as period labels. We talk of both a style of literature and a historical period as 'Victorian', whereas we are making a distinction if we use 'Augustan' rather than 'Hanoverian'. 'Restoration comedy' foregrounds the links with the political and social history of a period, while 'Romantic poetry' does not. Developments within some genres or some periods may more obviously call for extra-literary explanation than in others: any account of drama from Jonson and Middleton to Wycherley and Congreve has to discuss the closing of the theatres and the Interregnum; an account of the development of poetry from Shelley and Keats to Tennyson and Browning is not under a similar necessity to deal with the Reform Act or the Factory Acts (though, clearly, more or less thickly textured historical accounts may be given in both cases).

G. M. Trevelyan's offhand definition of social history as 'history with the politics left out' has become hackneyed from overuse, but one might adapt the phrase to say that literary history could be defined as history with the history left out. That is to say, the fundamental problem for all literary history is that, if it confines itself to literature, it has no way to go beyond a merely descriptive sequence of writings or literary forms. If, instead, it seeks to *explain* change in literary production, then (as the use of the sociological term 'production' already hints) it is likely to give explanatory primacy to some non-literary forces, usually found in one or another kind of social, economic, or intellectual history. Conventional literary history records various kinds of sequence—of authors, works, genres, styles, and so on—but it cannot, in its own literary terms, account for the causes and timings of the larger patterns that such sequences reveal.[23] Nonetheless, versions of literary history, in both its narrowly and broadly conceived forms, constituted the dominant way of organizing knowledge about literature in the nineteenth century, and, in more modern or sometimes simply more pedagogical guise, such histories have remained a staple element in the study of literature ever since.

In considering the ways in which the abundant literary histories written in the later nineteenth and very early twentieth centuries presented the literary past while exhibiting the constraints inherent in the genre, it may be helpful to transpose them into the terms of Nietzsche's celebrated essay 'On the Uses and Disadvantages of History for Life'.[24] The equivalent of the first of Nietzsche's three types, what he terms 'monumental' history, involves selecting those few masterpieces that still directly inspire us. This, we may say, is the least historical form of literary history: it is not denied that these masterpieces are in the past, but the principle of selection and the character of our relation to them presumes, in effect, that they are also contemporary with us. Work in this style tends to be both ruthlessly selective and piously celebratory. Literary history's equivalent of Nietzsche's second type, 'antiquarian' history, usually takes the form of peopling a tradition—most often a national tradition though the logic is the same if the unit is some other kind of group—with a large number of writers who share some common characteristics that are held to be distinctive of that group. Identifying with the expression of this tradition in the present, the antiquarian literary historian looks back 'with love and loyalty', extending these emotions to, but only to, all who partake of the tradition.[25] The third model is what Nietzsche called 'critical' history: largely negative or destructive, this affects to 'take the knife' to the accepted roots of the present, to cut them away, although, as Nietzsche observes, this is 'an attempt to give oneself, as it were, *a posteriori*, a past in which one would like to originate in opposition to that in which one did originate'.[26] Much of the ostensibly historical engagement with earlier literature undertaken by practising writers corresponds to this model.

A great deal of the appreciative criticism so evident in the second half of the nineteenth century, whether in periodical essays or longer studies, was, in effect, a version of 'monumental' literary history, enthusing over the beauties or insights of past writing in ways that presumed its universality. Much of the more scholarly or, by the closing decades of the century, the more pedagogical literary history exhibited the characteristics of Nietzsche's 'antiquarian' mode, especially when some unbroken thread of Englishness was traced from Chaucer (or, in some of the more strenuous claims for 'Old English', from *Beowulf*) through to the present. Although individual writers and critics might seek to downgrade or reclassify some traditionally revered figures from the literary past—'Dryden and Pope are not classics of our poetry, they are classics of our prose'[27]—there was no systematic attempt before 1914 to reshape commonly received literary history by applying 'critical' history's knife. Staying for the moment within these categories, it could be said that part of the shock value of T. S. Eliot's early criticism lay in the manner in which he treated 'critical' literary history as the only intellectually acceptable mode. Of course, it is wholly consonant with what Nietzsche says about 'critical' history's implicit attempt to 'give oneself...a past in which one would like to originate in opposition to that in which one did originate' that Eliot's reconstruction of 'tradition' should install a different kind of usable past in place of the derided pieties of the inherited account. Nonetheless, this sharply critical mode entailed a radically different relation to the literary past, one harder to assimilate to the conventional categories of continuity and celebration. Any such reshaping of the understanding of literary history was bound to have consequences for the relations between Literature and History considered as forms of knowledge or, as we mostly now think of them, disciplines.

In reading any critic, we become aware of the chronological perspectives within which they move—the habitual points of reference, the reliance on established period labels, and so on. Beyond this, we also sense the range of their historical responsiveness, the spurt of verbal vigour prompted by particular episodes or epochs, the modulations of affinity that emerge, often indirectly, in choosing this topic or that writer. But there is also another kind of temporal consciousness at work—namely, that involved in the implicit situating of both author and audience that underwrites any act of criticism. All the assumptions that help to sustain the confident assertions about 'now', 'today', or 'the present' are, necessarily, historical, as are all claims about what might be relevantly distinctive about this particular moment. Many of the elements involved in pitching an address to an imagined audience are historical, tacitly situating 'them' within stories of social change, educational level, intellectual fashions, and so on. Judgements about what needs saying *now*—whether because of the state of scholarship on the topic or the state of some larger public discussion—trade upon a sense of movement, of the relation of the present to the past.

As a preliminary to the detailed examination of particular instances in the chapters that follow, it may be worth setting out an elementary taxonomy of some of the main forms this historical presence in literary criticism may take, giving explicit propositional form to the points already mentioned discursively. First, there is bound to be some explicit or implicit relation to 'general history'. The mere use of chronology brings historical baggage with it. Period-specific descriptions and identifications cannot be avoided. Frequently these involve assumptions about the character of past societies, about the forms and drivers of change, or about the relation of literature to other social activities, and so on. Second, there is bound to be some explicit or implicit relation to a wider literary history. Literary analysis inevitably involves assumptions about styles and movements, about the rise and fall of genres, about predecessors and successors. The labels and classifications employed or alluded to will usually be drawn from the residues of earlier literary histories. Third, there is bound to be some explicit or implicit relation to the present. All critical writing involves decisions about what needs to be addressed, about the current understanding of an author or topic, about the characteristics of the implied reader, about the method of publication or dissemination, and so on. All of these matters involve placing the present in some broadly historical frame.

Beyond these three points, which can, as it were, be deduced from the character of literary discussion itself, critics may, and very frequently do, introduce other kinds of historical claims. For example, critics will often propose, explicitly or implicitly, historical accounts of particular themes, topics, genres, such as 'the reading public', 'the English language', 'the lyric', and so on. In addition, critics will often propose, explicitly or implicitly, various meta-historical claims, either about large-scale changes such as 'the transition from medieval to modern' or 'the rise of print culture', or about the nature and direction of qualitative changes such as 'the decline of taste', 'the fragmentation of the public', or indeed about the nature of whatever they choose to term 'modernity'.

At a more detailed level of scholarship, there will be aspects of the relationship between literary critics and professional historians that may become more or less prominent according to circumstance. These include cases in which critics draw on particular works of history, at first- or second-hand, in framing their descriptions of period-specific features or their characterizations of the dynamics of change; or cases where critics are involved in the establishment and regulation of the boundary between literary and historical scholars, whether in terms of syllabuses and educational arrangements or of literary journalism and reviewing.

Clearly, each of these aspects of the relation will take local and distinctive forms in particular settings, just as their relative prominence or subordination will vary also. No less obvious is the fact that the investigation of these matters will, in any given instance, involve a complex form of intellectual history in which familiar questions about critical method or practice will radiate out into explorations of professional identities, genres of writing, forms of public debate, political, religious, and cultural affiliations, and so on. The very practice of literary criticism, in other words, always already involves a wider intellectual history.

This is nowhere more evident than in the attempt, prominent in this period but repeated in various guises across the century, to deploy some radically revisionist version of literary criticism to underwrite a broader cultural critique. Here, too, it may be helpful to set out a small taxonomy of the way reinterpretations of favoured historical episodes and periods could furnish such weapons. If, for example, the aim was to mount a swingeing condemnation of the alleged standardization, mindlessness, and levelling-down of contemporary culture in inter-war Britain (not an unknown aim at the time), what interpretation of history—both literary history and 'general history'—would be useful to buttress and justify this critique? One could go back to, for example, the Victorian age, emphasizing the role of serious periodicals, the success enjoyed by great novelists, the standing of major cultural critics, and so on, all of which was debased by the consequences of mass literacy. Or to the eighteenth century, identifying the role of polite essays and coffee houses, the growth of writing as a profession, and a harmonious gentry-farmer country life, all of which was destroyed by the Industrial Revolution. Or to the Civil War and the Commonwealth, calling attention to its flowering of radical and popular ideas, all cut short and suppressed by the return of monarchy, the enhanced power of the court, the rise of science, and the founding of the Stock Exchange. Or to the Elizabethan age, seeing it as a time when all classes shared a common theatre culture, fired by a lively vernacular language, set against a backdrop of the energetic exploration of the globe, all of which was increasingly squeezed between the mounting pressures of royalism and Puritanism. Or to the Middle Ages, understood as an Age of Faith, where art was in the service of religious belief, underpinned by the acceptance of hierarchy and a stable unchanging rural order, all of which was undermined by the Renaissance, the beginnings of secular humanism, and the growth of trade.

It would be only a slight exaggeration to say that versions of *all* these routes could be found in the allegedly 'ahistorical' form of literary criticism developed in the interwar period. Part of the interest of the story that needs to be told here lies in the way certain specific and local revisions of literary history (largely poetic history) came to nourish and be merged with the broader critique of the alleged dominance of modern society by 'the economic'. By the middle of the twentieth century, literary critics in Britain had become habituated to the way in which the right reading of, say, an early Jacobean sonnet was alleged to constitute an act of resistance towards the prevailing economism of contemporary society, though this is in fact a highly peculiar contention, one that itself has, I am arguing, a specific history. In the late nineteenth and early twentieth centuries, readers would generally not have looked to critics to deploy literature against contemporary society in this way. There was no shortage of social criticism in the culture as a whole, but it was not looked for in the works of A. C. Bradley and Walter Raleigh, nor in those of Edmund Gosse and George Saintsbury. Eliotic criticism made the question of literary inheritance more vexed: he, as it were, challenged the reading of the will that other members of the family had been happy to accept.

In ordinary familial terms, we are always told that we cannot choose our ancestors, but of course artists and writers of all kinds do just that. It may not be easy to say exactly what is involved in drawing inspiration or sustenance from the work of a long-dead predecessor, what kind of continuity or resemblance is in play, what element of fantasy or self-delusion. Even so, most writers are also primitive literary historians, selecting and arranging a sequence of kin while excluding or disregarding the larger throng. But, again, this selecting and arranging of a literary past can take a more than individual form, an attempt to establish some kind of pattern—or, at the very least, of sequence—among a wide variety of earlier writers and literary forms. This is not so far removed from the enterprise that, in its more organized and academic aspect, we still call literary history.

Here again it may be helpful to discriminate in general terms some of the ways in which writers may attempt to draw inspiration from earlier exemplars.

We can, for example, distinguish at least three such modes: the first looks to those immediate predecessors who have inaugurated or expanded what now seem to be the most fertile and rewarding forms in which to write; the second looks to neglected or occluded predecessors whose achievement has only belatedly become fully legible in the present; and the third looks to the writing of a more distant period which can be represented as having some unobvious kinship with the present, unlike that of the intervening centuries.

Further subcategories can easily be elaborated. Not all of these manoeuvres entail attempting to destroy or reduce some established reputation in the present, but they necessarily involve some challenge to the accepted distribution of esteem. Part of the interest of the story to be explored in this book lies, I believe, in the way such literary-critical and literary-historical sallies came, in the decades between 1920 and 1960, to engage with, to challenge, and even, at the limit, to displace aspects of the narrative of 'general history' provided by professional historians.

Eliot's initially iconoclastic version of literary history appeared to make change endogenous yet also curiously trans-temporal, a matter of poet speaking unto poet across the centuries in a schema that was neither developmental nor really historical. Part of the long-term significance of Eliot's early criticism in particular was the way it broke the cosy link between belief in England's special historical glory and the cultural enshrining of Romanticism and its legacy. The monument in which this link had been enduringly embodied was the 'English Men of Letters' series, which, like Palgrave's *Golden Treasury*, gave disproportionate prominence to Romantic and Victorian writers (thirty-one of the thirty-nine subjects in the first series were from the eighteenth or nineteenth centuries; fifteen of the twenty-six subjects in the second series were from the nineteenth century).[28] The series implicitly assumed not just an immediacy of access to, and intimacy with, past writers, but also that Romanticism and its legacy represented the apogee of the national literary tradition, the epitome of the English sensibility. By treating the legacy of Romanticism as shallow and second rate, as a form of decadence in an almost Nietzschean sense, Eliot made the link between literature and modernity a profoundly uneasy one. Another way to put this would be to say that the dominant style of literary history in, roughly, the half-century before 1914 had not furnished some *alternative* narrative to that established in 'general history': it had not, for the most part, been a resource for criticism of the development and outcome of that general history. Eliot's early critical essays sketched an alternative form of literary history that fulfilled precisely this function.

Eliot did not do this alone, of course, and we now know a lot about the contribution of other literary figures, such as Ford Madox Ford, T. E. Hulme, W. B. Yeats, and Ezra Pound, as well as various extra-literary forces, not least the First World War (we should also note the more recent judgement that 'Eminent Victorians . . . is a criticism of the Whig interpretation of history'[29]). Ford's encompassing jeremiads had none of the pointed detail of Eliot's retrievals of distant models, but his irritable dismissal of Victorian moralism and sonorousness, and his hankering after 'the old feudalism and the old union of Christendom beneath a spiritual headship', opened spaces that others would fill with more attention to detail.[30] Similarly, Hulme made little contribution to literary history in the narrower sense, but his ruminative voyages across large stretches of European intellectual history certainly assisted others to place more specific literary developments as part of his vaguely adumbrated 'decline into humanism' from the Renaissance onwards.[31] Yeats, another major figure whom I shall not discuss, at one point located the lost 'unity of being' in the late Middle Ages; for him, the rot had set in by 1450. His A Vision (1925) was perhaps the limiting case of Symbolist mythography as history, appearing to push the story back to Byzantium.[32] Over the course of a long life, Yeats entertained a variety of meta-historical narratives, nearly all pointing to some form of recurrence or decline. In the 1930s he could be found endorsing what was by then one of the more familiar versions: 'The mischief began at the end of the seventeenth century when man became passive before a mechanized nature.'[33]

Pound was, of course, the really enabling collaborator as far as Eliot was concerned, his importance here lying above all in the way he anchored his large meta-historical gestures to knowledgeable and detailed commentary on the sequence of various verse forms. Pound famously urged that a properly modern poetry should be 'austere, direct, free from emotional slither', and he then parlayed the implicit aesthetic into a way of understanding and organizing history, albeit a kind of farceur's history: 'As for the nineteenth century, with all respect to its achievements, I think we shall look back upon it as a rather blurry, messy sort of a period, a rather sentimentalistic, mannerish sort of a period.'[34] Pound always enjoyed a spot of demotic dethroning, and it is tempting to dismiss such naughty-boy remarks as of no consequence other than for the practice of poetry. But such generalizations about 'a period' have a way of colouring broader understandings about the past, and one of the most remarkable intellectual developments of the 1920s was the bizarre marriage between Pound's 'hard' aesthetic and early adumbrations of the critique of 'mass society'. As time went by, Eliot's scarcely less offhand remarks about the seventeenth century were, as we shall see, interfused with the accounts put forward by earlier historical economists and economic historians in ways that came to underwrite an interpretation of fundamental social and cultural decline. More broadly, revisionist literary-critical narratives transposed familiar accounts of key periods in British history, such as the Civil War or the Industrial Revolution, into shifts in sensibility and thence into weapons of cultural critique in the present.

Perhaps partly as a consequence of the fashionableness of such literary-critical narratives, traditional literary history tended to be sidelined and then fell into disrepair. Such history had still been in rude health when, as late as 1909, David Nichol Smith, lecturing at Oxford on the familiar theme of 'The Functions of Criticism', could confidently declare: 'The kind of criticism which of late has been making the greatest advances, which alone may claim to have made any real advance, is, in one form or another, historical.' He instanced the names of several of the best-known literary historians of the day, such as George Saintsbury, Walter Raleigh, and W. P. Ker (he also, rather surprisingly, included A. C. Bradley in this list, though it seems unlikely that contemporary readers would have seen Bradley as any kind of 'historical' critic).[35] But from about 1920 onwards the fall from grace of such literary history was very marked. In the 1960s George Watson observed that no literary histories had been written to replace the older works by Saintsbury and Oliver Elton. 'Literary history', he concluded, 'has never had such a shamefaced air as in the half-century since the First World War'.[36]

In reassessing literary history, critics in the middle decades of the twentieth century were also addressing a shift in the place of poetry in the national culture. Until at least the late nineteenth century, poetry remained the most admired genre (the novel far exceeded it in popularity, of course), and even when subgenres such as epic or long narrative poems began to decline, the lyric retained its sway, confirmed in its pre-eminence by sources as different as Arnold's criticism and Palgrave's anthology. Up to 1914, proposals for the study of English literature at university still meant, above all, the line of English poets and poet-dramatists from Chaucer to the present. And it was still the case that poetry was very widely read and, occasionally, could still sell in large quantities, as the different cases of Rudyard Kipling and Rupert Brooke illustrated. Although many of these conditions continued to obtain in some form after 1918, both the popular and academic situation of poetry changed. Poetry was increasingly becoming a minority interest, one principally associated with the highbrow side of the new division of the brows. Moreover, it was clear that the poetry of earlier centuries was increasingly being read in an archaeological or academic spirit. This was the premise of Empson's *Seven Types of Ambiguity* (published in 1930): readers were constantly confronted with examples of poetry from more distant periods but now needed help to understand and appreciate them. And the old confidence that poetry taught a form of truth about life—a confidence still in rude health in Palgrave—was increasingly challenged by ideas such as those of I. A. Richards that saw poetry as a kind of 'pseudo-statement', functioning by emotive or evocative means rather than by propositional statement. Poetry continued to be the central genre for literary histories long after it had ceased to be the central genre for contemporary readers.

V

At the heart of the elevated claims made from the 1920s to the 1960s for the reading of literature were assumptions about the ways in which criticism, of the approved kind, enabled readers to possess and articulate an experience whose intensity and purity necessarily transcended anything available from 'everyday life', where such life was tainted with all the cramped or shallow character assumed to typify 'modernity'. Nearly all invocations of the extraordinarily protean term 'modernity' involve a more or less tendentious schematizing of historical change. One possible correlative of this cluster of assumptions was the implication that a desirable 'wholeness' of experience (as it was often termed) had in fact been available as part of everyday life in earlier periods, but that it had been lost or destroyed by processes of social change and so now needed to be recuperated or re-created through a certain kind of intensely attentive reading. There is a pastoral inflection to most such stories: the past is assumed to be simpler, more transparent, less dependent on 'technology' (understood, implausibly, as a novel phenomenon); responses to experience were more 'instinctive' then, less the result of analysis and debate; more 'natural' (blessed word). The whole perspective is shot through with ideas of 'community' as something different from, and better than, forms of social coexistence available in the present.

Inevitably, these historical characterizations drew on received views about some of the major periods of history, which were in turn often derived from widely selling history books of previous generations. To a surprising extent, some of the most radical critiques of 'mass society' or 'commercialism' in the middle decades of the twentieth century rested indirectly on pictures of the past drawn from such 'authorities' as G. M. Trevelyan and J. L. and Barbara Hammond or even J. A. Froude and Leslie Stephen. In turn, widely read works of literary criticism and literary history helped to disseminate such views to audiences—whether in universities or teacher-training colleges, in adult education or among the Penguin-reading public—who turned to literary criticism for illumination about how to live, a palatable form of moral philosophy as well as an easily assimilable form of history, all the more effective for not being hedged around with the increasingly professionalized protocols governing Philosophy and History as academic disciplines. Arguably, such criticism did damage by its promotion of an adversarial or redemptive function for literature, its perpetuation of an unanalysed binary opposition between 'culture' and 'society', and its casual homogenization of 'modernity'.

Part of the argument of this book, therefore, is that even the supposedly 'purest' or most formalist versions of literary criticism always, in practice, depended upon and secreted various types of historical understanding. My focus is on Britain: the history of the so-called New Criticism in the United States was a related but distinct development, operating in a very different cultural and institutional setting, and anyway the wider cultural role of American criticism in this period has been extensively studied by others. More specifically, I concentrate on a small number of the major critics who did most to shape this practice over the period in question, such as T. S. Eliot, F. R. Leavis, William Empson, and Raymond Williams. Though these are the figures I attend to in greatest detail, others have their parts to play, notably Basil Willey, L. C. Knights, Q. D. Leavis, and Richard Hoggart. This selection of names is itself entirely conventional, reflecting their various forms of prominence at the time. I would not wish to propose, least of all in a book derived from the Ford Lectures, that the necessary condition of doing any interesting literary-critical thinking in the period between 1919 and 1961 was an affiliation to the University of Cambridge, but its centrality is in this case unignorable. Apart from Eliot, these figures were all university teachers for at least part of their careers; and, apart from Queenie Leavis, they were all male. But institutional definition is not what unites my chosen critics: rather, there is an established intellectual and personal filiation that binds them'. Also, they, more than any other selection, came to stand for the great achievements of 'literary criticism' in what may now seem like its heyday, and they were undoubtedly among the group that most decisively influenced subsequent generations of academic literary critics. Other selections of critics from this period could, of course, be made, and the story that could be told would alter accordingly. For instance, a broader survey of journalistic criticism in the period might range from, say, Virginia Woolf, John Middleton Murry, and Desmond MacCarthy up to, say, Cyril Connolly, Rebecca West, and V. S. Pritchett, but that would be to write an entirely different book (though one that would have the merit of attending to more women).

However, if my cast are familiar, I like to think that my treatment of them is rather less so. I shall argue that, in order to understand some of the most prominent works by literary critics that fall between, roughly speaking, *The Sacred Wood* and *The Long Revolution*, it will not be enough to focus on shifts of critical technique or the pressures of academic literary studies, just as we shall fail to grasp some of the widely influential ways the English came to interpret their history if we confine ourselves to the work of professional historians.[37] We must also think about more indirect ways of finding meaning in time, about ways of situating the present, and even about how people, including literary critics, half-remember the history they read earlier in life ('Where got I that truth?', as Yeats asked in his poem 'Fragments' about one quasi-historical flourish). In intending this book to be *simultaneously* a contribution to twentieth-century British intellectual history and a study in the history of literary criticism, I realize that I run the risk of failing to satisfy the two most obvious communities of readers onto whose territory I am venturing. But here I take some comfort from Eliot's own acknowledgement that 'you cannot treat literary criticism as a subject isolated from every other subject of study; you must take account of general history, of philosophy, theology, economics, psychology, into all of which literary criticism merges'.[38] The truth is, as the following chapters attempt to illustrate, that there is no escaping from history. Critics must also be historians, whether they acknowledge that fact or not. This book explores the ramifications of that claim with respect to the one group of critics who are conventionally thought to be the least likely to confirm it.

I

Whig History and the Mind
of England

I

Writing in 1970 in the introduction to the volume of *The New Cambridge Modern History* that dealt with the decline of Spain and the Thirty Years War in the seventeenth century, the volume editor, the Oxford historian J. P. Cooper, urged fellow historians to resist the temptation to rely, as he put it, upon 'modern myths such as "dissociation of sensibility" or "the organic society", as keys to too many, or in these two cases to any, doors'.[1] Scepticism towards large explanatory concepts may scarcely have been unusual from a mid-twentieth-century academic historian, but the particular 'modern myths' Cooper identified as having exercised a seductive attraction over others are, in this setting, surely very striking, indeed extraordinary. Would most of those now writing or studying the history of the European seventeenth century be likely even to have *heard* of these two notions, let alone to be tempted to use them in structuring their accounts? Why in 1970 would *historians* have had to be cautioned against them, and what world of discourse did they come from in the first place?

The importance of these and related notions, and the reasons behind Cooper's felt need to issue a caution against them, will be central elements in the story this book has to tell. For the moment, having begun with the seventeenth century, another quotation referring to the same period suggests itself. 'It is necessary to insist upon the unique character of the seventeenth century which, just because it experienced the acute crisis of transition from the old to the new Europe (to the Europe, we might say, of 1914), is the most difficult of all centuries to understand.' This is, by any measure, a historical statement, one that lays claim to know a good deal about what constituted both the old and the new Europe as well as to more than superficial knowledge about the seventeenth century. The rest of the paragraph that it introduces ranges widely over the place of religion in the political and international disputes of the time, including the growth of Puritanism in England and of Lutheranism and Calvinism in continental Europe. Taken by itself, the paragraph seems characteristic of the work of one of those confident, generalizing historians in the first half of the twentieth century, such as H. A. L. Fisher or perhaps of slightly later, somewhat more specialized but still wide-ranging, scholars such as G. N. Clark.

Similarly, to propose 'a study...of the temper and mind of the period from Henry VIII to Cromwell' that would take account of 'influences and interests political, philosophical, theological, and social' is, clearly, to propose a major work of history. In this latter case, the proposal was part of an application that was put before a committee of senior historians, but they were, it seems, not persuaded. They observed of the work submitted in support of the proposal that they were unable to 'find evidence of a depth of knowledge sufficient to justify the candidate's philosophical and historical conclusions'. That, at least, was the public form they gave to their judgement. The candidate's backer, who had been present at the crucial meeting, reported the reasons for rejection in somewhat different terms. First, some of what he called the 'professorial old women' had been shocked by the lack of decorum detected in a quite other genre of the candidate's writing than that relevant to the application. But second, and perhaps more important, had been what he called 'the narrow angular opposition of the academic historians to any kind of research other than that which they themselves understand'. Presumably, the historians in question would not have described the grounds of their opposition in quite such reductive terms, though long experience in universities may make such a description seem both plausible and dispiritingly familiar.

At first sight, what we have here is a recognizable minor episode in academic politics in which a younger historian's attempt to combine an over-ambitious project with a heterodox approach is firmly squashed by the elders of the tribe. In this instance, the episode also has an Oxford connection, since it was part of an application for a Fellowship at All Souls in 1926, and we know that the 'academic historians' included Sir Charles Oman, at the time the Chichele Professor of Modern History, and E. L. Woodward, later to be Professor of International Relations. So far, so familiar, but what gives this particular episode a larger interest and significance is the fact that the candidate in question was T. S. Eliot, and the full details of this episode came to light only with the publication of the relevant volume of his letters in 2012.[2] In addition, the earlier quotation, about 'the unique character of the seventeenth century', is taken, not from one of the historians I mentioned, but from Eliot himself. It occurs in the piece of work that he submitted in support of his application, the typescript of the Clark Lectures that he had delivered at Trinity College Cambridge earlier that year (and that were to remain unpublished during his lifetime).[3] By the end of those lectures, Eliot was disavowing any intention to supply the place of what he called the 'general historian': his bailiwick, he insisted unconvincingly, was poetry, and he had not meant, as he put it, to 'trespass' on the territory of 'history, social or political'. But then, perhaps—to paraphrase another representative twentieth-century figure—he would say that, wouldn't he?

In 1926, the year of his application to All Souls, Eliot was 38 years old: after working in Lloyds Bank for a number of years, he had recently joined the publishing firm of Faber and Gwyer, and it was his senior colleague Geoffrey Faber, a Fellow of All Souls, who had proposed him for election. By this date, Eliot had already established himself as the leading avant-garde poet and critic of his generation (the alleged indecency of some of the poetry may have been what had caused the 'professorial old women' at All Souls to take fright). Before long, he was to achieve that pontifical sway over English letters that lasted at least until the end of the 1950s. Moreover, those styles of literary criticism that claimed to take their inspiration from Eliot became the dominant fashions in the study of literature in British and American universities between the 1930s and 1960s. This reputation and this influence, the standing and reach of which may now be hard to appreciate, gives an added edge to any reconsideration of Eliot's early critical prose that attends, instead, to its often fragmentary or covert character as an attempt to write a kind of history.

The question of the critic's bad conscience about historians will be a recurring topic in what follows, but we should first note the surprisingly sustained character of Eliot's engagement with history and historians in the early and mid-1920s. Writing to Ezra Pound in September 1923, Eliot defended his journal, the *Criterion*, against Pound's intemperately expressed charges of timidity and conformism. As an example of the journal's heterodoxy, Eliot instanced the hostility that he believed had been directed by the literary establishment against the Shakespearean scholar and rationalist J. M. Robertson as a result of his association with Eliot and his periodical. Writing to his mother in October 1923, Eliot cited Robertson and Charles Whibley as 'allies...of an elder generation'. But Robertson, Eliot complained to Pound, 'is NOT reviewed any longer by *The Times* or the bloomsbury [*sic*] press in consequence, and...although he is a whig the whig vermin will not associate with him'.[4] It is scarcely surprising that correspondence with Pound tended to bring Eliot out in such excesses as 'vermin', but his choice of adjective is surely striking. If in 1923 one were looking for a single disparaging adjective with which to describe respectable literary London and its fashionable Bloomsbury offshoot, especially if one were writing from the perspective of experimental post-*Imagiste* poetry and unsparingly rigorous literary criticism, the term 'whig' does not seem an obvious choice. A label originally deriving from English party politics, it had, of course, come more generally to be applied to a style of history-writing that told a story of constitutional and social progress, celebrating the native English gift for restrained liberty. So why, looking around the influential literary editors and reviewers in London in the early 1920s, would Eliot, in writing to one of his closest confidants, choose to disparage these particular vermin as 'whig'?

One simple, even simplistic, way to answer the question would be to invoke the contrasting party-political label and to say that it was because Eliot identified himself as a 'Tory', and anyway that an element of datedness or archaism about so using these terms appealed to him. There is obviously some truth to this, though in 1923 Eliot had yet to fully elaborate that high-and-dry reactionary and Anglican persona that characterized so many of his public performances in the second half of his life. But the narrowly political reference seems an inadequate explanation for his choice, especially in the early 1920s, not least because by that date the term was far more current to describe a form of history than a form of politics. As I shall illustrate, Eliot used the term 'whig' with some frequency, and the association between an interpretation of history and a range of wider cultural attitudes lay at the heart of this usage.

Eliot's *Kulturkampf* against what he at one point termed 'the contemporary degeneracy that one loathes' was conducted on many levels.[5] That his *poetry* involved a kind of dislocation of time has become a standard characterization, but the engagement of his *criticism* with history in the narrower and more conventional sense tends to be neglected. In this chapter, I want to suggest that, in the early and mid-1920s in particular, Eliot found himself drawn into the task of reconfiguring the relation of the English to their past, and that this involved him in attempting to dispossess the 'whigs' of their ownership of that history. His chosen terrain for these endeavours was, for the most part, literary history, but, as he increasingly emphasized, it was impossible to maintain a strict demarcation between literary history and what he and his contemporaries usually referred to as 'general history'. In other words, if one wanted to challenge the late-Romantic aesthetic represented by Georgian poetry and its admirers, one was eventually driven to becoming a historian of the seventeenth century.

II

One of the difficulties involved in characterizing the historical framework around which so much of Eliot's early criticism was elaborated is deciding just how seriously to take it. By this I do not just mean the problem, familiar to readers of his writing more generally, of knowing when he is mocking various manifestations of misplaced earnestness or even parodying certain conventional styles and ways of going on. I mean that it is frequently unclear whether his apparently historical assertions are intended to be true claims about the past or whether they are more a device, a kind of rhetorical flourish, intended to endow unfamiliar or outrageous claims about poetry with some added authority. When, for example, he writes: 'And the sixteenth century was a chaotic period which apparently has little to show for itself, but was doing the work that made the seventeenth century possible', we would do well not to judge him by the chastest protocols of academic historiography.[6] In thinking about his critical writing during its most fertile decade, we should always remember the element of cultural experimentation and role-playing in both his writing and his life, in addition to the demands of ambition as this particular recent immigrant tried to make a name for himself in literary London. Still, the more closely we scrutinize his critical writings, the more we see they are shot through with historical (or perhaps meta- or even pseudo-historical) assertions, and so, while not forgetting Old Possum's taste for tricks and disguises, it is important to try to take the measure of these assertions.

There have been numerous interpretations of the development of Eliot's career and reputation. Here I shall simply assert—I have tried to provide the supporting evidence elsewhere—that his standing as a critic initially rested on the review essays he wrote for the *Athenaeum* and the *Times Literary Supplement* between 1919 and 1921.[7] These pieces—several of which reappeared in his first collection, *The Sacred Wood*, published in 1920 and others in *Homage to John Dryden* in 1924—memorably make the case for literary criticism understood not as a statement of personal preferences or as a rapturous enthusing over literary beauty, but as the strenuous application of intelligence. Can they also be said to have encouraged contemporary English readers to understand aspects of their history in unfamiliar terms? For the most part, his essays do this only indirectly, glancingly, almost invisibly. It certainly cannot be said that Eliot rewrites 'general history' in any familiar or recognizable form; it cannot even be said that he provides a coherent, joined-up alternative to the established kinds of literary history at the time. Nonetheless, I want to suggest, a form of history or quasi-history is what some of his early criticism also provides.

It is well known, of course, that in the *second* half of his career Eliot elaborated a variety of historical or quasi-historical views as part of his increasingly conservative social criticism.[8] Those later views have a place both in Eliot's biography and in the wider intellectual history of the period,[9] but they provide less of a challenge than his earlier work precisely because they were so explicit, so self-consciously conservative, and so largely extrinsic to his literary criticism. It is in his prose of the years from 1919 to 1927 that the most interesting and complex questions arise about the presence of various kinds of historical thinking and assumption in even the purest forms of literary analysis. Or rather—to put at least one card on the table in advance—this may be to say that there are no 'pure' forms of literary analysis.

In his prose of these years, Eliot is a 'historian' in the way that T. E. Hulme was a historian, which is to say both not one at all and somebody whose thinking increasingly revolved around a revision of the widely accepted secular stories about the path of progress in thought and sensibility since the Middle Ages. Hailing a posthumous collection of T. E. Hulme's writings in 1924, Eliot celebrated him as 'the antipodes of the eclectic, tolerant, and democratic mind of the end of the last century', a conjunction of qualities for which 'whig' became one of his favoured shorthands.[10] As early as his 'Reflections on Contemporary Poetry', when he was attacking the idea of poetry as a 'cry from the heart', Eliot wrote that 'I am inclined to believe that Tennyson's verse is a "cry from the heart"—only it is the heart of Tennyson, Latitudinarian, Whig, Laureate'.[11] Classifying Tennyson as a 'Whig' was deliberately transgressive, of course, but it is revealing that Eliot chose this historical term with which to condense so many of his antipathies. In a celebrated exchange with Middleton Murry in 1923, Eliot excoriated that blend of Romanticism and Liberalism that claimed to steer by no more fixed authority than 'the inner voice', adding: 'It is a voice to which, for convenience, we may give a name: and the name I suggest is Whiggery.'[12] Again, it may at first seem curious that Eliot should use this term derived from English history to designate that congeries of attitudes that constituted the opposite of his classicism. But for Eliot the term connoted all that he detested about nineteenth-century national self-congratulation, including (as his attack on Murry made clear) a faith in individuals, a lack of principles, and a belief in Muddling Through.

Macaulay, most celebrated of Whig historians, was a particular bugbear. Eliot frequently inveighed against 'the influence, for the most part pernicious, of Macaulay on literary and other opinion in England'.[13] For example, in 1923 he declared: 'The style of Macaulay is an eighteenth-century style debased by a journalistic exuberance and theatrical emotion.' Carlyle's style may have had its weaknesses, 'but if open licence is better than concealed depravity, his style is healthier than Macaulay's'.[14] 'Theatrical emotion', 'concealed depravity': these are scarcely minor failings or confined to the more technical aspects of writing history. And the emphasis on 'concealment' pointed to something that particularly irked Eliot about Whig history. 'Some of the most satisfactory historians', he ruled in a later unpublished piece, 'are those whose bias is unconcealed'.[15] It may be partly because his 'bias' was so little concealed that the Victorian historian whom Eliot relied upon with the fewest reservations was J. A. Froude, whose *The Reign of Elizabeth* was the text Eliot recommended for 'historical background' when he gave his first course of lectures on 'Elizabethan Literature' in 1918–19.[16] By contrast, when reviewing a reissue of G. P. Gooch's *English Democratic Ideas in the Seventeenth Century* in the *Criterion* in 1927 Eliot complained: 'It is one of those liberal-historical treatises which appear wholly impartial and are in fact extremely biased.... The tendency is Republican and the author appears to be in sympathy with religious movements in so far as they are rebellious.'[17] (Gooch's book has more recently been described as 'a defence of Protestant individualism as the basis of modern egalitarian ideas'.[18]) After this, it comes as no surprise to find that the most authoritative modern account of early twentieth-century English historiography briskly characterizes Gooch as 'a confirmed whig'.[19] By contrast, the historians whom Eliot cultivated, such as Charles Whibley, Kenneth Pickthorn, and Charles Smyth, were all strongly identified as anti-Whig—which is clearly what Whibley meant when he recommended Pickthorn to Eliot as 'a sound historian with sound views'.[20]

Eliot's parallel engagement with the question of how literary history might be written began earlier and was more extensive than is commonly recognized. Remarkably, no fewer than five of the reviews he wrote for the *Athenaeum* between April and August 1919 were about such works.[21] Predictably, he finds shortcomings in all of them, chiefly those written by professors, and especially those written by American professors. Where the authors attempt to sketch in the relevant general history, they merely produce, claims Eliot, 'a jumble of stage properties in [the] background'.[22] And yet something on this scale is essential, for, as he tellingly observes (in a sentence that serves as an epigraph to this book): 'The historian of literature must count with as shifting and as massive forces as the historian of politics.'[23] The beginnings of a recipe for better literary history emerge from the least unfavourable of these pieces, a review of a volume of George Saintsbury's *History of the French Novel*: 'Mr Saintsbury is a master of the literary history—a form of writing which demands qualifications of its own. The literary historian needs critical gifts, but his task is not that of the critic. He needs a sense of values, but he has little occasion to exercise it beyond the mere indication of the place of the great...', and so on.[24]

In the course of the early and mid-1920s, Eliot toyed with ways to replace conventional literary history with accounts that were driven by the critic's 'sense of values'. At the same time, as part of his own spiritual development, he took his distance from almost all post-medieval literature, since it had all been corrupted by the taint of 'humanism'. An extreme but revealing illustration of his radically revisionist handling of literary history is provided by a lecture that he gave in Cambridge in 1924 but never published (it was published for the first time as part of the online *Complete Prose* in 2014). Entitled, modestly but misleadingly, 'A Neglected Aspect of Chapman', the lecture ranged back to Dante and forward to Dostoevsky. Chapman, like Donne, is criticized for 'an internal incoherence, as of an era of transition and decay'. Eliot proposes, invoking Hulme, to 'call the period which includes Chapman and Dostoevski the humanist period'. 'My point is', Eliot underlined, 'that Chapman and Dostoevski and ourselves are all part of a modern world and that Dante belonged to another and perhaps a wiser one'. And he drove home the revisionist moral: 'I know that the Elizabethan literature is usually regarded as a golden age, instead of an age of decomposition,' but he insisted that Chapman (and Donne) must be seen as part of that long development, coming down to the present, 'which accepted the divorce of human and divine, denied the divine, and asserted the perfection of the human to be the divine'.[25] The lecture was, by Eliot's own admission, hurriedly composed and more than usually scrappy—two days before he was due to deliver it, he described it to Richard Aldington as 'still in very rough shape', a judgement borne out by the evidence of the unpolished typescript; writing to Virginia Woolf several days later he reported that the lecture was 'unworthy of subsequent publication'—but it presented in correspondingly stark form the concerns that were agitating him as he struggled to reshape his, and his culture's, literary inheritance.[26]

In the end, he did not write a general literary history himself—indeed, Eliot, notoriously, did not write books: he wrote essays, lectures, and reviews, and then made books out of a selection of these shorter forms. The three most sustained pieces of prose he wrote were his Ph.D. dissertation, his Clark Lectures, and his Norton Lectures in 1933, and it is telling that, first, all three were instances of what Larkin later termed 'required writing', and, second, that two of them remained unpublished in his lifetime. But, although in the case of the Clark Lectures that decision may have reflected more than even his usual level of self-criticism and dissatisfaction, there is a case for saying that they constituted the most sustained piece of history that Eliot wrote in the first half of his career, and it is for what they tell us about the historical character of his thinking at this point that I want to use them here.

The Clark Lectures present themselves as an investigation into the character of 'metaphysical poetry'. By this, Eliot means not just the work of those early seventeenth-century writers conventionally labelled, following Dr Johnson, 'the Metaphysicals'. Rather, he structures the lectures around comparisons between the poetry of three periods—that of Dante and his associates in the thirteenth century, that of Donne and certain other poets in the early seventeenth century, and that of the followers of Baudelaire, especially Laforgue and Corbière, in France in the late nineteenth century. 'It is these moments of history,' he writes, 'when human sensibility is momentarily *enlarged in certain directions* to be defined, that I propose to call the metaphysical periods'. They are periods when 'the revolution of the sphere of thought will so to speak throw off ideas which will fall within the attraction of poetry, and which the operation of poetry will transmute into the immediacy of feeling'.[27] Even these little bits of preliminary throat-clearing suggest that an enquiry into those 'moments of history when human sensibility is momentarily *enlarged in certain directions*' and into those periods when 'the revolution of the sphere of thought... throw[s] off' certain ideas is no narrowly literary enterprise.

Furthermore, focusing on the poetry of three periods cannot be a merely definitional or taxonomic exercise: it is bound to involve some implied story of the transitions from one to another, and hence a trajectory of some sort. In the Clark Lectures, the connections and contrasts are neither left wholly implicit but nor are they given fully historical status either. Insofar as there is a single thread, it is provided by his phrase 'the disintegration of the intellect'. Quite what this means is never clear; it seems to have more to do with the separation of thought from feeling than any more encompassing break-up, though the culturally pessimistic implications of the phrase were obviously congenial to Eliot. At one level, the lectures are a remarkably high-handed confection of literary and intellectual history even by the standards of this notoriously high-handed critic. We are offered sketches of transitions in sensibility between centuries, even epochs, with considerable citation of philosophical and religious history to buttress the claims he makes principally on the basis of noting certain contrasts in poetic styles. They effectively assert the superiority of the unified sensibility of the thirteenth century, where feeling was allegedly suffused with the deeply held beliefs of a philosophically articulated religion, over the seventeenth century, or at least Donne, where traces of various thought-worlds are present but not fully integrated, and that period in turn was superior to the nineteenth century, where the examples of Tennyson and Swinburne demonstrate what he called 'a further stage in the disintegration of the intellect, the further separation of sound, image and thought'.[28]

But the moments of confident assertion or calculated outrageousness, so familiar from Eliot's early criticism, should not lead us to overlook those passages where he seems suddenly seized by a kind of self-consciousness or embarrassment about the extent of his bare-faced trespassing on the historian's domain, prompting him to issue nervous disclaimers. For instance, at the end of the fifth lecture (of eight), he suddenly says of his contrasts between the work of Dante and of Donne: 'The differences involve a certain theory of the disintegration of the intellect in modern Europe.' But then Eliot immediately retreats, stressing that he is concerned 'primarily with poetry, not with modern Europe and its progress or decline'. He then cannot resist adding a final sarcastic flourish to mark his distance even more emphatically, insisting that it is not for him to identify whether this 'disintegration' is good or bad: 'to draw its optimistic or pessimistic conclusions is an occupation for prophets and makers of almanacks, of whom I am not one.'[29] In reality, even the Eliot of this date is not averse to donning the mantle of the prophet when it suits him, but the function here of this lordly wave of the hand is to turn away in advance any expectation that he could be doing something that, he wants us to understand, is best left to quacks and hacks. Of course, the mannered disclaimer would not be necessary had he not in fact been offering just such large-scale characterizations of a species of cultural decline. It is hard to know whether to attach any significance to the fact that he does not at this point suggest that concern with 'modern Europe and its progress or decline' might reasonably be considered an occupation, not for 'prophets and makers of almanacks', but for *historians*.

Sometimes he does not even apologize: he hurries on like the nervous guest who does not wish to draw further attention to a faux pas. Observing the difficulty of tracing the continuity of the type of conceit characteristic of Donne in the work of the next generation, he immediately says: 'It is only by grasping the movement of the whole period, from Elizabeth to Cromwell, as an integrity, that one can form any conception of the conceit or of this type of metaphysical poetry.'[30] Such a self-interruption might have seemed less disruptive if he had written that one had to 'grasp the movement of the whole period from (say) Jonson to Marvell' or some other representative writers. But by insisting so emphatically that it is *only* 'by grasping the movement of the *whole* period, from Elizabeth to Cromwell, as an *integrity*' that one can 'form *any* conception' either of the conceit or of metaphysical poetry, he sets the historical bar unreachably high (and may seem to call into question the feasibility of the project of his lectures). In fact, the effect of blurting out this admission is to draw attention to the very lack in his lectures of any sustained attention to social, political, or economic history—the kind of thing that would constitute an understanding of the period 'from Elizabeth to Cromwell'. There is a truth here that Eliot seems to want simultaneously to acknowledge, apologize for, and erase.

We encounter another instance of this half-recognition of the claims of 'general history' as Eliot approaches the end of his final lecture. He anticipates that some of his audience will be dissatisfied with his failure to have supplied a 'neat and comprehensive definition' of the metaphysical poets of the seventeenth century, and then affects to remind them of the contract between lecturer and audience: 'But I think I warned you in advance, that

I did not intend to define the seventeenth century, or the first half of it—for to do that I should have had to draw in the background much more completely, with the figures of James, and Charles, and Hooker, and Laud, and Hyde and Strafford.'[31] But surely no member of the audience could, after seeing his announced title or still less after attending his first lecture, have expected him to do *that*. It is often a mark of the guilty that they rebut a charge that has not yet been laid against them. Whether out of an unease at addressing a largely academic audience on this occasion or out of his own sense of the impossibility of separating literary history from general history, Eliot keeps disowning an obligation of which he nonetheless feels the force.

This tension surfaces again in a peroration in which he at last frankly acknowledges that 'you cannot treat literary criticism as a subject isolated from every other subject of study: you must take account of general history, of philosophy, theology, economics, psychology, into all of which literary criticism merges', and so on.[32] But each time, in these final pages, that he protests his innocence, he in effect confirms his guilt. He insists that he has only been concerned with 'the progressive deterioration of poetry, in one respect or another, since the thirteenth century', but he at once concedes that this is 'probably only one aspect of a general deterioration'—suggesting that the company of those 'prophets and makers of almanacks' is not so easy to shake off.[33]

The European frame of Eliot's criticism was one way of relativizing English parochialism, just as his cultivation of the more recondite or remote features of literary and intellectual history was a way of undercutting the temporal parochialism that saw the Victorian period as the culmination of cultural progress. (As he was to express it later: 'It is the endless task of men of letters to disturb the provincialism of their particular place and time.')[34] Eliot knew that he was addressing a readership whose self-understanding very considerably depended on forms of historical identification, and his early criticism involves a series of oblique assaults on the received celebratory story. Seen thus, his Clark Lectures may be said to constitute a kind of anti-Palgrave. Part of the drama of the development of Eliot's literary-historical thinking in the 1920s lies in the way in which his brilliant recasting of the central notion of Imagism as a means of identifying the superiority of Elizabethan and Jacobean poetry hardens into an assertion about poetry's necessary dependence on religious, and indeed eventually ecclesiastical, orthodoxy. But from the outset there is in Eliot's prose also the half-guilty acknowledgement that such a recasting of literary history would need to be underwritten by a larger rewriting of 'general history' than he could provide.

After Eliot had delivered his Clark Lectures, he had them bound in a typescript, to which he added a brief preface (this was presumably the form in which they were submitted in support of his All Souls application). Here he announced, as applicants do, that the 'completed book' of his lectures would be far more thorough and well documented, adding (as, again, applicants tend to do):

> The completed book on *The School of Donne*...is intended as one volume of a trilogy under the general title of 'The Disintegration of the Intellect': the other two volumes will deal with *Elizabethan Drama*, its technical development, its versification, and its intellectual background of general ideas; and with *The Sons of Ben*—the development of humanism, its relation to Anglican thought, and the emergence of Hobbes and Hyde. The three together will constitute a criticism of the English Renaissance.[35]

This makes it sound as though Eliot had embarked on a major piece of critical intellectual history not unlike, say, Basil Willey's *Seventeenth-Century Background*. But it is worth remembering that, where the announcing of never-written books is concerned, Eliot had form. The three books he was not writing in 1926 were different from the two he was not writing in 1924, as announced in the preface to *Homage to John Dryden*,[36] and different again from the three he was not writing in 1928, as announced in the preface to *For Lancelot Andrewes*.[37] All three statements involved a certain amount of posturing and perhaps even more than the usual amount of authorly self-deception when announcing future projects (none of these volumes, needless to say, was ever written). Still, this sequence of unwritten books neatly charts Eliot's development across the mid-1920s, away from what he came to regard as an overly pure concentration on poetry as poetry in *The Sacred Wood* and towards, as he put it in the 1928 introduction to the reissue of that volume, a focus on 'the relation of poetry to the spiritual and social life of its time and of other times'[38]—or, in other words, a strengthening conviction that what was needed was a more extended engagement with large-scale intellectual and cultural history. It cannot be said that Eliot ever pursued that engagement in any systematic fashion, continuing instead to throw out sweeping pseudo-historical judgements such as this from his Norton Lectures:

> The history of every branch of intellectual activity provides the same record of the diminution of England from the time of Queen Anne. It is not so much

the intellect, but something superior to the intellect, which went for a long time into eclipse; and this luminary, by whatever name we may call it, has not yet wholly emerged from its secular obnubilation.[39]

The precise meaning of this cloudy assertion suffers from some obnubilation of its own, but it does suggest that there were moments when Eliot was willing to allow that a state of relative cultural or intellectual health may have persisted even beyond the Civil War and the Restoration.

III

I have thus far deliberately stayed away from the most obvious and best-known, as well as most influential, example of Eliot's historical or meta-historical claims from these years. But when seen in the context of the preoccupations I have just been discussing, this claim falls into place as one of Eliot's more provoking flirtations with a form of revisionist historical narrative. The claim in question was first formulated in the *Times Literary Supplement* of 20 October 1921. In a review essay loosely hung round H. J. C. Grierson's anthology *Metaphysical Lyrics and Poems of the Seventeenth Century*, the reviewer (still at that point anonymous, of course) asserted that in Donne and other so-called 'Metaphysical Poets' there is a quality that can also be found in Chapman—namely, 'a direct sensuous apprehension of thought, or a recreation of thought into feeling'. The reviewer briefly contrasted an example of this style with passages from Browning and Tennyson, and then went on:

> The difference is not a simple difference of degree between poets. It is something which had happened to the mind of England between the time of Donne or Lord Herbert of Cherbury and the time of Tennyson and Browning.... We may express the difference by the following theory: The poets of the seventeenth century, the successors of the dramatists of the sixteenth, possessed a mechanism of sensibility which could devour any kind of experience.... In the seventeenth century a dissociation of sensibility set in, from which we have never recovered...[40]

In the half-century or so after its first appearance, this claim became part of the furniture of literary and intellectual discussion in Britain. As early as 1925, Edwin Muir could observe that 'Mr Eliot's diagnosis of the increasing psychological debility of English poetry since the time of the Elizabethans and their immediate successors is sufficiently well known...'. Identifying the 'dissociation of sensibility' as the root of the decline, Muir added: 'That this analysis is accepted as a truism by intelligent people today is due chiefly to Mr Eliot.'[41] But, although the idea has been endlessly, and often critically, discussed in subsequent scholarship, perhaps even this great volume of commentary has not quite identified the peculiar character of the *historical* claim being made here. Obviously, Eliot is implicitly establishing an affinity between the poetry of the early seventeenth century and contemporary poetry influenced by Symbolism and *Imagisme*, thereby downgrading pretty much all poetry between the mid-seventeenth and the early twentieth centuries. But to explain this by claiming that 'something... happened to the mind of England' during the intervening period does seem to be using an extremely large and unwieldy historical sledgehammer to crack a relatively modest literary nut.

Similarly, the assertion that 'in the seventeenth century a dissociation of sensibility set in, from which we have never recovered' involves a polemical surplus almost comic in its excess. The provocative form of these assertions may seem designed to make the professional historian bridle. 'The mind of England' has not been, shall we say, a favoured unit of analysis in modern historiography. It is also noticeable that Eliot does not even gesture towards an explanation of the change, certainly not in political, social, or economic terms: the dissociation simply 'set in'. Poets possessed the 'mechanism' up till the mid-seventeenth century and then it was lost. Still, the claim cannot just be dismissed as the semaphore of the hurried reviewer or the axe-grinding of the critic who favours one type of poetry over another and wishes to furnish his preference with some weighty legitimation, though both those descriptions may say something true about the review in question. Beyond all that, the structure of Eliot's claim evidently involves movement from a kind of wholeness to a kind of fragmentation: what had been fused in a unity was thereafter sundered into separate parts and not only in poetry. That the change, as represented, is to be regretted is clear; as in most such meta-historical claims, wholeness carries a positive charge, separation connotes a fall.

Eliot cannot be held wholly responsible for the extraordinary afterlife of this idea in literary and cultural discussion of the next forty years; it belonged, he later reflected somewhat disingenuously, among those 'few notorious phrases which have had a truly embarrassing success in the world'.[42] But nor was he entirely innocent in the matter of its longevity; after all, he reprinted the review essay in which it occurs several times, first in the slim volume of 1924, then in his *Selected Essays* of 1932, and then again in the revised and expanded edition of that collection in 1951, by which time he was well aware that, partly as a by-product of his own unmatched cultural standing, his sweeping yet offhand claim had come to be treated as a serious contribution to the understanding of history.

IV

'Mr Eliot' was an unignorable presence in English literary culture from the late 1920s to the early 1960s. To describe that presence as 'pontifical', the regulation adjective, risks suggesting that his authority rested on one particular institutional identity, but it does not exaggerate its reach. Certainly, any discussion of the ways in which understandings of history were expressed through literary criticism in these decades needs to take the measure of Eliot's role, not least because others so often cited him, deferred to him, criticized him, misrepresented him. Thus far, we have considered his engagement with history in the prose written in, roughly, the decade leading up to his formal conversion to Anglicanism in 1927.[43] In moving on to address, much more briefly, his later career, we encounter a double difficulty. First, there is the fact—and it surely is a fact, not merely a statement of aesthetic preference—that his later work on the whole lacked the intensity and sharpness of his best criticism, especially that written between, say, 1919 and 1923. And, secondly, there is the mediating presence of his reputation: what 'Mr Eliot' was alleged to think becomes, in these later years, almost as important in contemporary cultural discussion as what he actually thought. Of course, 1927 did not mark any kind of clean break in Eliot's work: one can, if so minded, detect signs of an Anglo-Catholic sensibility before 1927 just as easily as one can demonstrate continuities with his earlier writing thereafter. But both Eliot's role and the character of his writing did change once his confessional affiliation became a defining public identity, and we need at least to note, however briefly, the consequences of that change for his dealings with history.

In some ways, the slightly pompous, stilted character occasionally detectable in his later prose could be said to have gone along with the expression of rather more conventional or predictable views. The provocative ironies and wilful obliquities of the earlier prose give way to a form of statement that is more eirenic and more cautious, as well as simply more of a 'statement'.

It is also notable that his later views, though presented as those of 'a man of letters', derive less directly from the practice of his literary criticism.[44] In particular, his later social criticism does not seem to depend so closely upon the kind of revisionist literary history that had underpinned his earlier polemical flourishes. Nonetheless, his later social criticism needs to be attended to, partly to correct any onesidedness in my treatment of the earlier writings (where I did not dwell on their religious inclinations, such as they are), and partly because his later views were such important points of reference for literary critics writing in the 1940s and 1950s.[45]

In one obvious respect, Eliot's work became more explicitly historical after 1927. To define oneself as an 'Anglo-Catholic' was to take one's stand upon history. As a confessional identity, this strain within Anglicanism depended upon making a case about the continuity of the 'Catholic Church in England', a continuity that, according to the most strenuous accounts, stretched from Augustine to the present. Anglicanism, on this view, was not created by Henry VIII, even if it was during his reign that the yoke of subjection to Rome was removed (an argument that, in turn, pushed English Roman Catholics to the margins of the national society thereafter). And so it was not in the strict sense a 'Protestant' church: its theology and liturgy drew upon the teachings of the sixteenth-century reformers but it blended these with older traditions, especially in matters of church governance and of ritual. Cranmer and Elizabeth played important parts, but so did Richard Hooker and such early seventeenth-century divines as Lancelot Andrewes and William Laud. Anglo-Catholicism was, therefore, an intrinsically historical identity that could involve, depending on context, emphasizing various historical reference points: 'the ideal of the primitive church; the medieval English church; the English High Church tradition, particularly as it developed from the earlier seventeenth century; and, of course, the contemporary Western Church, as centred in Rome.'[46] Eliot engaged with all these sources at different moments, but an obvious strand of continuity with his earlier literary writings was the primacy he gave to the late sixteenth and early seventeenth centuries.

Anglo-Catholicism could trace its own genealogy back to the Tractarian movement of the 1830s and 1840s, but it particularly flourished in the early decades of the twentieth century, reaching its peak of influence in the interwar years (just as religious observance and church membership more generally were beginning what was eventually to be a precipitous decline).[47] It is important to remember its prominent and partly official position during these years, since it meant that Eliot did not think of himself as speaking from a dissident or iconoclastic position: indeed, he came to be recognized as a leading Anglo-Catholic layman, and that entailed writing with a somewhat different literary voice. At the same time, his meditations led from literary history to ecclesiastical history and then on to more sociological questions about the character of 'community' and 'culture' in the modern world. His earlier pronouncements about 'order' had tended to be formal or doctrinal; now he made efforts to specify some of the necessary social conditions for the kinds of 'order' he was recommending. 'Tradition' became 'social tradition', requiring recourse to different aspects of history.

'The Church of England is the creation not of the reign of Henry VIII or of the reign of Edward VI, but of the reign of Elizabeth', since she attempted to 'find a mean between Papacy and Presbytery'. This is Eliot, writing in 1926, the year before he was received into the Church of England, controverting the popular assumption about the beginnings of Anglicanism. He went on to analyse the differences between the sermons of Hugh Latimer and those of Lancelot Andrewes in best Anglo-Catholic manner, suggesting that the key lay not in their different audiences or occasions: 'It is rather that Latimer, the preacher of Henry VIII and Edward VI, is merely a Protestant; but the voice of Andrewes is the voice of a man who has a formed visible Church behind him. . . . Andrewes is the first great preacher of the English Catholic Church.'[48] The bulk of the essay is devoted to insisting on Andrewes's superiority to Donne, not least in his greater intimacy with the traditions of the medieval church. It has some claim to be Eliot's first significant attempt to revisit ecclesiastical history for contemporary polemical purposes. Perhaps by the very purest Anglo-Catholic standards it could still seem a little too 'Protestant' in not tracing the 'English Catholic Church' back to Augustine, but at this point Eliot's attention was focused overwhelmingly on the late sixteenth and early seventeenth centuries.

When, alerted by the new preoccupations of the piece on Lancelot Andrewes, the editor of *Theology* wrote to its author inviting him to contribute to his journal and proposing in the first instance a piece on a new biography of Archbishop Bramhall, Eliot, in accepting, indicated that the two further figures he was particularly keen to write about were Hooker and Laud.[49] The review essay on Bramhall combined some of his earlier manner with his more recent concerns. Yet again, Eliot disclaims any standing as a historian: 'With the purely historical matter I am not competent to deal; Bramhall's life includes an important part of the history of the Church and the history of England.' But, as even the second half of that sentence indicates, he is not shy about making historical claims. One of the most striking comes in the course of his undisguisedly hostile account of Bramhall's opponent in philosophical controversy, Thomas Hobbes, including this remarkably dismissive sneer: 'Thomas Hobbes was one of those extraordinary little upstarts whom the chaotic motions of the Renaissance tossed into an eminence which they hardly deserved and have never lost.' No less striking is the calculated snub to liberal historical assumptions contained in the gloss to his use of 'Renaissance':

> When I say the Renaissance I mean for this purpose the period between the decay of scholastic philosophy and the rise of modern science. The thirteenth century had the gift of philosophy, or reason; the later seventeenth century had the gift of mathematics, or science; but the period between had ceased to be rational without having learned to be scientific.[50]

So much for the 'rebirth' of Western thought.

Eliot spelled out some of his assumptions about the specific character of English history in two articles on 'The English Tradition' contributed to *Christendom* in 1940.[51] One central theme was the way in which social and religious life could not be clearly separated: 'The civil history of England, and its religious history, are the same with only a difference of emphasis and detail', and hence 'the chief common defect of most histories of England is that they are written with an inadequate understanding, an unexamined bias, or a lack of interest, in respect of religious forces'. He instanced the parish system to illustrate the indivisibility of church and society, but it is noticeable that, in elaborating on its dependence on communal norms of landholding and tithe-paying, he stretched the point in a potentially radical direction:

> a form of tenure of land suitable to an agricultural society, in which man's dependence upon the fruits of the soil created a responsible relationship, becomes grotesque when it applies to the subterranean stores of coal and minerals which are irreplaceable, and also when it applies to the ground ownership of urban land used for habitation or industry.[52]

The contention that the usual rights of private property did not apply to mineral resources and urban land was a view with a long radical pedigree in English political thought, stretching back through Fabian and New Liberal thinkers to such figures as Henry George or the more radical followers of J. S. Mill in the Land Tenure Reform Association in the 1870s.[53] (Major

Douglas's 'Social Credit' theory, which aroused considerable interest in the 1930s among literary intellectuals, including Eliot, elaborated some not dissimilar ideas about the social bases of capitalist wealth.) Eliot does not in fact commit himself to any specific policy consequences of this claim, such as common ownership or even special taxation of land values, but what seems striking is, first, how relatively familiar this sentiment was in the social thought of the 1930s, and, second, that it could equally well sit alongside political opinions that were identified as conservative as those identified as radical.

In these articles Eliot also spells out a view of the different phases in the intertwining of church and society in English history. For example, the Erastianism detectable in the eighteenth century partly reflected, in his view, the low spiritual temperature of the eighteenth-century church and partly the close social relations between the clergy and the governing class. 'The most important change in the nineteenth century was surely the displace-ment of High Church by Anglo-Catholic, the consequent dissociation from the Tory Party, the recruitment of Anglo-Catholics from various political groupings, and their critical attitude, inspired by their increasing attention to problems of social justice, to both of the political parties.' At this point, he shows no sign of disapproving of this development or of being made at all uncomfortable by this ecumenical co-habitation with those of a radical pol-itical persuasion. Indeed, the 'critical attitude' is what, in one sense of the phrase, he favours, since he sees the main failing in English history to have been the assumption that 'we were Christians in an indefectibly Christian society'—that is, that in England the union of society and religion had been assumed to be so natural and so close that the ways in which in recent centuries religion had started to be sidelined or overruled had not been suf-ficiently appreciated.[54] 'We' now had to do better, a task which relied upon a more adequate grasp of the relevant social and religious history.

V

Eliot's claim about a 'dissociation of sensibility' became, as already noted, something of a literary-historical orthodoxy in the next three or four decades, utilized and discussed in countless books and articles—hence J. P. Cooper's warning, quoted earlier.[55] But Eliot was, as ever, ahead of his commentators in registering reservations. His 1947 British Academy lecture on Milton is celebrated for its partial retraction of the charges he had earlier laid against the poet, but, in the course of his reconsideration of his great predecessor, Eliot slipped in some significant historical observations. He noted that attitudes towards Milton's poetry cannot but be affected by attitudes towards his politics and his theology, and that these are not merely of antiquarian interest. 'The fact is simply that the Civil War of the seventeenth century, in which Milton is a symbolic figure, has never been concluded. The Civil War is not ended: I question whether any serious civil war ever does end.' He then goes on to offer this reflection on his own earlier claims about a 'dissociation of sensibility':

> If such a dissociation did take place, I suspect that the causes are too complex and profound to justify our accounting for the change in terms of literary criticism. All we can say is, that something like this did happen; that it had something to do with the Civil War; that it would even be unwise to say that it was caused by the Civil War, but that it is a consequence of the same causes which brought about the Civil War; that we must seek the causes in Europe, not in England alone...[56]

Eliot's Milton lecture is often cited as an example of his more concessive, eirenic later manner, as he smooths away the rough edges of his earlier, more spikily performative prose. But in some ways this passage could be seen more as an extension and hardening of his original claims than a retraction of them; it certainly seems to make them more rather than less historical. First, it is worth noting that in his original 1921 review essay he had not explicitly linked the 'dissociation' to the Civil War at all, which is not mentioned at that point. 'Something happened to the mind of England between the time of Donne or Lord Herbert of Cherbury and the time of Tennyson and Browning.' Not only was the change spoken of entirely in terms of poetry, but the timescale gestured towards seemed to run from the first half of the seventeenth century to the middle of the nineteenth. Secondly, the 1947 passage explicitly denies that the changes involved can be accounted for in terms of literary criticism; they are now clearly to be understood as part of a much wider historical process, which includes the causes 'which brought about the Civil War'. And, finally, it is not something that happened only to 'the mind of *England*': the causes must be sought in Europe.

The upshot of this reformulation is to make the idea of a 'dissociation of sensibility' much more historical, and more clearly something that happened in the seventeenth century. We are left to wonder what at this point Eliot took the causes of the Civil War to have been. His 'dissociation of sensibility' might, just conceivably, be grafted onto a story that foregrounded, say, the decline of Aristotelianism, the rise of Puritanism, and the beginnings of the new science; it would surely sit rather oddly with a story that emphasized, say, the rise of mercantile interests, the economic difficulties of the gentry, and the excesses of an out-of-touch court.

Or perhaps not. For, if we want a really remarkable but telling illustration of the impact of Eliot's quasi-historical claim, we may jump ahead seven years from his British Academy lecture to the unlikely setting of the 1954 summer school held by the Communist Party Historians' Group. The theme of the school was 'The Rise and Decline of Capitalism in Britain', and one of the speakers was Christopher Hill on the topic 'Ideas and the State 1660–1760'. Everything about the occasion may seem to be utterly remote from the sketchy thoughts on poetic history of a young poet and critic at the beginning of the 1920s, but in fact we learn from the recently examined records of this group that in his paper Hill 'sought to assess the effect of ideologies and cultures on the way the country was governed, with reference to T. S. Eliot's idea of "integrated sensibility" '.[57]

Commenting three years later still in 1957 on the influence of Eliot's idea of a 'dissociation of sensibility', Frank Kermode noted that 'enquiries into the dissociation had long ceased to be conducted entirely in terms of literary criticism. Almost every conceivable aspect of seventeenth-century life had been examined by scholars anxious to validate the concept, though it is true that the investigators were usually historians of literature by profession.'[58] The caveat in Kermode's last clause recurs to the theme of the relation between literary history and general history, and he speculated that the idea of 'a pregnant historical crisis...was attractive because it gave design and simplicity to history; and because it explained in a subtly agreeable way the torment and division of modern life'. Kermode had no doubt that 'Mr Eliot's extraordinary persuasiveness', which had led to the idea enjoying such success in the previous three decades, would mean it would continue 'to exert a powerful influence for a long time yet'.[59]

Here, Kermode was more successful as a historian than as a prophet, since Eliot's idea soon ceased to enjoy an active life among either critics or historians, partly as a result of the decline of his influence more generally from the 1960s onwards, partly for other reasons—but that, as historians like to say, 'is not my period'. Kermode was, nevertheless, surely right to attribute some of the power and longevity of Eliot's notion to the way in which it 'gave design and simplicity to history', and that design, we may say, involved, however obliquely, a fundamental repudiation of the Whig interpretation of history. The presence of some such archetypal trajectory in Eliot's later social thought has often been remarked, but its roots in his earlier attempts to engage directly with the work of historians have attracted much less attention. As we have seen, these attempts involved him in a rather nervous negotiation of the boundary between literary criticism and history whenever he seems to be proposing any large-scale historical story, a pattern that recurs with revealing frequency in his early prose above all. Over and over again, Eliot appears to propose some large historical generalization, only to pull back from it—not so much by modifying the generalization as by disowning the intention to trespass on the territory of the general or professional historian, categories he tends to equate. But this oscillation may not be entirely attributable to Eliot's notorious slipperiness, for there is in fact no way to draw a hard and fast boundary between literary history and general history. Literary history, as I suggested in the Introduction, always presumes a selective kind of general history and at the same time threatens to modify or even supplant it. Indeed, literary-historical orthodoxies have a way of becoming part of the narrative of general history in the next generation, just as the textbook commonplaces about historical periodization and change are, in their turn, presupposed by subsequent literary histories, however revisionist.

Eliot's ideas entered the bloodstream of English literary and intellectual life in the mid-twentieth century; the subsequent chapters of this book will illustrate some of the ways in which those ideas were absorbed, modified, and challenged in the work of later critics. That work, too, testified, in its own way, to the constant overlap or slippage between literary and general history. In the final sentence of *Romantic Image*, Kermode attempted to look even further ahead to the time when poets would have rediscovered Milton: 'And by the time they have done that, the dissociation of sensibility, the great and in some ways noxious historical myth of Symbolism...will be forgotten, except by historians crying their new categories and still unheard persuasions.'[60] The idea of a 'dissociation of sensibility' did eventually disappear from view, but in the meantime some of the most influential historical 'categories' and 'persuasions' in mid-twentieth-century Britain were disseminated by critics trespassing across the border between literary and general history for their own purposes. For that reason, the developments discussed here cannot be understood simply in terms of the work of one or even a few individuals. They were, I am tempted mischievously to say, about something that had happened to the mind of England.

2

Scrutinizing the Present Phase
of Human History

I

All accounts of the distinctiveness of the present are, implicitly if not always explicitly, historical. Simply to identify a period as 'the present phase of human history' is to begin to sketch a larger interpretation, bringing in questions of periodization as well as, ultimately, of explanation. This chapter focuses on the work of a critic who, perhaps more than any other during this period, reached a wide audience with an interpretation that presumed, as he put it in an arresting statement, that 'the present phase of human history is, in the strictest sense, *abnormal*'.[1]

F. R. Leavis suffers under the handicap of being, it is generally reckoned, a known quantity. Few figures in the history of criticism attain a broad cultural standing unless they can also draw on creative work in other genres, usually poetry, yet the name of Leavis, who published no fiction or poetry of his own, became a widely circulated cultural counter during his lifetime, and it still brings with it an unusually large baggage-train of preconceptions. Where his dealings with the past are concerned, those preconceptions are easy to pillory, perhaps to travesty. He thought, didn't he?, that life used to be better; then things went badly wrong; and now they are worse than ever. No dates or events need to be mentioned in such a summary, since Leavis's view is understood to be more encompassing and less specific than that.[2] He held, didn't he?, that literary and intellectual life in contemporary Britain is irredeemably shallow and corrupt; the only connection to 'finer living' that is now available comes through the properly intense engagement with the work of a severely narrowed canon of great writers such as George Eliot and D. H. Lawrence, plus the occasional glimpse of a healthier way of life to be had by reading about the 'old wheelwright's shop'.

The fact that this schematic summary is not *wholly* wrong is part of what makes a reconsideration of Leavis's engagement with history such a difficult undertaking. He undoubtedly wins the prize as the most controversial English critic of the twentieth century, and during the 1950s and 1960s in particular he enjoyed a celebrity, or notoriety, that is accorded to few university teachers in any field. But Leavis's dealings with the past were, I want to propose, more interesting, and in some ways more surprising, than the familiar caricature suggests. For example, on closer examination it turns out that the notion of 'the organic community' played relatively little part in Leavis's thinking. Most of the references to it come from one slight early book, *Culture and Environment*, a primer for schools that Leavis later recorded was written in a week in 1933, with substantial contributions by his former pupil, Denys Thompson, who remained more committed to an explicit ideology of ruralism than Leavis did.[3] The representativeness of this quotable tract has been exaggerated by later, largely hostile, critics. Neither Leavis's analysis of the defects of contemporary society nor his partly implicit interpretation of the course of English history depends upon this nebulous and increasingly disregarded notion, though in Chapter 1 we saw the editor of a volume of the *New Cambridge Modern History* still warning fellow-historians in 1970 against the temptations of the idea (or 'myth', as he called it) of the 'organic community'. Here I agree with Christopher Hilliard, in what is the best recent examination of 'the *Scrutiny* movement', that, considered as 'a utopia in the literary sense', a device for criticizing one's own world, 'Elizabethan and Jacobean England...organized *Scrutiny* thought to a much greater degree than the organic community did'.[4]

One claim about Leavis that seems in no danger of being challenged is that his early work was heavily influenced by T. S. Eliot. The indebtedness of such books as *New Bearings in English Poetry* (published in 1932) and *Revaluation* (1936) to the work of 'a certain critic and poet' was acknowledged at the time and has been amply confirmed by subsequent scholarship. Obviously, I do not propose to question the existence of that general debt. But part of what Leavis is said to have taken over from Eliot was his account of history, especially the fact of, and the working-out of the consequences of, that 'dissociation of sensibility' that Eliot alleged happened in the mid-seventeenth century. This, it is argued, not only shaped the *literary* history that Leavis presented in those two books and related writings, but also determined his interpretation of subsequent centuries as one long fall from the time of an 'undissociated' sensibility.

In *Education and the University*, published in 1943 but drawing on pieces published in *Scrutiny* over several years, Leavis certainly made the study of the general history of the seventeenth century, seen as the 'key passage in the history of civilization', the centrepiece of his proposed course in English: 'It is at one end in direct and substantial continuity with the world of Dante, and it shows us at the other a world that has broken irretrievably with the mediaeval order and committed itself completely to the process leading directly and rapidly to what we live in now.'[5] A note of insistence is hardly a rare element in Leavis's prose—'enforce' was, after all, one of his favoured verbs—but the adverbial intensification here is striking: 'broken *irretrievably*', 'committed itself *completely*', 'leading *directly* and *rapidly*'. Both the absoluteness of the change and the directness of the connection with the present are strongly emphasized, as though the focus on the study of this century might otherwise seem arbitrary or inconsequential. In any event, the established scholarly view is summarized by Richard Storer, in the most detailed study to date of *Education and the University*, when he writes: 'This reading of history was clearly derived from Eliot's early essays.... What Leavis was proposing was in effect a broad study of the "dissociation of sensibility".'[6]

Although there is clearly some truth in this claim, the development of Leavis's historical thinking followed, I would argue, a less predictable and less purely Eliot-inspired course than such a summary suggests. Any such reconsideration will be consequential for understanding the larger role of Eliot and Leavis as cultural critics in the mid-twentieth century. As I noted in the Introduction, at a time when the ethos of professional history encouraged chaste and detailed studies grounded in official documents, the broad and forceful interpretation of history at the heart of the work of these literary critics and their associates played a powerful part in diffusing an understanding of a contemporary cultural identity that was closely tied to an account of the national past. I shall return to the larger story at several points in this book, but that significant outcome needs to be borne in mind as we re-examine Leavis's formative historical assumptions more closely.

In his *Literary Englands*, David Gervais made a bold attempt to rescue Leavis from charges of reactionary ruralism, in the course of which he observed pertinently:

In suggesting that Leavis gave a doctored version of pre-industrial England, I do not mean to imply that he also gave an unhistorical one. I would prefer to say that he chose to dwell on particular aspects of English history which for him summed up what was essentially English, and then let them stand for the whole.

'I would *prefer* to say that he *chose*...and then *let*...': there is a lot of volition involved here, a lot of selecting from among other possibilities. And surely that 'letting them stand for the whole' fatally damages the case for the defence: to *choose* to *let* them do this is precisely what renders his account *un*historical. History itself, after all, allows us no such leeway. For this reason, Gervais seems to me nearer the mark when he says of Leavis: 'The past for him is not a vast collection of data but a moral force.'[7] Quite so, but that makes for a peculiar kind of dealing with the past, and it suggests why Leavis has such complex relations with both literary history and 'general history'.

II

The place to start may be the historical framework, or framework*s*, of Leavis's thinking *prior* to the publication of *New Bearings* in 1932. According to Leavis's later recollections (of which there were several, not entirely consistent, versions), he read Eliot's first collection of critical prose, *The Sacred Wood*, soon after it came out in 1920, but he and other readers did not really grasp its significance until the publication of Eliot's second prose collection, *Homage to John Dryden*, in 1924.

> *The Sacred Wood*, I think, had very little influence or attention before the Hogarth Press brought out *Homage to John Dryden*.... It was with the publication in this form of those essays (the Hogarth Press had recently published *The Waste Land*) that Eliot became the important contemporary critic. It was the impact of this slender new collection that sent one back to *The Sacred Wood* and confirmed with decisive practical effect one's sense of the stimulus to be got from that rare thing, a fine intelligence in literary criticism.[8]

The evidence from contemporary reviews and other sources suggests that Leavis was here understating the early impact of *The Sacred Wood*, and indeed of the review essays in *The Athenaeum* in 1919–20 on which it was largely based,[9] though it may be right that it took the republication of the three more celebrated review essays in *Homage to John Dryden* to bring home to Leavis himself the full significance of the reorientation of literary history that Eliot was proposing. But, even if that was the case, the historical dimension of Eliot's criticism features less prominently in Leavis's early work than one would then expect. Even when we reach *Education and the University*, it is not in fact obvious that Leavis's emphasis on the seventeenth century should be understood exclusively in terms of his debt to Eliot.

The only direct access we have to Leavis's historical thinking in the first half of the 1920s is through his unpublished Ph.D. thesis of 1924 on 'The Relationship of Journalism to Literature: Studied in the Rise and Earlier Development of the Press in England'. This has been a somewhat under-exploited source, and one reason for that may be, to put it in mildly provocative terms, that it is bound to strike the modern reader as a markedly *un*Leavisian piece of work.[10] It is true that there is a preoccupation in the thesis with the question of the historical development of the reading public, but it is not written in the distinctive style evident from Leavis's earliest *published* work onwards: it contains little by way of close literary criticism; it scarcely discusses poetry; and it does not evince the moral passion or the cultural aggression so familiar from his mature writings. Instead, it is a broadly positive, rather conventional literary-historical account of the importance of the forms of topical or occasional writing he calls 'journalism' in the development of English literature in the seventeenth and eighteenth centuries.

The dissertation implicitly contends against the Romantic model of the isolated literary genius, asserting instead that good literature can be written only when it is 'on terms of intimacy with the life of the day'. Leavis argues that it is not until the Restoration and the early eighteenth century that the conditions start to exist to sustain a genuine reading public. That public allows for the development of the profession of the man of letters, and the prose of Dryden and L'Estrange or, later, Addison and Steele shows the benefit of being in touch with a definite public. This also prompts the beginning of the novel: 'In Defoe's work art blossoms out of the life of the community.'[11] The dissertation certainly does *not* presume that the peak of literary vitality had been represented by the 'unified' Elizabethan public, with all subsequent periods being part of a long decline. Instead, it argues that it is from the late eighteenth century that the reading public starts to fragment: thereafter, as he puts it, 'no code of urbanity could win general allegiance', as it had done in the days of the *Tatler*.[12] There is a loose form of literary sociology at work here, though it does not go far beyond what could be found in Leslie Stephen's Ford Lectures, *English Literature and*

Society in the Eighteenth Century. The dissertation stops before the end of the eighteenth century, and, although an epilogue suggests a rather jaundiced view of much of the 'journalism' prevalent in contemporary society—'a deluge of printed matter pours over the world'—Leavis manages, even so, an oddly democratic, upbeat conclusion, suggesting it is good for the writer to be 'forced to address a wider public, to speak to everybody in the language of all'.[13]

In the preface, Leavis acknowledged that, apart from the material in the fourth chapter on the growth of the reading public in the late seventeenth century, the dissertation did not involve uncovering hitherto unused sources, but depended rather upon the standard published authorities. He particularly chose to record his debt to Courthope's *History of English Poetry* (published in six volumes between 1895 and 1910), to Beljame's *Le Public et les hommes de lettres en Angleterre au dix-huitième siècle*, first published in 1881, and to the works of Leslie Stephen, notably those Ford Lectures. Perhaps the work of general history most frequently quoted in the body of the thesis is Trevelyan's *England under the Stuarts*, published in 1904, while considerable use is also made of the volumes in the late-nineteenth-century 'English Men of Letters' series. As a scholarly aside, I would just mention that Leavis's account bears some similarity to the much more celebrated version of the period in Jürgen Habermas's *Habilitationsschrift* thirty-five years later on the development of 'the public sphere', which, interestingly enough, also draws on Trevelyan and Stephen for much of its view of the coffee-house culture of early eighteenth-century England.[14]

Scholarly work is never entirely determined by the authorities it relies upon, but it is worth remarking how traditional, even conservative, many of Leavis's main authorities were. Courthope's history, for example, was devoted to showing how the 'national spirit' was expressed throughout English literature and how it should be 'the object of all patriotic endeavour to strengthen the established principle of authority in matters of taste, and to widen its base so as to meet the needs of our imperial society'.[15] The Whiggish character of this literary history is hard to miss: as Chris Baldick claims in his survey of criticism in the period: 'The argument of Courthope's *History* maintains consistently that the great poets have harmonized the tendencies of the national spirit just as the English Constitution itself perfectly balances the claims of Liberty and Authority.'[16] Similarly, Trevelyan's *England under the Stuarts* proposes that 'never perhaps in any century have such rapid advances been made towards freedom' as in the seventeenth, while Trevelyan's biographer, David Cannadine, describes the work as a celebration of the 'classic Whig themes of religious toleration and constitutional progress'.[17] Most revealing of all, for reasons I shall return to, is the character of Beljame's now-forgotten book. This provides a very positive, indeed Whiggish, account of 'the gradual growth of an enlightened and interested public'. By the time of Pope's death, it argues, 'a public has been established; the writer's trade has become a liberal profession; the man of letters has won for himself the place in society which he occupies to-day'. Pope's literary success meant that he could refuse patronage, and so he deserves to be saluted for 'having invested the literary profession in England with the rank and dignity it enjoys to-day'.[18] Beljame, writing in France at the end of the 1870s, clearly admired Victorian literary culture and looked for its roots in the early eighteenth century.

One indication of the largely traditional character of Leavis's account is to be found in the responses of the dissertation's first two readers. The early files of the Cambridge Board of Graduate Studies have only recently been catalogued in the university archives, and Leavis's file contains his examiners' reports.[19] The thesis was examined by Sydney Roberts, a specialist on eighteenth-century literature who later became the head of Cambridge University Press and Master of Pembroke, and, as the external, the 79-year-old George Saintsbury, a prolific literary journalist who had become a prolific professor.[20] The examiners' reports are only moderately praising, and they both note the lack of original research in much of the thesis, though they clearly recommend the award of the degree, and Saintsbury seemed to think that, properly revised, it might be deserving of publication. It is interesting that, although Leavis was struggling to make his way in the academic world in the 1920s and early 1930s, he never did publish this work, and the modern reader of it would have to say that that was a wise decision. For my present purposes it is also worth remarking that the thesis indicated no indebtedness at all to Eliot's criticism. This is perhaps not surprising, especially if we take at face value Leavis's later recollection of only really having registered the historical importance of Eliot's critical work with the appearance of *Homage to John Dryden*, since that slim volume was not published until late November 1924, some weeks after Leavis had been examined on his thesis. The important point, however, is that the framework derived from Beljame and Stephen predated anything Leavis could have taken from Eliot's account of the seventeenth century, and as a result it continued, in a slightly awkward manner, to coexist alongside that account thereafter.

The enduring presence of these early points of reference in Leavis's later work is evident in various ways. Let me just illustrate by taking his essay on the ostensibly very different theme of 'Sociology and Literature', which was published over twenty years later and was then reprinted in *The Common Pursuit* seven years later still, in 1952.[21] Here, Leavis had occasion to reproach the German sociologist Levin Schücking for various forms of ignorance. Warming to his theme, Leavis argues that, even when Schücking was on what should have been his strongest ground, 'the economic history of literature', he 'doesn't mention Beljame's admirable book, nor does he the work of A. S. Collins'. To each of these proper names Leavis attaches a footnote. In the first, after giving the full title of Beljame's book, he calls upon the Library of Sociology, edited by Karl Mannheim, to publish a translation of it.[22] He opens the second footnote not with details of Collins's book, but by writing: 'Nor does he appear to know Courthope's *History of English Poetry* or Leslie Stephen's *English Literature and Society in the XVIIIth Century*, both of which are half a century old.' He then launches into a paean of praise to Stephen's book, as illustrating 'the possibilities of a "sociology of literary taste"' far better than Schücking had.[23]

Two observations may be relevant here. First, it is striking that so many years later Leavis is still taking as his reference points for the social history of literature exactly the same books that provided the framework for much of his Ph.D. thesis at the beginning of the 1920s, books that had themselves appeared some decades earlier still (over six decades earlier in Beljame's case). He has now added Collins's *The Profession of Letters*, published in 1928, which is inspired by the same authorities; the book expresses a particular debt to Beljame's 'brilliant study' and relies a good deal on Trevelyan's *British History in the Nineteenth Century*. Collins draws a more declinist moral from the most recent phase of the story by insisting that, with the expansion of the reading public, quality has fallen: 'For where the master is mediocre, so must the servant be. And the public is mediocrity's vast embodiment.'[24] Second, although the general *Scrutiny* partiality for the 'old Cambridge' of Henry Sidgwick and Leslie Stephen is well attested (both Leavises wrote admiringly about them), the praise for Stephen's last, somewhat thin, book is striking, even a little puzzling. But praise for Stephen's book remained an article of faith with the Leavises. Leavis himself indulgently claims that 'in the ready fulness of ordered knowledge and with the ease of a trained and vigorous mind he [Stephen] really *does* something' in that book, though presumably what Leavis mainly appreciated was its demonstration, or at least assertion, that the growth of the reading public in the eighteenth century affected the literature written for it.[25] Writing as late as the mid-1950s, Queenie Leavis was recommending Stephen's Ford Lectures as 'a stimulating model for handling the sociology of literature in a given period', and into the 1960s, when claiming that Stephen's lectures had 'directed my work as a post-graduate student', she was still insisting on it, with characteristic excess, as 'a book that cannot be overpraised and has never been superseded'.[26]

More generally, it would seem that Leavis had carried a set of historical assumptions over from his doctoral work in the early 1920s and was now presenting them as part of an argument about the impossibility of any sociology of literary taste that is not based on the prior exercise of a properly discriminating literary criticism, though this had not been something he had insisted on or, really, exhibited in his own dissertation (and, it would have to be said, is not much exhibited in Stephen's book either). In any event, it seems to have been Leavis's passing remark in his 1945 review essay that led to the translation of Beljame's book, which was published in English in 1948. It is also worth noting that so positive was Beljame's account of the rise of the profession of the writer that the critic Bonamy Dobrée, in his introduction to the English translation, felt obliged to strike a more sceptical note, emphasizing that scarcely any serious writers in modern Britain, aside from the outright bestsellers, could make a living from their writing alone. So we have the curious sight of Dobrée, a critic who had publicly recorded his reservations about the supposed far-reaching significance of the 'dissociation of sensibility', being the one to challenge Beljame's upbeat Whiggish account, whereas Leavis, in other ways so pessimistic about the course of recent history, seemed still to accord the book an unqualified endorsement.[27]

In the same review essay in 1945, Leavis develops a more general complaint against historians for their lack of inwardness with literature as a potentially rich source of evidence. He softens this charge a little when discussing another work extensively used in his dissertation, Trevelyan's *England under the Stuarts*, which, says Leavis, 'I re-read with gratitude at fairly frequent intervals'. Even although 're-read' was another of Leavis's favoured verbs, this still seems a rather surprising thing to claim at this date, over a decade after the assaults on Whig history by Lewis Namier and Herbert Butterfield, especially about a book that was somewhat old-fashioned even at the time of publication forty years earlier. Leavis acknowledges that the book's 'appreciation of seventeenth-century civilization [is]...a seriously limited one', but then adds: 'And one would be agreeably surprised to find a historian who was essentially any better provided with the kind of quali-fication under discussion' (that is to say, a properly sensitive reading of litera-ture used as evidence).[28] Again, it is hard to avoid the suspicion that Leavis had grafted his later conception of the role of literary criticism onto a largely unreconstructed narrative of English history derived from traditional Whiggish sources, a framework that was in most respects pre-Eliotic. In add-ition to Trevelyan's sunny narrative of progress, both Stephen and Beljame tell a positive story about the development of the reading public in the early and mid-eighteenth century, and so chart a significant advance from the late-Elizabethan period, whereas Eliot's scheme had seemed to posit a continued decline in sensibility throughout the post-'dissociation' period.

In similar vein, we shall struggle to find much evidence of Eliot's histor-ical framework elsewhere in Leavis's early writings. His first significant published work involving historical or social criticism was his 1930 pamphlet *Mass Civilization and Minority Culture*, but here the focus is on recent devel-opments, principally from the beginning of the twentieth century, above all the spread of literacy, the rise of the 'yellow press', and the consequent debasement of standards. There is nothing about the seventeenth century and only passing mention of the Industrial Revolution. In his other Minority Press pamphlet of 1930, on D. H. Lawrence, he enthusiastically endorsed Lawrence's ragings against the dehumanizing power of 'the machine' and the consequent loss of intimacy with the rhythms of the physical world; he also threw in some of Spengler's vatic pronouncements about the relation between abstract intellectualizing and cultural decline. Though he later had reservations about his Lawrence pamphlet, its themes recur throughout his early *Scrutiny* contributions and he was happy to reprint his 'mass civiliza-tion' pamphlet more than once, right up to the late 1940s.[29]

So, if we try to take stock of the relationship between Leavis's early social criticism in the 1930s and 1940s and Eliot's historical ideas, the picture is complex, involving explicit homage and substantial indebtedness, yet also other, perhaps incompatible, allegiances and implicit repudiation. It is, of course, the case that the broad historical framework within which *New Bearings* situates its studies of contemporary verse can be seen as Eliotic in temper, especially in emphasizing the low place of poetry in what Leavis calls 'the modern world', though there is relatively little of historical substance to support this claim. *Revaluation*, published in 1936, clearly presupposes

Eliot's reorientation of literary history, especially in its focus on 'the line of wit' from the Metaphysicals, but again Leavis's chapters remain close to the poetry, offering little by way of wider historical analysis and saying nothing about any major change or caesura in English history.

Moreover, at various points in Leavis's writing in the early 1930s we can again detect the ghostly presence of the pre-Eliotic historical framework inherited from his doctoral research. For example, his 1932 pamphlet *How to Teach Reading* explicitly contrasted the disarray of contemporary culture with that of the *eighteenth* century, which, he writes, 'enjoyed the advantages of a homogeneous—a real—culture', one in which Johnson's appeals to 'the Common Reader' represented an appeal to 'the competent, the cultivated in general'.[30] Similarly, in an article of the same year entitled 'What's Wrong with Criticism', he insisted that in the age of Johnson taste was 'in the keeping of the educated who, sharing a homogeneous culture, maintained in tradition a surer taste than any that is merely individual can be'.[31] Indeed, as J. A. Smith has shown in a recent article in *Essays in Criticism*, the essential good health of the eighteenth-century reading-public becomes a staple of the Leavisian indictment of the contemporary scene, and along the way Pope's poetry is rescued from Arnoldian disdain.[32] *Scrutiny*'s overall account of the eighteenth century may have been ambivalent and sometimes inconsistent, to be sure, but it did not provide unequivocal confirmation that in the mid-seventeenth century 'something had happened to the mind of England'.

In summary, the comparison between Eliot's and Leavis's handling of history in their work of the relevant periods might be expressed as follows. Eliot's early historical gestures are high-handed and offhand in almost equal measure. The intent to provoke is manifest. Many of his comments involve startling reworkings of literary history, redirecting attention, revising judgements. In the course of the 1920s, his literary manner becomes more intransigent, as dandyish posing yields to an almost ecclesiastical hauteur. The disdain for the present is certainly not hidden, but in his early work it is not itemized at any length, either. Eliot's claims have a way of foreshortening history, absorbing the peaks of the mid-thirteenth or early-seventeenth centuries into a timeless contemporaneity. The authority of his superior sensibility is his, and his readers', sufficient guide, though, as we saw in Chapter 1, this is shadowed by a nervous acknowledgement of the claims of 'general history'.

Leavis's critical judgements aspire to a drastic finality of tone, yet his supporting historical claims also often betray an edgy defensiveness. In characterizing the state of modern society, Leavis offers a far more extensive, and concrete, sociology of error than Eliot ever does, returning with wearying frequency to a number of clinching instances. Yet the tone of incredulity that he cultivates when discussing these examples is amplified by both exasperation and nervousness, as though the widespread inability to recognize emptiness or fatuity were both inexplicable and threatening. Leavis's historical accounts are far fuller than Eliot's, in part because he constantly essays an assessment of the quality of life of various social groups in different periods. Where Eliot might cite a couplet as indicating a sensibility beyond the reach of subsequent generations of poets, Leavis will marshal selective readings from social and cultural analysis to support the insights literature gives of the finer living available for various classes in earlier periods.

The most obvious common element, beyond the shared reliance on certain literary touchstones, is that both sketch an account of cultural decline. But their articulation of the nature and timing of loss is divergent. Eliot is chilly about the present, consistently dismissive of the Romantic and Victorian generations, selectively lofty about the eighteenth century; it is the Elizabethan and Jacobean playwrights and poets who stir him to creative engagement, while only an idealized version of medieval Christianity eventually attracts his unrestrained endorsement. Leavis, alert to fresh signs of corruption in the present, is driven to a greater attentiveness to recent periods of history to account for contemporary decline. He has a lot to say about the late-Victorian and Edwardian years, in which the beginnings of mass culture (and its causes) can be identified; he has a good deal to say, not all of it negative, about the social history of the eighteenth and early nineteenth centuries, where an effective reading public coexists alongside the early forms of commercial and industrial society; his seventeenth century overlaps with Eliot's at some points, but he has far more to say about joint-stock companies and Bunyan and somewhat less about metaphor and belief; he has practically nothing to say about the Middle Ages. Leavis calls upon the likes of Trevelyan and the Hammonds to buttress his case; Eliot tends to make a historical point by mentioning a neglected play by Chapman.

From the 1930s onwards, Leavis had increasing reservations about Eliot's development, and the gap between their historical frameworks, as between their critical perspectives more generally, widened still further. But, already by the early 1930s, we can see the melding of several historical stories, animated by an antipathy to a selectively described modern world and united only by their shared insistence on there having been some greater vitality, some more intense form of experience, located in the literature of one or more earlier periods.

III

Writing in 1931, Leavis commended Eliot, Richards, and the young Empson for being 'alive ... to the exciting strangeness of the present phase of human history'.[33] But what, in that case, did Leavis identify as the 'present phase of human history' and in what did he think its 'exciting strangeness' consisted? Writing two years later, Leavis and Thompson declared, in the disconcerting statement with which I began, that 'the present phase of human history is, in the strictest sense, *abnormal*'.[34] Here the strangeness has been dramatized and, so to speak, upgraded. It will surely, we are bound to feel, require an unusually powerful as well as original interpretation of history to substantiate these arresting claims.

Anyone hoping to extract such an interpretation of history from Leavis and Thompson's little handbook, *Culture and Environment*, will be disappointed. Its focus is the present: insofar as it sketches a process of change, it is a very recent process—and the account is sketchy indeed. In identifying certain developments in English rural and small-town life, it ranges no further back than three or four decades. George Sturt, author of *The Wheelwright's Shop* and similar works, is the main witness, and Sturt largely recounts changes that have happened in rural and small-town Surrey in his adult lifetime, essentially since the 1880s. Insofar as we, now, may place these changes as part of a wider social and economic history, as Leavis and Thompson do not, they are more about the impact of electricity and the internal combustion engine than about the steam power of the Industrial Revolution. Sturt's villagers, at least as Leavis and Thompson see them, continued in their old ways until the end of the nineteenth century. In using the villagers' assumed fulfilment in their work as a device of social criticism, *Culture and Environment* is preoccupied not with poverty and exploitation but with emptiness and standardization, as allegedly seen in the contemporary American suburb. They cite the 'motor coach, wireless, cinema and education' as the agents of destruction, not factories, steam power, and capital.[35] The fear is that

Farnham, where Sturt lived, is becoming a version not of Manchester but of Muncie, Indiana.[36] The two books that frame their story are that unlikely pairing, Bunyan's *Pilgrim's Progress* and Robert and Helen Lynd's *Middletown*, their 1929 study of social life in Muncie.

The discussion moves quickly to 'the place of advertising in a modern economy', where 'modern' is unspecified but clearly post-Victorian, and largely exemplified by the USA, and thence on to the question (which is, one feels, always for Leavis the real question) of the reading public. 'Classes moderately advanced in training might be asked to consider the probable concomitants of a change from the Bible, the Prayer-Book, Bunyan, Shakespeare and Milton as the main influences upon our emotional vocabulary to newspapers, advertisements, best-sellers and the cinema.'[37] (It is hard not to feel that these advanced classes might have been asked whether there is any reason to think that the ancestors of all those who now go to the cinema actually did read Milton.) Such historical gestures as the book does contain are vague in the extreme: Sturt's references to 'the old order' are casually endorsed, suggesting a timeless mode of life that was alleged to have lasted into the 1890s or even 1900s, but that now had only a vestigial or partial existence. The old order is purely English in this recension: professional historians might be inclined to generalize about a 'preindustrial order' across Europe, but Leavis and Thompson make no mention of any such larger picture. This is old England, and especially old Farnham, and, more especially still, the old wheeelwright's shop.

The present is a curiously disinherited place in Leavis and Thompson's account; there is no going back, yet something has been lost. They do not attempt to reconcile us to our loss—quite the contrary. They write to keep alive the awareness of what was vital and desirable in what has been lost, even though it was surrounded by much that does not deserve to be lamented. It is a minatory, hortatory use of the past, and a not very specific past. As so often in this kind of cultural criticism, the surest indication of 'modernity', that so doubtful and deceitful category against which I warned in the Introduction, is the growth of a kind of self-consciousness, the loss of an immediate or 'natural' intimacy with one's society.

Culture and Environment was a primer for schools and adult education classes; its aim was to bring students to understand what it calls 'the general process of civilization', and it identifies the USA as 'where the process of Western civilization has gone furthest'.[38] But the book did not indulge conventional anti-Americanism: like the larger *Scrutiny* critique, of which it was an early expression, the preoccupation was not with such hackneyed targets as Hollywood or Manhattan, but with the mid-west. Conformity was the concern, not outlandishness. (I would just remark in passing that, for this reason, it is curious that Leavis never seems to have taken the measure of Tocqueville.) In the recommended reading, almost all the titles refer to the present: there is no work of history in the bibliography. In suggesting how pupils' awareness of change could be educated, the principal authorities cited are, once again, Bunyan, Sturt, and the Lynds. Strikingly, Leavis and Thompson then say: 'Obviously, too, in the teaching of cultural history a historian would be able to co-operate, though he would have to be energetic as well as intelligent, for his formal historical training would not have helped him much, and there are few useful books.'[39] It is revealing that the most 'a historian' is allowed to do in 'the teaching of cultural history' is to 'cooperate'; his formal training almost disqualifies him, and anyway 'there are few useful books'. (I shall leave aside the further possible implication of Leavis's phrasing here that intelligent historians are rarer than hen's teeth.) Change, one might think, is the province of the historian by definition, but here, at the earliest stage of Leavis's career as a social critic, historians are, slightly sorrowfully, relegated to an auxiliary role, at best.

Given the vehemence of Leavis's early denunciation of a civilization that was in thrall to 'the machine', one might expect his historical energies to have been concentrated on the period of the Industrial Revolution. Certainly, it would not be difficult to assemble a substantial anthology of references to this supposedly transformative episode, and, if we focus on his swelling endorsement of D. H. Lawrence, including the latter's dark view of modern English history, or on Leavis's later opposition to the technocratic optimism of C. P. Snow, then the coming of industrialism might be represented as the pivot on which his understanding of history principally turned. Yet, the more closely one examines his writings from the mid-1930s to the mid-1950s—his high period that saw the publication of, among other works, *Revaluation, Education and the University, The Great Tradition, Mill on Bentham and Coleridge, The Common Pursuit*, and *D. H. Lawrence, Novelist*—the more striking becomes the *lack* of any sustained historical attention to the Industrial Revolution. It is not so much that across these decades the outlines of Leavis's view of history undergoes any dramatic alteration: the fallen state of the modern world remains a given. It is more that, when sketching in the general historical setting within which literary history is to be placed, his attention is, in practice, focused elsewhere.

As so often with Leavis, the animating energy for these historical forays arose out of teaching. The intensity of his engagement with the education of those reading English at Downing—and I put it like this to underline how far removed his efforts were from mere preparation for the Tripos—is well attested, but he never thought of this task in narrowly professional or disciplinary terms. The aim was to develop in students the capacity to evaluate cultural change, a capacity that had to be grounded, could *only* be grounded, in the identification of what 'made for life' in the finest literature. But, while such literary-critical responsiveness was, as it were, the *method* by which the capacity for such judgement was cultivated, the *matter* on which that judgement was to be exercised was nothing less than the life of whole societies, which is surely one reason why a significant number of his former students went on to make careers in social anthropology, including, in the late 1940s and early 1950s alone, Paul Baxter, Godfrey Lienhardt, Peter Lienhardt, David Pocock, and Malcolm Ruel.[40] The Leavisian student had to know enough to be able to compare one phase of social life with another, and this meant being in some ways both more and less than a historian. With these pedagogical concerns to the fore, we can see how Leavis mapped out two main periods for which students needed this peculiar form of historical education. They were, roughly identified, the seventeenth and the nineteenth centuries, though the relation of these two periods to Leavis's central preoccupations was subtly different. The difference can be most economically illustrated by comparing two texts that explicitly address the question of history in pedagogical mode, *Education and the University* and *Mill on Bentham and Coleridge*, both of which belong to the 1940s.[41]

IV

Even considered purely in terms of literary history, the seventeenth century was an unavoidable focus. If the peak of English literary achievement was to be found in the late-Elizabethan and early Jacobean period, then clearly a historical story had to be told of how the social conditions that had sustained this unique flowering changed and with what effects. At one point, Leavis did couch the need for such a larger explanation in quasi-Eliotic terms:

A serious attempt to account for the 'dissociation of sensibility' would turn into a discussion of the great change that came over English civilization in the seventeenth century—the change notably manifested in the decisive appearance of modern English prose during the early years of the Restoration. Social, economic and political history, the Royal Society, Hobbes, intellectual and cultural history in general—a great and complex variety of considerations would be involved.[42]

The use of the conditional has a curiously distancing effect here—these are the sorts of considerations that 'would' come into play if one were minded to pursue this sort of question.[43] Leavis implies that he knows what the history would look like—that Royal Society-influenced prose is a standard reference point for him—yet, as the rest of the paragraph moves on, the chief upshot of this 'great change that came over English civilization' seems to amount to Rochester's verse being less 'fine' than Carew's. In Leavis's criticism, 'general history' often seems in this way to play the role of minder to his literary history, hovering in the shadows, to be invoked to deter disagreement though never fully produced.

Still, no critic writing after Eliot—at least no critic who took Eliot as seriously as Leavis did—could escape the idea that the seventeenth century was at the heart of the larger story of how what could loosely be called 'the medieval world' gave way to what might even more loosely be described as 'the modern world'. So it was not just, or even mainly, that no student of English literature could avoid trying to understand how the age of Shakespeare and Donne turned into the age of Pope and Richardson, though in Leavis's hands that question alone opened the way to an extensive social history. But it was, rather, that no apprentice diagnostician of the quality of life in successive phases of English history could avoid analysing what separated the world of the mid-sixteenth century from the world of the mid-eighteenth century.

This broader view of the seventeenth century as marking in some sense the origins of the modern world starts to become more of a presence in Leavis's work in the course of the 1930s. Such historical texture as it has in these early years clearly owes something to the work that went into L. C. Knights's *Drama and Society in the Age of Jonson*, eventually published as a book in 1937 but partly published in *Scrutiny* before that (see Chapter 3), and thus to R. H. Tawney's seminal work of 1926, *Religion and the Rise of Capitalism*. (It is not clear when Leavis first read Tawney's book; the first mention of it in *Scrutiny* seems to be by Knights in 1935, although his saying 'it is probably unnecessary to refer to' Tawney's book may suggest that it was already well known in *Scrutiny* circles.)[44] Part of the interest of the story of the development of this framework in the 1930s and 1940s lies, I would argue, in the way in which Eliot's literary-historical pronouncement gets absorbed, and modified, into a larger story about the beginnings of a modern society based on a capitalistic economy, but, by the time of the essays that make up *Education and the University* at the beginning of the 1940s, it is clearly the latter emphasis that predominates.[45] Indeed, Leavis explicitly uses Tawney's phrase to describe the seventeenth century in terms that condense its function in this larger historical story: 'the notion of society as an organism gives way to that of society as a joint-stock company', complete with footnote to *Religion and the Rise of Capitalism*.[46]

Moreover, the pedagogic purpose in his proposed syllabus of the central paper on the seventeenth century is to encourage students to develop the capacity to appraise whole societies and arrive at some estimate of progress or decline in the quality of life they represent. The recommended reading is geared to this purpose. Thus, the student should start to think about progress by reading Macaulay's third chapter, and 'all students' would read Tawney's *Religion and the Rise of Capitalism* and Basil Willey's *The Seventeenth-Century Background*, plus E. A. Burtt's *The Metaphysical Foundations of Modern Science*. The task for students would be to explain how, as he puts it, 'the England of the seventeenth century became the England of today'. Interestingly, in his list of topics for detailed study, all the rest of which are substantive developments in the seventeenth century itself, he includes 'the reaction against Whig history'—which is clearly a different kind of topic: reflexive, methodological, and tied to the present. (By 1968, Wallace Robson could regard this account as dated: Leavis 'was writing in the full tide of the "reaction against Whig history", and it was natural that he should describe the English seventeenth century in the way that he did', though Robson may exaggerate the Eliotic character of Leavis's account when he says: 'There is a danger that students doing this course might come to see the past of English literature, and the past of English history, exclusively through Anglo-Catholic spectacles.'[47]) All this is explicitly geared to enabling the student to address the question of whether the earlier century was 'a better or worse place to have been born in'.[48] Leavis's account suggests an emphasis on the rise of capitalism well before the Industrial Revolution rather than on the way poets ceased to feel a thought as a sensation. It is hardly surprising that one correspondent should have responded by observing that there did not seem to be much *literature* in Leavis's proposed course, noting in slightly pained tones that Leavis's discussion 'seems to show more concern for history'.[49]

Even when addressing literature, the framework is of a familiar historical kind: 'For instance, attempting to explain the decisive appearance of modern prose in the first decade of the Restoration, a student would find himself invoking something like the whole history of the century, political, economic, social and intellectual.'[50] This is Leavis's recycling of the familiar claims based on Sprat's account of the founding of the Royal Society, though, as David Hopkins has recently pointed out, he was relying on the 'misleading excerpts' from Sprat published in Joel Spingarn's 1908 anthology *Critical Essays of the Seventeenth Century*.[51] Be that as it may, Leavis emphasized the attempt to reduce 'all things as near the Mathematical plainness' as possible, taking this ambition to be an index of much wider changes. Overall, the most one can say is that Leavis's early cultural criticism conjoined his *Middletown*-inspired critique of contemporary society to a Tawney-inspired critique of the transition to capitalism in the seventeenth century and used the amalgam to put historical stuffing into Eliot's sketchy remarks about changes in poetic sensibility.

Insofar as Eliot himself was to put more flesh on his account of the seventeenth century in subsequent writings, as he certainly did, his emphasis was chiefly political and ecclesiastical, part of the hardening of his conservative identity from the late 1920s onwards, rather than any further elaboration of this change in 'sensibility'. There are clearly points of congruence between Eliot's and Leavis's social criticism in the 1930s, above all in their shared reliance on Tawney's account of the decline of religious or moral constraints on selfishness, but the tenor of their respective writings was by now rather different. Insofar as Eliot broadens his criticism from the late 1920s onwards, his targets are principally Whiggism, Romanticism, Liberalism, and ultimately secularism and democracy; in his later work, the seventeenth century is prized above all for Anglican doctrine and ecclesiastical prose. Leavis has a more continuous historical story in mind, one that, loosely speaking, links the rise of science, the Agricultural and Industrial Revolutions, the growth of mass society, with all its standardization, advertising, and cheap press, right up to the decline of values in the present. When in his later work Leavis repeats, as he does more than once, the point that 'modern prose appeared so decisively in the first decade of the Restoration', he glosses the underlying causes of this as inaugurating 'the triumphant advance towards the civilization, technological and Benthamite, that we live in'.[52]

Perhaps here it is helpful to think of Leavis as constructing his historical case backwards, so to speak, beginning with the characterization of the present in the work of the Lynds, moving back to the recent loss of settled local communities in Sturt, moving further back to the impact of the Agricultural and Industrial Revolutions in the Hammonds, and then back further to Willey and Burtt on the origins of modern science, and then back further still to Tawney and Knights on the early impact of mercantile capitalism. There may have been hints of aspects of this scheme in a variety of earlier writers, notably Arnold and Lawrence, but perhaps none of the major critics developed such a connected historical story.

Nor, in Leavis's view, had professional historians provided an adequate account. The historical economists had pioneered analysis of the transformative effects of the Industrial Revolution, but, on the whole, historiography in the age of Tout and Pollard and their successors encouraged, as I observed in the Introduction, an austere abstention from such transhistorical judgements.[53] Emphasizing the role that an initial training in literary criticism would have in forming the powers of judgement more generally and thus in enabling students to evaluate the quality of life in earlier periods, Leavis hoped it would develop 'a maturity of outlook such as the study of history ought to produce, but even the general historian by profession doesn't always exhibit'.[54] The shortcomings of professional historians are a constant refrain throughout the literary-critical cultural history of the half century after 1920, and it may be that the kinds of broad historical interpretation carried by *Scrutiny* and later the volumes of the *Pelican Guide to English Literature* did much to fill this alleged void. But, given the influence of the kind of historical understanding promoted by the literary criticism of this period, it is important to remember how distant many of its sources were from the few throwaway remarks to be found in Eliot's 1921 review essay. As I observed earlier, the interpretation of English history that animated Leavis's cultural criticism melded several not easily compatible perspectives, including some that may now seem surprisingly traditional in character.

V

The place in Leavis's pedagogy of thinking in large historical terms about the *nineteenth* century was rather different, and it may be a useful first step to recognize that the period that was really at issue was the Victorian age rather than the century as a whole. We should not forget how close and intimate a relation this was for Leavis himself. When he was born, Victoria would still be on the throne for another six years; when he took the Preliminary examination for the History Tripos in the summer of 1915, at the end of his first year at Cambridge, not only had the Great War yet to be fully felt or analysed as marking an epochal change, but historical and general culture had not yet received the perspective-shifting impact of publications such as *Eminent Victorians* or *The Waste Land*. Moreover, the political culture into which Leavis grew up was still absorbed with attempting to work out and apply a critique of what were perceived to be the individualist principles dominating Victorian England. Both the line of celebrated social critics from Carlyle to Morris and the later cohorts of New Liberal and Socialist thinkers had elaborated an account of the governing assumption of Victorian society that foregrounded a cluster of related abstractions: laissez-faire, political economy, individualism, Utilitarianism, and so on.

One way to begin to think about Leavis's relation to this picture would be to say that for him English literature embodied the *contrary* of these abstractions, and the fact that it did so in concrete, particularistic terms was, he held, the basis of both its power and its unique relevance. The abstract, calculating instrumentalism that a long line of critics had identified at the heart of what was represented as official or dominant nineteenth-century attitudes provided the intellectual foundation for those contemporary expressions of reductive and quantitative thinking that *Scrutiny* never ceased to excoriate. Insofar as a single eye-catching label for this nexus of attitudes recurred, it was 'Benthamite', a label that, given the apparent specificity of its referent, required a supporting historical story. Leavis's story about this was, essentially, the received turn-of-the-century story, the story propagated by Dicey and given more biographical and intellectual depth by Stephen and Halévy. In general terms, it must presumably have been the validating power of literature's opposition to the cast of mind identified in this way as dominant in Victorian England that accounted for the extraordinary esteem in which Leavis held *Hard Times*, Dickens's most diagrammatic fiction. But it is of a piece with the quasi-historical dynamic that I am pointing to here that the central figure, the character whose name became a kind of fictional metonomy for a whole culture of calculating heartlessness, should have been—indeed, *had* to have been—a Utilitarian, namely, Mr Gradgrind.[55] The ungainly composite Leavis came to use to damn all that was amiss with contemporary society—'technologico-Benthamite'—installs itself in his lexicon only in the 1960s and 1970s. But the demonizing of 'Benthamism' has a longer history in his work, one that can be traced back to the rapid deterioration at the beginning of the 1930s in the relation of both the Leavises to I. A. Richards, identified as Bentham's modern representative.

In this connection it is significant that for the second number of *Scrutiny* a long review essay was commissioned on recent books about Bentham, including, notably, one by C. K. Ogden. Ogden was well known to be Richards's collaborator and to share his scientistic enthusiasm for analysing the operations of language, so there may have been some aggression involved in choosing as reviewer the young Cambridge philosopher and political theorist Michael Oakeshott, who could be predicted, as both a Hegelian in philosophy and a conservative in politics, to be unsympathetic to this approach. In his review essay Oakeshott was duly unsympathetic to Ogden's claims for Bentham as an important philosopher and analyst of language, reiterating the traditional view that his significance lay, despite the weakness and confusions of his thinking, in his influence in the sphere of legal reform and political practice. This, averred Oakeshott, was the standard picture derived from Mill and amplified by Stephen and Halévy, and it was the true view: 'It appears, then, that Mill's estimate of Bentham's genius is, with certain reservations, more accurate than the view with which we are now presented.'[56] The break with Richards was consolidated by D. W. Harding's devastating 'Evaluation' in the fourth number, which was followed by Leavis's own very disobliging long review essay on *Coleridge on Imagination* two years later, where he characterized Richards as 'an avowed Benthamite'.[57]

A sketch of the intellectual history of Victorian England was, therefore, already in place in Leavis's thinking by the early 1930s, but it was not to receive its full elaboration until the mid-1940s. There was, of course, a caricature of Victorian literary history already at work in his earliest books such as *New Bearings* and *Revaluation*, which largely involved taking over Eliot's charges that nineteenth-century verse had retreated to a sentimental fairyland. In some ways, the two caricatures complemented each other: it was precisely because the dominant Utilitarianism was so mechanistic and heartless, and so in command of the everyday world, that writers had withdrawn to a balmier region of sentiment and fancy.

Part of the interest of Leavis's long introduction to his edition of Mill on Bentham and Coleridge lies in his unsteady acknowledgement of the oversimplification involved in this familiar picture.[58] At the same time, the structuring role assigned to a generalized notion of Utilitarianism is, though modified in detail, never abandoned. The initial stimulus to furnish students with detailed guidance on how to address 'the Victorian background' came from the establishment of a new paper in the English Tripos on 'George Eliot and her setting', and this is a reminder that so much of Leavis's interpretation of history took shape as a form of intellectual map-making for pedagogical purposes. Already in June 1946, he was writing to his former pupil Gordon Cox, explaining the guidance he had just given 'the finishing 1st years' on how to approach the nineteenth century (presumably a recommendation about vacation reading in preparation for their work on George Eliot). The letter makes the structure of his view starkly clear: on the one hand, there is the Utilitarian 'line', running from Bentham through J. S. Mill to Beatrice Webb, the Fabians, and on to I. A. Richards in the present; on the other, there is the Coleridgean line, best embodied by Matthew Arnold but also other Victorian 'sages', coming down in the present to T. S. Eliot. The page of suggested reading he had prepared for his students contained this revealing indication of how the 'lines' functioned in his own mind:

> For anyone wanting to explore, a full account of Utilitarianism is to be found in E. Halévy's *Growth of Philosophic Radicalism* and of J. S. Mill in Leslie Stephen's *English Utilitarians*. But there's no need to plunge: what's important is to grasp the significance of the line from the 17th century 'Political Arithmetic' (see Tawney—and note the complex of social, economic, political, and intellectual considerations) to Bentham and on to Richards and Ogden (*Science and Poetry*, I.A.R.; D. W. Harding's critique of I.A.R. in *Determinations*, Oakeshott on *The New Bentham* in *Scrutiny* I, 2; F.R.L.'s review of *Dr Richards, Bentham and Coleridge*, *Scrutiny* III, 4; and various other reviews of R in S).[59]

The 'line' from Tawney's account of economic reasoning in the seventeenth century to the 'Benthamism' of I. A. Richards could not be clearer; the major part of Leavis's understanding of the nineteenth century fell into place as part of this story.

Leavis's key move is to propose Mill's two essays as a uniquely valuable point of access to the age. These essays are, to use one of his favoured positive terms, 'classical', and Leavis clearly evinces some admiration for the quality of Mill's mind. But his role here is as 'a great representative figure of Victorian intellectual history', and as the account progresses it emerges that his representativeness consists principally in both being and not being a Utilitarian—for that, it could be said, is also how Leavis characterizes Victorian culture as a whole. For example, while declaring that George Eliot 'was never a Benthamite' despite working on the *Westminster Review* (which by that date had changed its intellectual complexion since its high Philosophic Radical days, though Leavis does not acknowledge this), but 'the atmosphere of the intellectual milieu to which she belonged—a milieu very central to the Victorian age—was in a general sense Utilitarian'.[60] It is this last assumption that underlies so much of Leavis's treatment of the nineteenth century and his symbolic uses of that century in contemporary controversy.

But, if John Stuart Mill's *Autobiography* 'gives, in its classically representative way, a most important part of the intellectual history of the nineteenth century', the story is carried on in Beatrice Webb's *My Apprenticeship*, which he claims is still not fully recognized as 'one of the classics of English literature'. (The fact that Webb treated the novel as a rich source of social understanding further recommended her to Leavis.) The story of the young Beatrice Potter's education and self-education shows, suggests Leavis, that some of the familiar representations of the Victorian age need to be handled with care. For example, he observes that the Potter family home, though that of a wealthy businessman, was not philistine: 'in fact, the first part of *My Apprenticeship* serves as a most effective reminder of the actual concrete complexities simplified in Matthew Arnold's threefold classification, which (like Arnold's methods in general) had its point and its efficacy because there was a public capable of appreciating it—one, that is, not exhaustively describable as Philistine or Barbarian.' The point about the coexistence of various publics is a good one, perennially relevant, though for the most part it was not one that Leavis applied reflexively to his own implied readership. But this caution is only partially extended to the other overused label, 'Utilitarian'. The extreme individualism of Spencer's politics 'is a tribute to the strength of the Utilitarian tradition'—one casual indication of the stereotypical understanding of Utilitarianism that Leavis so often falls back on. Beatrice Potter's mother is tarred with the same brush, where her version of 'Utilitarianism' is defined in terms of '*laissez-faire* individualism' and where most of the illustrative names Leavis supplies are those of political economists.[61]

At this point, Leavis embarks on a short riff on the kind of reading the student should do to understand this 'Utilitarian' tradition. What the student will get from Halévy is 'the coming together of what is represented by the name of Adam Smith with what may be represented by the name of Newton'. In addition, 'the history of the central part played by Philosophic Radicalism in the movement of agitation, political education and organized pressure that led up to the Reform Act of 1832 is to be found in Halévy's book'. It is revealing that Leavis moves immediately from this sketch of the historical formation of 'the Benthamite ethos' to an identification of I. A. Richards as the contemporary embodiment of it. Indeed, Leavis uses Mill's attempt to combine Bentham and Coleridge as a stick with which to beat Richards's alleged 'replacement' of Coleridge by Bentham, for he sees Richards's whole theoretical enterprise as just 'cloth[ing] an essentially Benthamite spirit'. Leavis's dealings with history rarely disguised their contemporary controversial animus.[62]

But as this section of Leavis's discussion proceeds, it becomes even harder to pin down quite what he understands by 'Utilitarianism'. When summarizing Bentham or Mill's critique of him, the referent seems fairly clear: a body of theorizing elaborating the sovereign status of the principle of utility in morals and politics. But elsewhere the sense becomes much more elastic: 'What may fairly be called a Utilitarian ethos was pervasive, and can be found in representative figures who would not have called themselves Utilitarians', his chosen illustration being Macaulay, an ironic choice given Macaulay's celebrated attack on the unimpeachably Utilitarian premises of James Mill's *Essay on Government*. It is hard by this point not to feel that he is using the term as a synonym for a kind of practical hard-headedness and commitment to material progress. It might negatively be understood as a robust approach to human affairs characterized by what he called (speaking of Mill on Bentham but also by extension of Richards's failings) 'its indifference to essential human interests'. And this broad-brush treatment becomes even more salient as he moves into his paean to *Hard Times*: 'Gradgrind and Bounderby give us, in significant association, two aspects of Victorian Utilitarianism.'[63] This, as Donald Winch has pointed out, is a curious misreading of the intellectual identity of the latter character, but Leavis pushes it further: Bounderby 'is "rugged individualism"', and thus he clearly represents 'the tendency of James Mill's kind of Utilitarianism'.[64] The moral of the novel, as summarized in the almost contemporaneous section on it of *The Great Tradition*, is held to be 'the confutation of Utilitarianism by life'.[65] By this point, the term seems to have broken almost entirely free of its actual historical referent and become what it so often was in Leavis's later writings, a generalized swear-word.

Even so, Leavis is not yet done with the actual history. The New Poor Law of 1834, he declares, was the

> symbolic embodiment of all that was most rationally and righteously inhuman in orthodox Utilitarianism, with its implacable Malthusian logic. Utilitarianism,

in fact, provided the sanction for the complacent selfishness and comfortable obtuseness of the prosperous classes in the great age of Progress: they were protected by righteous rationality from the importunities of imaginative sympathy.[66]

We may leave aside the unwarranted insistence that Malthusianism was an inherent part of 'orthodox Utilitarianism' and concentrate instead on the slight tonal arrest indicated by the insertion of the phrase 'in fact' at the beginning of the second sentence. If the phrase were removed, the sentence becomes purely expository or declarative: with the phrase inserted, it acquires a slightly more argumentative note, as though urging a view that might be rejected or overlooked initially. There is a hint of the prosecuting barrister's tone in summarizing the charge that Utilitarianism was not merely a theoretical system, but that it had damaging consequences in the world: 'Utilitarianism, *in fact*, provided the sanction . . .'. And the qualities it allowed to flourish do make a serious charge-sheet: 'complacent selfishness and comfortable obtuseness', a lack of 'imaginative sympathy'. The task of a literary education might almost seem to be framed as a corrective to the failings allegedly characteristic of the Victorian prosperous classes.

For the first twenty pages of his essay Leavis has purported to show how 'the kind of field that coordinates itself round John Stuart Mill' would be his recommended route by which the literary student might arrive at an understanding of the Victorian age more generally. Only in what is in effect a brief coda (the final two pages) does he consider the figure 'to be set over against Mill' for this purpose—namely, Matthew Arnold. Here we get a glimpse of an element that is Victorian but not Utilitarian, and the key lies in the fact that Arnold is not 'a systematic thinker' and so should not be 'judged by inappropriate criteria'. Instead, what is to be celebrated in Arnold—it is clearly a profession of faith in the more general value of the literary critic—is 'the flexibility, the sensitiveness, the constant delicacy of touch for the concrete in its complexity, the intelligence that is inseparably one with an alert and fine sense of value'.[67] For all Leavis's sympathetic treatment of Mill in the preceding pages, these few phrases remind us what has been lacking in all writers steeped in 'the Benthamite ethos'. Of course, 'Leavis on Mill and Arnold' might seem to be reproducing the structure of 'Mill on Bentham and Coleridge', except that Leavis is more unabashedly partisan, clearly identifying with Arnold. And this contrast continues to structure his view of English intellectual history in which the governing philosophy of the nineteenth and twentieth centuries is set over against those 'essential human interests' that are represented by literature.

Leavis's introduction is a relatively learned piece of intellectual history in its own right, one with more explicit reference to existing scholarship than was usual in his writing. In this way is revealing of the frame of reference he brought to his understanding of the nineteenth century. Perhaps he was only being realistic in recognizing that, in the mid-1940s, literary students attempting to get to grips with the 'background' of the Victorian period might begin with such recognized surveys as Trevelyan's *British History in the Nineteenth Century* and Oliver Elton's *Survey of English Literature 1830–1880*.[68] I have already remarked on Leavis's continuing partiality for Trevelyan's work, and his recommendation to his students to use the nineteenth-century volume as their basic textbook smuggled in attitudes of its own. Published as long ago as 1922, the book expressed an antipathy to what Trevelyan termed 'the strange world in which we live today'.[69] As David Cannadine has noted in his biographical study, the book celebrated English exceptionalism, turning the Whig story into the national story, but giving it a pessimistic twist: 'At some point in Britain's late-nineteenth-century history, Trevelyan lost his Whiggish confidence in ordered progress and continuing reform.' And Trevelyan's gloomy diagnosis extended to that most Leavisian of themes, the reading public: 'In the seventeenth century, Members of Parliament quoted from the Bible; in the eighteenth and nineteenth centuries from the classics; in the twentieth century from nothing at all.'[70] English students were getting a pretty clear sense of the direction in which history had moved.

It is also clear that Leslie Stephen still provides the basic outlines of the relevant intellectual history, above all in his three volumes on the English Utilitarians.[71] Stephen's account was to some extent modified by the more detailed historical research of Halévy on the eighteenth-century sources of Benthamism and on the closely related contributions of classical political economy. The other works cited shed an interesting light on the historical perspectives Leavis brought to the discussion. Among older studies cited are Graham Wallas's *Life of Francis Place* and J. A. Hobson's study of *John Ruskin, Social Reformer*, now supplemented by G. D. H. Cole on *The Life of William Cobbett* and Benjamin Lippincott on *Victorian Critics of Democracy*, as well as G. M. Young's *Victorian England*. Sources for more general historical issues include Firth's commentary on Macaulay's *History*, J. M. Robertson on *Modern Humanists*, and Herbert Butterfield on *The Whig Interpretation of History*. It may seem as though students of English are being advised to read very widely in works of history, though the list has, on closer inspection, a very distinctive colouring, combining the Edwardian progressive critique of the intellectual roots of laissez-faire with the sceptical examination of the older Whig story. Some of Leavis's recommended reading, which clearly represented the bulk of his own reading on these topics, appeared a little dated by 1950, and, unsurprisingly, it remained pretty much undisturbed thereafter by the great expansion of work on the political and social history of the Victorian period.

Overall, Leavis displayed a complex ambivalence towards the nineteenth century. In some respects, he shared the antipathy, common in educated circles from the late nineteenth century onwards, towards the alleged individualism and utilitarianism that had shaped policy and attitudes in the mid-Victorian period. Like other social critics during the interwar years, he looked for ways first to isolate and then to supplant what was represented as the one-sided application of the supposed 'laws' of political economy. Leavis, in other words, did not altogether disown the caricature of Victorian England as having been in the grip of a peculiarly reductive conception of human agency, one based on the model of *homo economicus*, a conception that then allowed all the more generous or elevated ideals to be overridden in the name of the selfish pursuit of material gain. For all of Leavis's early imprecations against 'the machine', which had allegedly destroyed a more 'natural' relation with the environment, his picture of the nineteenth century does not focus on industrialism as such. For the most part, he does not indulge in Ruskinian denunciation of squalor or Morrisian condemnation of injustice: his target is, rather, the natural marriage of philistinism with economism. Ideas, rather than social and economic history itself, are his preferred historical medium.

Yet, at the same time, Leavis also looked back on other features of Victorian culture with admiration or even longing. Compared to the peculiarly debased nature of the present, the existence of a reading public that could bring commercial success to such manifestly serious writers as George Eliot deserved respect. Moreover, the excesses of acquisitive individualism had been denounced and to some extent checked by the sheer quality of the social criticism of the great Victorian sages. Though his complete assessments of figures such as Arnold or Mill fell far short of idolatry, he not only gave due recognition to the force and pointedness of their analyses of the excesses of Victorian commercialism, but he also bemoaned the impossibility of such serious writing having real sway with a serious public in his own time. And, of course, it was a *Scrutiny* maxim that the 'great reviews' of the nineteenth century were far superior to anything that existed in the middle decades of the twentieth century. 'It was still possible to write for the reading public as a whole,' intoned Gordon Cox, a second-generation Scrutineer in 1938, and the Victorian periodicals 'played the major part in creating for the writers of their age that informed, intelligent and critical public without which no literature can survive for very long, and which is so conspicuously lacking to-day'.[72] The sentiment may now seem the small change of *Scrutiny* polemic, but the continuity with the assumptions of Leavis's dissertation is striking.

As so often when history is being mobilized in the service of social criticism, it all depends on the depth of focus. When Leavis was taking the long view of social change from the late sixteenth century onwards, the nineteenth century could figure damningly as the culmination of the rise to dominance of economic categories that began in the seventeenth century. But when focusing the lens for a close-up, anatomizing the vulgarities of interwar literary culture in the twentieth century, then the Victorian period could seem to represent a land of lost content, where a serious reading public sustained serious writers publishing in serious journals. In this book I am arguing, among other things, that literary critics are always, by default, second-hand historians, especially when they aspire to be social critics, too; but it is no part of my case that the historical assumptions that can be teased out of their work need necessarily be seen as either consistent or persuasive.

3

Science and Capitalism
as 'Background'

I

The two previous chapters focused on some of the explicit and implicit forms of history present in the work of two critics who were indisputably major figures in twentieth-century British culture. But it is a commonplace of intellectual history that figures of the second rank can often prove to be the most illuminatingly representative of patterns of thought and assumption in a particular period. This chapter will mainly deal with two such figures whose writings were to have a widespread impact between the 1930s and 1960s, and who illustrate the ways in which the tricky category of 'background' in literary studies can actually be a medium for transmitting some very substantive understandings of history—even, in these two cases, understandings of the part played by such major forces as science and capitalism in forming modern societies. These two examples will, in addition, provide further illustration of how, in the interwar period, what were presented as scholarly reinterpretations of seventeenth-century literature could also operate as forms of contemporary cultural criticism. Of course, figures of the second rank do not always make for exhilarating reading, so readers may have to be patient until the larger implications of the analysis can be brought out in the final section of the chapter.

No one, I assume, would now want to argue that the English critic Basil Willey belongs in any imaginable first rank, though he was a scholar of considerable standing in his own day who latterly held at Cambridge what some people regarded as the premier chair of English in the country (some people at Cambridge, anyway). But Willey has an important if limited place in my story, partly because his version of 'background' became the way in which generations of readers in literary studies and beyond imbibed an understanding of the development of English thought from the seventeenth to the nineteenth centuries, and partly because his work exhibited a distinctive blend of literary criticism and intellectual history.

We may begin with a deliberately mundane source, a review of one literary scholar by another. The quotation comes from a 1934 review of Willey's first book, *The Seventeenth Century Background*, by his Cambridge colleague L. J. Potts, a figure whom history has scarcely deigned to put in any rank at all.

> During the last fifteen years the attention of critics has been increasingly focussed on the Seventeenth Century. When the reaction against Victorianism was at its height it was to Elizabethan drama and the poets of the Romantic Revival that we went for inspiration, and to 'our excellent and indispensable Eighteenth Century' for a steadying influence. But partly owing to the pioneer work of Professor Grierson and Mr T. S. Eliot, it has become clear that a revolution took place in the Seventeenth Century involving deeper issues than those of the Sixteenth, Eighteenth, or early Nineteenth; and until the nature of this revolution has been sufficiently expounded it is unlikely that the centre of interest will shift or disperse.[1]

With a contemporary's alertness to shifts in fashion, Potts here distinguishes the general reaction against Victorianism of the first two decades of the century from the historical change that had taken place since then. This latter perspective is associated particularly with the work of Eliot, and, as the review progresses, Potts repeatedly represents Willey's book as working within the framework supplied by Eliot. For example, he argues that Willey 'extends to [Sir Thomas] Browne Mr Eliot's well-known and profound statement that "a thought to Donne was an experience: it modified his sensibility"', but that shortly afterwards the beginnings of that rationalism that reached its full expression in the eighteenth century put such a 'unified sensibility' beyond reach.[2]

So far, so Cambridge; but even the more Olympian perspective of Sir Herbert Grierson, Regius Professor of Rhetoric and English Literature at Edinburgh, yielded at least one similar conclusion. In reviewing Willey's book, he also noted its treatment of Sir Thomas Browne: 'Mr Willey groups him with the Metaphysicals in virtue of his "unified sensibility" (the popular phrase today), the way in which his thought is steeped in feeling.' Grierson clearly felt that by this date it was unnecessary to identify either the author or the import of the quoted phrase about the 'unified sensibility', but his slightly sniffy aside about its being 'the popular phrase today' acquires an added piquancy when one remembers that Eliot's dictum first began life in a review of Grierson's edition of the Metaphysicals. Still, Grierson was likewise identifying the Eliotic inheritance of Willey's book, even if he rightly noted its larger contention that the present generation no longer needed to accept scientific rationalism as the apogee of human progress.[3]

It is not altogether surprising that contemporary reviewers saw *The Seventeenth Century Background* as an application of Eliot's celebrated historical claim. From the outset, the book rather nervously paraded its Eliotic associations. He is the only writer quoted by name in the foreword (from a book published in the same year—Willey was clearly keeping up with Eliot's publications). The foreword ends with an acknowledgement that one chapter had already been published in the *Criterion* and 'I am indebted to the editor of that review'—the unnamed editor, of course, being Eliot. T. E. Hulme is quoted twice in the opening chapter, and reference is also made to Julien Benda's *La Trahison des clercs*, both known at the time to be touchstones of the Eliotic creed. By the early 1930s, Eliot's authority was entering its papal phase, and such obeisances from a slightly younger scholar might seem unremarkable. The influence of his claim about a 'dissociation of sensibility' was a significant element in this standing, but what is curious about Willey's book, when more closely examined, is the way it infuses Eliot's notion with a historical interpretation of a rather different provenance. This other strain becomes evident even in the discussion of Sir Thomas Browne that reviewers had picked out for its Eliotic character.

Admiring Browne for the way he could both embrace the 'new philosophy' and cling to the old religious, quasi-magical, sensibility, Willey writes:

> He had, in fact, what Mr T. S. Eliot has called the 'unified sensibility' of the 'metaphysicals'.... It meant the capacity to live in divided and distinguished worlds, and to pass freely to and fro between one and the other, to be capable of many and varied responses to experience, instead of being confined to a few stereotyped ones.[4]

As this theme is developed, it becomes clear that Willey is actually making a point against later specialization: 'the major interests of life', he writes, 'had not as yet been mechanically apportioned to specialists, so that one must dedicate oneself wholly to fact or wholly to value'. The 'metaphysical' mind could hold all these styles of thought 'in a loose synthesis'. Although this is a different, and in some ways more hackneyed, point than Eliot's, Willey nonetheless treats them as equivalent. 'As in Mr Eliot's celebrated instance of Spinoza and the smell of cooking, Browne thinks of Gorgons when he is discoursing of crystal and fuses them into a whole.' (Willey cites *Homage to John Dryden* as the source of Eliot's remark, which may suggest he had drafted this passage before the relevant essay was republished in *Selected Essays*, but which anyway bears out the point made in the Chapter 2 about the influence of the essays in the form of that slim Hogarth Press volume.) And, although Eliot's text would have been well known to likely readers of his book in 1934, Willey seeks to go further in grafting Eliot's terms onto his own argument. In the passage partly quoted by Potts, Willey writes: 'Mr Eliot has rightly pointed out that "a thought to Donne was an experience; it modified his sensibility"; this is largely true of Browne as well, and both owe it, I believe, to the scholastic tradition, in which "fact" and "value" had not yet been sundered by the mechanical "philosophy".'[5] This is surely a curious, and curiously philosophical, rendering of Eliot's celebrated claim, with a rather different history attached to it. Willey makes the claim essentially one about the modern divorce between fact and value, whereas Eliot (insofar as one can give a clear meaning to his famously gnomic remarks) seems to have had a form of poetic responsiveness in mind, the cognitive power of a certain kind of poetic image.

As Willey's book progresses, it extends its central theme beyond individual figures such as Browne to embrace the whole movement of English thought and literature over two centuries. Indeed, by introducing a chapter on Descartes into a book that otherwise confines itself to English writers, it is able to sketch the consequences of the wider move towards the Enlightenment. The 'Cartesian spirit' encouraged the view, argues Willey, that only that which could be demonstrated with something like mathematical certainty could be true. This entailed the downgrading of religion and poetry, which, he claims, 'spring from quite other modes of knowing', and so by the beginning of the eighteenth century 'religion had sunk to deism, while poetry had been reduced to catering for "delight"'. But just as these larger vistas are opening up, we are pulled sharply back to Willey's informing preoccupation:

> The Cartesian spirit made for the sharper separation of the spheres of prose and poetry, and thereby hastened that 'dissociation of sensibility' which Mr Eliot has remarked as having set in after the time of the Metaphysical poets. The cleavage then began to appear, which has become so troublesomely familiar to us since, between 'values' and 'facts'; between what you *felt* as a

human being or as a poet, and what you *thought* as a man of sense, judgement, and enlightenment.[6]

The gentle agreeableness of Willey's prose cannot altogether obscure the slides in argument here. Where Eliot's point had originally been about types of poetry, it is here turned into a story about the 'separation of the spheres of prose and poetry'. The passage is silent on causal or explanatory claims, but the suggestion is that this led to the cleavage between facts and values (not Eliot's theme), and that *that*, in turn, is then equated with a divide between feeling, the province of the human being or poet (here loosely, and rather implausibly, equated), and thought, including judgement. In its structure the argument is a familiar one, much rehearsed in nineteenth-century literature, and here rephrased in terms that appear to owe something to I. A. Richards's recent pronouncements on the divide between statements of fact and the 'pseudo-statements' of feeling and evaluation. The whole argument and scale of the book seem to have far outrun Eliot's dictum; in fact, it seems to be reinterpreting Eliot's claim in order to embrace a quite different, and in some ways more conventional, historical story, one in which, as we shall see, the otherwise unnamed phenomenon of what came to be recognized as the 'Scientific Revolution' played a central part.

Looking back almost thirty-five years later, Willey himself clearly came to feel that the Eliotic provenance of his first book had been somewhat exaggerated. He was quick to insist that 'I have no wish to under-rate the debt which, like the rest of us at that time, I owed to him,' and then went on:

> But I can honestly say that if any one book suggested to me the leading idea of *The Seventeenth Century Background* it was Whitehead's *Science and the Modern World*. I can even remember the place and time when the flash of illumination came to me: it was, of all incongruous circumstances, while sitting reading Whitehead over a cup of morning coffee in Lyons's shop in Petty Cury. There and then it dawned on me that 'Truth' was not all of one kind; that 'scientific truth' was not the whole of truth; that poets and divines had access to regions of it which were closed to mathematics and physics; and that the intellectual history of the seventeenth century could be seen as the struggle of scientific truth to emancipate itself from religion and poetry and to claim for itself unique validity. In the light of that idea I wrote my book.[7]

According to Willey, *The Seventeenth-Century Background* was largely written between June 1932 and July 1933, though it drew on the lectures he had been giving for some time on 'Seventeenth Century Life and Thought'. He does not say when he had his epiphany in the tea shop; Whitehead's book was published by Cambridge University Press in 1926 and attracted a good deal of attention, so Willey may have read it some years before he started to write his own study.

Reading Whitehead's book now, it is easy to see why Willey was drawn to it. Combining his very considerable authority as philosopher and mathematician with an accessible style, Whitehead attempted to elaborate an 'organic' view of mind and nature that rescued humankind from what he called the 'dead end' of scientific materialism, restoring religion and the aesthetic as central forms of experience. Whitehead made clear that it was the science and mathematics of the seventeenth century that constituted the great rupture with the past. Outlining the elements of what he termed 'the mechanistic theory of nature, which has reigned supreme ever since the seventeenth century', Whitehead argued that 'the history of thought in the eighteenth and nineteenth centuries is governed by the fact that the world had got hold of a general idea which it could neither live with nor live without'.[8] The Romantic reaction of the late eighteenth century marked the point at which the poets rejected this world view, a rejection most powerfully expressed by Wordsworth. 'The nature-poetry of the romantic revival', Whitehead writes,

> was a protest on behalf of the organic view of nature, and also a protest against the exclusion of value from the essence of matter of fact.... The romantic reaction was a protest on behalf of value. [Thereafter,] the literature of the nineteenth century, especially its English poetic literature, is a witness to the discord between the aesthetic intuitions of mankind and the mechanism of science.[9]

The effect of Whitehead's argument was to make the seventeenth century, rather than either the Renaissance or the Industrial Revolution, the true birth of the modern world. In fact, the Industrial Revolution is accorded only a rather contingent and minor role: it drew on the discoveries of science and it helped to further the application of mechanistic philosophy to society, but it did not, in Whitehead's narrative, mark the key division between two epochs. He does make one passing reference to the way in which political economy encouraged the treatment of human beings as employable machines, adding: 'The internal history of England during the last half century has been an endeavour slowly and painfully to undo the evils wrought in the first stage of the new epoch.'[10] If there is a later divide of comparable significance to the seventeenth century, it is his own lifetime, which sees the development of relativity and quantum physics and the consequent break-up of the Newtonian view of the universe.

Whitehead's book was based closely on his Lowell Lectures of the previous year and it contains practically no footnotes or references to existing scholarship on the many topics he covers. Where matters of 'general history' are concerned (as opposed to the philosophical and scientific ideas to which the bulk of the book is devoted), he gives the impression of merely referring to the received wisdom. There are, however, two explicit citations of historical works, and these may suggest something about the role of a figure who was clearly a point of reference for Whitehead and his readers, since they are both to W. E. H. Lecky, one to his *History of Rationalism* and one to his *History of European Morals*, published in 1865 and 1869 respectively.[11] These two books affirmed the strongly progressive character of free thought in liberating early modern Europe from superstition, and, according to a later estimate, 'for the next fifty years they formed an indispensable element in the creation of the historical background to British thinking', a claim that might be supported by noting that, by 1914, the *History of Rationalism* was in its twentieth printing and *European Morals* in its seventeenth.[12] Whitehead's treatment made clear that Lecky represented the world view, or background, his own book was intended to overturn.

Whitehead's revisionism was the historical scheme that the young English scholar imbibed with his coffee, but, as always, it was absorbed into a pattern of thinking and sensibility derived from other sources. In the opening chapter of *The Seventeenth-Century Background*, the book that laid the foundation of his scholarly reputation, Willey considered the decisive break that the 'new philosophy' of the seventeenth century made through its 'rejection of scholasticism'. The reader is invited to consider the effects of this change in terms that are characteristic of the apparent mildness of Willey's writing:

> We have to be on our guard, I think, as much against those who represent the rejection of scholasticism as pure loss, as against those who regard it as pure gain. It is only because for three hundred years almost everybody has united to extol it as pure gain that we may be forgiven for leaning a little (as Aristotle advises) toward the opposite side, so as to restore the true mean. With this reservation let us boldly declare that the rejection [of scholasticism] was not wholly disastrous.[13]

Willey's sense of literary 'boldness' was clearly less than Napoleonic: after emphasizing that for three centuries this rejection of scholasticism had been unanimously celebrated (and after then nervously sheltering behind Aristotle), he comes right out with it and risks his all with the judgement that, 'with this reservation', the rejection was 'not wholly disastrous'. Neither the form nor the substance of the judgement seems designed to court instant notoriety. But there may, in fairness, have been more than Willey's own literary timidity involved in this apparent bathos. Why might even this adverbially qualified negative phrase have seemed 'bold'?

The first chapter positions the book as part of this recent reassessment of the supposed 'victory' of science over religion in the seventeenth century. Willey notes that 'Catholics and Neo-Thomists' such as Jacques Maritain have contributed to this reassessment, together with T. E. Hulme and Benda, and younger figures such as the Catholic historian Christopher Dawson. He then declares that sentiments such as Dawson's condemnation of the Renaissance as the source of 'the present chaos in Western civilization' can 'now be uttered in all soberness and with compelling force, whereas at almost any time during the past three hundred years they would have seemed a mad flouting of the dominant optimism and progress-worship'. These figures did indeed regard the rejection of Scholasticism as, simply, 'disastrous'. But Willey emphasizes that the topic has also been treated by philosophers of science, such as Whitehead and E. A. Burtt, while of pressing significance for anyone working, as Willey did, in the fledgling Cambridge English school were I. A. Richards's explorations of forms of 'truth' in *Mencius on the Mind*. It is this impressive consilience of authorities that emboldens Willey to suggest that, while we should no longer approach the question with any 'antecedent prejudice in favour of the modern', we should not undervalue the achievements of modern science, either.[14]

By this point, Willey's own allegiances have begun to emerge more clearly, as when he writes: 'Insofar as the rejection of scholasticism led to an undue elevation of empirical "truth", and an attribution to it of a special privilege to represent "reality", it was a disaster.' Since the temperature of Willey's writing rarely rises above the tepid, such a declarative statement stands out: 'not wholly' a disaster, perhaps, but in its main and most obvious consequence 'it was a disaster'. A disaster, moreover, through whose consequences we were still living. There could be no simple going back: few could want scholasticism to be revived in toto:

> But its great value must be preserved somehow: its testimony to the primacy of the 'truths' of religious experience. We may not want these 'truths' theologically and metaphysically expressed; but we do want to be able to experience reality in all its rich multiplicity, instead of being condemned by the modern consciousness to go on
>
> > Viewing all objects, unremittingly
> > In disconnection dead and spiritless.[15]

(Willey does not identify this embedded quotation, which is, characteristic-ally, from Wordsworth's *Excursion*.) By this point, his prose has become somewhat less than even-handed, we may feel: the 'primacy' of religious experience is the thing, and this is what 'the modern consciousness' prevents us from realizing.

An interesting aside reveals something of the historiographical tradition against which Willey saw himself as struggling. Having given a sympathetic account of Joseph Glanvill's efforts to defend belief in an afterlife and other forms of supernaturalism (including the existence of witches) against the new rationalism, Willey writes: 'Thus we get the queer spectacle of a Fellow of the Royal Society lashing his age for a type of "unbelief" which Lecky and others celebrate as one of the finest triumphs of the scientific movement.'[16] Lecky here once again serves as little more than a handy metonym for a whole tradition of historiography from the eighteenth and nineteenth centuries that celebrated the advance of reason against superstition, a tradition, Willey implies, whose day is done. In its place, we now understand that the 'great value' of scholasticism 'must be preserved somehow'. But how? What, in the arid desert of 'modern consciousness', could allow us 'to experience reality in all its rich multiplicity'? The answer, in 1934, was not far to seek: litera-ture, especially (for the English) English literature; and more especially still (for those of Willey's disposition) those writers who struggled to unite intel-lect and feeling; and most particularly of all (especially for all hard-walking, Lakeland-loving, boyhood-yearning English literary scholars), Wordsworth.

The triumph of the scientific world view had been fatal for poetry, which, it was claimed, then languished until the end of the eighteenth century. 'What the cold philosophy did destroy was the union of heart and head, the synthesis of thought and feeling, out of which major poetry seems to be born.' This is one of the places where we can see the residue of Eliot's Imagist sketch being reworked, but now, directly contrary to Eliot's own literary preferences, as a vindication of Romantic 'inspiration'. In Willey's view, it fell to Wordsworth, above all others, to re-create that union. But today, he writes in one of his most outspoken expressions of cultural pes-simism, even that has passed: the beliefs about man and nature that Wordsworth's poetry embodied have evaporated. 'The poetic tradition founded by Wordsworth is probably now dead and superseded.' Only a pass-ing reference to Lawrence might seem to suggest some small glimmer of hope: 'It is significant to reflect that Wordsworth and Lawrence were mak-ing their protest against some of the effects of the very science which Browne was trying to vindicate. Browne wanted to plant us in the universe [the phrase quoted from DHL] so that we might have science; Wordsworth and Lawrence, that we might forget it.'[17]

It is curious to find a work that was to be so widely used as a textbook survey of seventeenth-century thought concluding with a chapter entirely devoted to the work of one Romantic poet. But it is more curious still to find a scholar widely identified as elaborating the historical basis of Eliot's view of the failings of poetry between the Metaphysicals and the French Symbolists expressing such sentiments. Where Wordsworth and the Romantics more generally represented for Eliot the root of the decadent sentimentalism that marred Victorian and Edwardian verse, Willey ends up emphatically identifying the pantheistic nature-worship of Wordsworth as a poetic peak against which subsequent failure is to be measured.[18]

Willey also shared the tendency, evident in so much critical writing after Arnold, to see poetry and religion as serving very similar functions. 'Since the scientific movement began, and numinous experience has become less and less accessible, Scripture and the liturgies have preserved a range of experiences which have been increasingly threatened by modernity in its various manifestations, and might have been altogether lost.'[19] The presence of that deceptively usable word 'modernity' in this sentence is, as so often, an indication of the presence of meta-history or quasi-history. But, insofar as it is a historical story, it is again structured round the same binary: science has triumphed and driven out religion or poetry or value (these three being often equated by Willey), and so the Bible must be clung to in order not to 'cut the last thread that links us with a lost world of feeling'. This assertion appears to rest on an Arnoldian conception of the Bible as being valuable because it represents 'records of religious experience' rather than as being true, the Word of God, a further illustration of how Willey, a lifelong Methodist, could fuse various strands in his intellectual inheritance. In a memoir of his former teacher, John Beer similarly characterized Willey as 'a man who wished to remain true to everything he knew and to everything that his wide-ranging sympathies taught him'. For Willey, 'the permanence of Christian values, outlasting the decay of historically founded dogmas, lay in their relevance to permanent human needs'.[20]

II

In 1940, in his second major work, *The Eighteenth-Century Background*— creativity in the matter of titles was not his *forte*—Willey managed the unusual feat of writing a book about eighteenth-century thought without explicitly mentioning the Industrial Revolution.[21] The nearest he comes is when, at the conclusion of his discussion of, once again, Wordsworth, he mentions that 'for many a sufferer from the strange disease of modern life, looking up from amongst the dark Satanic mills of the industrial age, the authority of the Wordsworthian Nature-religion has seemed absolute'.[22] The reference could hardly be more formulaic; the phrases are not set off as quotations, but this unacknowledged blending of Arnold's 'Scholar-Gypsy' with Blake's 'Jerusalem' signals a sensibility Willey feels he can rely upon his readers to share. What is more surprising is the way Willey takes his distance from the modern secular forms of this 'nature-religion', when one might expect him wholeheartedly to identify with it:

> Vestiges of the Wordsworthian impulse still survive in the activities of bodies like the National Trust or the Society for the Preservation of Rural England, and amongst the hordes of hikers and cyclists who wander weekly over the countryside in search of they know not what (I have recently seen Wordsworth and Dorothy praised as the 'first hikers').

These people, he is clearly suggesting, with some condescension, merely have the outward part of the open-air creed: they have lost the religious impulse that filled it for Wordsworth, and so the joy the countryside gives them is simply that of 'physical and nervous regeneration rather than of spiritual assurance'.[23] Willey allows us to infer that he is still in touch with that religious impulse, which helps underwrite his cultural pessimism and enables him to take such a lofty view of the 'hordes', who are only doing what he himself also did with enthusiasm.

Willey may be an example of the extremism that so often lurks behind the chaste embrace of the *juste milieu*—in his case a conservative, religious rejection of the modern world. Generations of student readers (and others) were provided with a map of English literary and intellectual history since the seventeenth century that bore the marks of a sensibility shaped by the fraught encounter in the late nineteenth and early twentieth centuries between the English educated classes and their experience of what they perceived as a commercialized, reductive, landscape-destroying 'modernity'. (In this respect, it is curious that Willey does not write more about Ruskin, fellow votary of the religion of the Lakes and of reverence for creation. There is no chapter on him in any of Willey's books and no essay on him in his *Festschrift* either.)

By this point, Eliot's notion of a 'dissociation of sensibility' has been transmuted into something altogether more conventional, but perhaps also more usable. We get a glimpse of the process by which such transmutation can be absorbed into the disciplinary bloodstream by turning again to a humble, workaday review, this time in that most scholarly of English Literature journals, *Review of English Studies*, a couple of decades after Willey's first book had been published. Reviewing a study of 'the cultural revolution of the seventeenth century', the reviewer notes that the first half of the book

> is an attempt to find out just what constituted the seventeenth-century 'dissociation of sensibility'; the phrase is used, not in Mr T. S. Eliot's original meaning of the gap between sensation and reflection in the poetic process, but in the way that Professor Basil Willey has used it, to imply a dichotomy between thought and emotion, and hence between reason and faith.[24]

The matter-of-fact assurance of the allusions, the calm acceptance of the peaceable coexistence between Eliot's and Willey's versions of this quasi-historical scheme, are eloquent testimony to the capacity of the revisionist gestures of one generation to become the literary-historical commonplaces of the next.

Following Chatto's publication of *The Seventeenth-Century Background* in 1934, Willey became one of the commercially most successful of the impressive stable of literary critics published by that house between 1930 and 1970. Even though the book was animated by the wider preoccupations that I have identified thus far, outwardly it retained its modest air of being a serviceable survey. Using the same unassuming format, *The Eighteenth-Century Background* explored attempts in that century to find meaning and value in the universe through the exaltation of 'nature'. In his third book, *Nineteenth Century Studies*, published in 1949, Willey's Coleridgean affinities became more overt, as he explored the attempts of a series of 'moralists' from Coleridge to Matthew Arnold to ground their ethical convictions in a series of unstable syntheses of religion, history, and culture, while his fourth book, *More Nineteenth-Century Studies* (1956)—the modesty of his titles could be hard to distinguish from a kind of sublime egotism—pursued similar themes in discussion of 'a group of honest doubters' from Francis Newman to John Morley.

The central preoccupation of these four major books might be said to be the encounter between English intellectual and literary sensibility of the centuries between 1600 and 1900 and various attempts to revise, reimagine, or replace the animating beliefs of traditional Christianity, especially by finding similar sources of joy and consolation in the intense experience of nature and poetry. Willey reported one of his colleagues teasing him, with some shrewdness, by saying 'all your books have really been about Wordsworth'.[25] This was pardonable exaggeration—his books were 'about' much else—but after his retirement Willey came to acknowledge, in his revealingly named memoir, *Spots of Time*, the kernel of truth in the comment:

> Wordsworth has so pervaded my life that I can hardly distinguish what is his from what is my own. It is not so much that I have learnt from him (though of course I have done so), as that he has given expression to the imaginative experiences which were already mine, unexpressed and inexpressible, before I knew him. . . . [Willey's father read *The Prelude* to him in his early teens] . . . almost everything I have written since has been an acknowledgement, whether explicit or implicit, of my debt to Wordsworth.[26]

Willey also shared a passionate devotion to the Lake District, the setting of many walking holidays and, later in life, the location of his country retreat. As he wrote in *Nineteenth Century Studies*: 'The whole course of English thought and letters in the nineteenth century would have been different if this island had not contained the mountain paradise of Westmorland and Cumberland. The Lake District was part of its religious creed.'[27] The same could be said for Willey himself, notwithstanding his continued adherence to his inherited Methodism.

Reviewing *Nineteenth Century Studies* in 1949, Harold Laski had no doubts about how to characterize it in political terms. He bestowed some praise, but, in a comment that was applicable to Willey's work as a whole, he suggested the effect of the book was to encourage that 'obsessive nostalgia' detectable in the position of T. S. Eliot, which ended up opposing necessary social change in the present.[28] Interestingly, other critics could seem somewhat uncertain about how to characterize Willey's work in disciplinary terms. Graham Hough, reviewing the same book, emphasized the distinctiveness of Willey's approach. He described Willey's two earlier books as 'almost a genre of their own, unique and difficult to describe', and concluded his review by saying: 'It is Professor Willey's distinction to have discovered a new kind of criticism, which discusses neither philosophy nor imaginative writing in themselves, but the residual deposit of philosophy that goes to form the imaginative apprehension of an age. In this field he is alone.'[29] Even allowing for the *politesse* a recently appointed lecturer in Cambridge might wish to show to the recently elevated professor, this suggests some of the instability in the notion of 'background', neither 'real history' nor 'pure literary criticism'. J. C. Maxwell, reviewing the book in *Universities Quarterly*, was somewhat more critical, and pointed out that 'historiography receives surprisingly little attention', an observation that serves to remind us that the writings of modern historians are also largely absent from Willey's work.[30] This is 'background' as determined by a foreground of literature: perhaps it is not surprising that so few historians at the time recognized it as a form of history. Nonetheless, Willey's work had an extensive and enduring impact on the way many readers who were not professional historians understood the intellectual history of the preceding three centuries. Perhaps partly because they were not in thrall to any of the political or critical fashions of his time, his books proved uncommonly durable. *The Seventeenth-Century Background*, for example, sold steadily for almost thirty years before it was, rather remarkably, chosen in 1962 to be one of the ten initial titles in Penguin's launch of its ambitious 'Peregrine' imprint, in which format it sold many thousands for years thereafter.[31]

III

The routes by which something that is foreground for one enquiry or discipline becomes background for another are many and not always obvious. If we are to understand how a version of 'background' rather different from Willey's came to be developed by critics in the 1930s and 1940s, we have to begin by recognizing the long-drawn-out engagement of such critics with the place occupied in contemporary culture by economic theories and categories. In the 1930s, the determining power of economic activity seemed a pressing problem both practically and theoretically.[32] Contributors to *Scrutiny*, for example, constantly sought to challenge the standing and legitimacy of economists' concepts.[33] Leavis's deliberate estranging of the familiar phrase 'the standard of living' as 'the standard of life' was not an isolated instance. Having denounced the deadening passivity and fantasy-feeding qualities of film, 'now the main form of recreation in the civilised world', Leavis returned to the task: 'It would be difficult to dispute that the result must be serious damage to the "standard of living" (to use the phrase as before).'[34] Similarly, Thompson declared that he would be more willing to take politicians seriously 'if they showed any capacity to discuss with intelligence the nature of a "high standard of living"'.[35] Moreover, in the early and mid-1930s, Leavis and the *Scrutiny* circle recognized, as literary critics of the previous generation had not had to, that the most significant challenge to contemporary society's complacent view of itself (which they parodied as 'Wellsian optimism') now came from Marxism. Leavis and his associates were never willing to accord any legitimacy to Marxism's endowing of economic forces with explanatory priority: 'There can be no doubt that the dogma of the priority of economic conditions, however stated, means a complete disregard for—or, rather, a hostility towards—the function represented by *Scrutiny*.'[36] An important part in the Scrutineers' polemics against the current dominance of economic categories was played by their claim that Marxism shared in and expressed this dominance rather than offering a genuine critique of it. For obvious reasons, these disputes intersected with another important development of these years in which the seventeenth century, for so long the centre of a celebratory narrative about English constitutional history, became the battleground on which social and economic historians now fought over the origins of capitalism.

Surprising as it may at first seem, one of the most influential contributions to these debates took the form of a study of Jacobean drama. L. C. Knights's book *Drama and Society in the Age of Jonson*, published in 1937, enjoyed considerable standing among intellectuals on the non-Marxist left for some decades.[37] Raymond Williams recalled that he 'read and re-read' it through the late 1940s and early 1950s; E. P. Thompson later spoke of it as a 'truly seminal' work.[38] F. W. Bateson called it 'the most ambitious attempt since Buckle and Taine to relate English literature to the social background'—which is itself an interesting genealogical line to invoke, going back to the most sociological of nineteenth-century historians of ideas.[39] Conditions in publishing at the time meant that, although Knights's book, like Willey's, was a work of detailed scholarship, both were reviewed widely in the general press, the more improbable reviewers stretching from Elizabeth Bowen in Knights's case to Guy Burgess in Willey's.[40] And in the 1960s Knights's book, too, was given a new and influential lease of life by being included among the first set of titles to appear in Penguin's new widely selling Peregrine imprint. Given my general theme, it is worth mentioning that Knights, like Willey and Leavis himself, had switched from History to English during his undergraduate years at Cambridge, obtaining a distinction in Part II of the English Tripos in 1928. He later recalled (in an unpublished memoir) that studying History in the mid-1920s overwhelmingly meant constitutional history, and he claimed that he did not hear the name of Tawney till some years later.[41] Knights became one of the founding editors of *Scrutiny* in 1932 and wrote for it extensively in the 1930s.

The chapters in the first half of *Drama and Society* are collectively titled 'The Background'. This, as I have already remarked, is a dead metaphor to which we have become so habituated that we scarcely register either its pictorial origins or the implicit claim to set off or throw light on something that is, implicitly, more important in the 'foreground'. What may be less obvious is that, deployed in this way in works by literary scholars, 'background' also becomes a way of negotiating shifts in the received understanding of the relevant history. Although Knights does not signal the fact, his book in effect attempts to dislodge the constitutional historians from their central position in the historiography of the seventeenth century: 'Political history', he remarks as an aside, 'is responsible for many false perspectives'.[42] Instead, he turns to the work of the so-called historical economists of the late nineteenth and early twentieth centuries, such as William Cunningham and W. J. Ashley, together with economic historians such as George Unwin, Ephraim Lipson, and, above all, R. H. Tawney. In doing so, he was implicitly challenging the Whig version of material progress celebrated by Macaulay and his successors. 'Until comparatively recent times,' observes Knights, 'it was usual for historians . . . to discuss this process of change in terms of "progress"'. He then goes on to caution against installing the mirror image as a new orthodoxy: 'I do not mean of course that one should substitute for the Whig view a nostalgic glorification of the more remote past'—something, we may feel, that is more easily said than not done.

Knights acknowledges that there are already signs that the traditional Whig interpretation of the seventeenth century is undergoing revision: 'historians are already abandoning the simple Whig view.'[43] His footnote here refers to Butterfield's polemic, and it is relevant to my argument that literary critics, especially the *Scrutiny* circle, seemed more alert to the significance of Butterfield's critique than did the culture at large in the 1930s. Butterfield's little book received only limited attention during the first decade or so after its publication in 1931; it was the far greater success of his *Christianity and History* in 1950 that led to the reissue of *The Whig Interpretation* in 1951 and its subsequent centrality to the methodological controversies of the 1950s.[44] Knights was calling for a historical approach that would contrast both with Whig history and with Marxism: it would centrally involve asking questions about the *quality* of human living in various periods. The reliance on concepts of 'progress' will, he contends, 'hinder the kind of discrimination and evaluation that is relevant to the study of history'.[45] When the opening chapter of the book had first appeared as an article, its subtitle was 'Notes for the Historian of Culture'. It is noticeable that he can tacitly assume that this evaluative form of 'the study of history' is most likely to be promoted by certain kinds of literary critic.

The medium with which the critic works is language, and this goes to the heart of Knights's case about the relationship between literature and 'the economic ordering of society' in Elizabethan times. That case is reinforced by a quotation from Leavis: 'Shakespeare did not create his own language.'[46] This language grew out of a way of life, predominantly agricultural, and that idiom gave its users 'advantages in habits of perception and discrimination, in emotional and intellectual organization—in sensibility'. Knights then goes on, in a passage that is too long to quote in full, to elaborate by way of contrast:

> What those advantages were is revealed by comparison with that 'impersonal language that has come, not out of individual life, not out of life at all, but out of necessities of commerce, of parliament, of board schools, of hurried journeys by rail'. They were the advantages that spring from 'living at first hand', in close touch with 'primary production'. Today, unless he is exceptionally lucky, the ordinary man has to make a deliberate effort to penetrate a hazy medium which smothers his essential human nature, which interposes between him and things as they are; a medium formed by the lowest common denominator of feelings, perceptions, and ideas acceptable to the devitalized products of a machine economy.[47]

If, as is often said, a critic's quality is most surely indicated by his choice of what to quote, this choice from Yeats's *Essays* may not speak well for Knights. The embedded quotation is a characteristic expression of Yeats's romantic aversion to the modern world, but it may be too much a grumpy medley of crotchets to help Knights's argument.[48] Nonetheless, the argument is reiterated in emphatic terms: 'The claim that I am making', he asserts, 'is that the essential life of a period is best understood through its literature'.[49]

The first half of Knights's book combines an impressive synthesis of the work of economic historians with a detailed examination of sources from the period commenting on the new economic conditions. This array of learning is intended to substantiate the striking claim that the years between 1590 and 1620 saw the beginnings of the economic system that has endured ever since. 'It was during this period that modern forms of commercial and industrial enterprise took shape.'[50] This is again one of those places where the deceptive term 'modern' is allowed to do too much work. Although Knights was presumably well aware of the vast changes that took place in the three centuries after 1620, he is nonetheless implicitly asserting a unity to that whole period, a unity defined by the unfettered dominance of 'the economic'. Moreover, his language reveals that the point of reference that determines the whole shape of his argument about the seventeenth century is in fact a hostile conception of the *nineteenth* century. 'Medieval economic activities,' he writes, 'were not guided by purely economic considerations— as these were understood in the nineteenth century'; or, again, he notes that the Jacobean period saw 'the increasing dominance of newer forms of activity which look forward to the nineteenth century'.[51] In so many settings in the early part of the twentieth century, such formulaic references to 'the nineteenth century' could serve as a placeholder for the supposed excesses of economic individualism.

The nub of Knights's account of the Jacobean dramatists, to which the second half of the book is devoted, is that the best of them could call upon the categories of traditional morality in responding to the excesses of the new economic behaviour of the early seventeenth century. Their responses were embodied in dramatic literature that retains its power not just because of this ability to draw on the resources of an established morality that has since been lost—their moral sensibilities had not yet been dulled by familiarity into regarding aggressively acquisitive behaviour as normal—but also because their responses were not those of an embattled minority, as was the case for modern authors. Rather, they drew confidence and vitality from being part of a broader popular culture. Jonson and company could share the responses of 'the journalists and moralists of the common people, whereas the few poets and novelists who count at the present day not only cannot share, they are inevitably hostile to, the attitudes of suitable readers of the *Star*, the *Sunday Express*, or the *Tatler*'. Judged by these titles, Knights's notion of the modern version of 'the common people' does seem strikingly elastic. Such contemporary contrasts are pursued with characteristic *Scrutiny* relentlessness: for example, even those in the early seventeenth century who remembered little of the plays they saw were at least 'not doomed to pass their lives in the emotional and intellectual muddledom of the readers of the *Daily Mail*', and so on.[52] In any event, the best of the Jacobean dramatists, Jonson above all, are treated as a resource for the critique of the economic order that has prevailed ever since.

He spells this out in his discussion of Jonson's *The Devil is an Ass*, a play that 'goes beyond economics and questions of expediency. Since it is the work of a great artist it cuts beneath the superficial follies, the accidental forms, and goes to the root of the disease, shaping the material in the light of an humane ideal that is implicit throughout.' Economics is here lined up with 'disease', the 'superficial', and the 'accidental', against 'great art' and 'an humane ideal'. 'Humane' *means* 'more than economic'; art, it seems, *cannot* give a positive picture of 'acquisitive' economic activity. 'If this book establishes anything it should be that the reactions of a genuine poet to his environment form a criticism of society as least as important as the keenest analysis in purely economic terms.'[53] 'At least as important' is a form of mock modesty here: since 'the essential life of a period is best understood through its literature', literary criticism constitutes the most important form of social criticism. By its very nature, literary criticism will counterpose 'an humane ideal' against 'the purely economic'; by returning to the great drama of the early seventeenth century, we are put in touch once more with ways of experiencing the social world that predate the conception of 'the purely economic', and we are thereby helped to relativize the category itself.

Clearly, this argument relies heavily on the premise that it is the economic order that has defined 'modern' society since the early seventeenth century, but that it did not do so before then. This is where Knights's struggles with the category of 'the economic' ('Of course I called myself a socialist. But I had no head for economic theory'[54]) land him in particular difficulties:

> To say that the qualities embodied in Shakespeare's English had an economic base, is to remind ourselves that making a living was not merely a *means*, and that the 'economic' activities which helped to mould that supremely expressive medium fostered qualities (perceptions and general habits of response) that were not 'economic' at all. We remind ourselves, in short, of the dangerous facility with which the word 'economic' tempts us to beg the essential questions.[55]

The same contrast between the past and the present is being smuggled in here. By implication, making a living *is* now 'merely a means': the 'economic' *is* divorced from other aspects of life. Once again, modernity is characterized by the existence (and in some versions, the dominance) of the 'purely' or 'narrowly' economic—which is what 'the economic', he is implying, has come to mean.

And this is why, in Knights's view, the drama of the Jacobean period possesses such value in the twentieth century. His book is intended 'to show

how, in a few great plays, "that living body of assumptions as to the right conduct of human affairs" helped to nourish qualities that we can admire' (in this instance the embedded quotation was taken from Tawney's *The Agrarian Problem in the Sixteenth Century*).[56] Jonson, in particular—he is in effect the hero of the book—still speaks to 'us' because he 'is one of the main channels of communication with an almost vanished tradition', a tradition that judged economic behaviour in individual moral terms. In the nineteenth century (always present as a negative reference point) the notion of an impersonal economic system had established itself, but in the early seventeenth century the focus was still on the failings of individuals. 'The diagnosis', writes Knights, 'was moral rather than economic. Or, to put it another way, the dramatic treatment of economic problems showed them as moral and individual problems which in the last analysis they are.'[57] In other words, Knights is arguing, the plays remind us that the notion of the autonomy of the economic sphere is illusory: there are no 'purely economic' problems of any human consequence.

It is worth remarking that one of the authorities Knights particularly relied on was the now largely forgotten book by H. M. Robertson entitled *Aspects of the Rise of Economic Individualism*, published in 1933. The book is subtitled *A Criticism of Max Weber and his School*, and it attempts to demolish what it takes to be the thesis of Weber's famous essays on 'The Protestant Ethic and the Spirit of Capitalism'.[58] But, as Talcott Parsons, who had translated Weber's work, pointed out, Robertson misdescribed Weber's claim. Robertson tried to show that Weber's thesis about the Protestant notion of 'the calling' was not sufficient to account for the rise of an economic and social system, but *that*, Parsons insisted, had not been Weber's claim. Weber had been pointing to a psychological homology between the rational asceticism of the new religious discipline and the abstemious accumulative drive of early capitalist practice.[59] As Robertson's title indicated, *his* central concern was with an entire economic system held to have reached its purest form in the nineteenth century. Knights's other great source, as I have indicated, was Tawney, but, despite many subsequent references to 'the Weber–Tawney thesis', Weber's argument, as Peter Ghosh has recently reminded us, was also quite different from Tawney's, both in its focus and in its level of abstraction, since Tawney concentrated on empirically describing the retreat of religion and morality from regulating economic activity.[60] Although Knights makes a couple of passing references to Weber's work, his own framework combines the perspectives of Robertson and of Tawney, both of whom, it is worth repeating, define the problem in terms of accounting for the rise of an economic system symbolically represented by Victorian Britain.

IV

In a later article entitled 'Bacon and the Seventeenth-Century Dissociation of Sensibility', published in *Scrutiny* in 1943, Knights summarized a new orthodoxy: 'The last twenty or thirty years have seen a revolution in our attitudes towards the seventeenth century' was his confident opening, echoing the remarks by L. J. Potts quoted at the beginning of this chapter. This change was partly due to reinterpretations arising out of more detailed historical research, where historians had 'pushed back the beginnings of the Industrial Revolution and demonstrated a direct line of connexion between the commercial and industrial enterprise of Elizabethan and early Stuart times and the greater changes of the eighteenth century'—or, in other words, the work of those economic historians I mentioned earlier. The net effect of these enquiries had been to displace 'the picture of political development as drawn by the Whig historians', which focused on the constitutional struggle between liberty and autocracy, with accounts that instead emphasized 'the part played by economic pressure'.[61]

But Knights acknowledged that the change was not merely the by-product of historical research: 'it is due primarily to a shift in evaluation intimately related to the needs and interests of the present.' 'We can see this most clearly', he declared, in a somewhat surprising turn, 'in recent literary criticism', instancing the revaluing of the Metaphysical Poets and some of the Elizabethan and Jacobean dramatists. In other words, his central theme, he announces, is nothing less than that 'dissociation of sensibility', from which, 'as Mr Eliot remarked in his brilliantly suggestive essay, "we have never recovered"'.[62]

Having discussed Bacon's work in some detail in the body of the article, Knights returned to his theme by way of conclusion. In helping to promote the divorce of reason from the feelings, Bacon 'points forward to the conscious and unconscious utilitarianism of the nineteenth century of which we ourselves are the embarrassed heirs'—embarrassed, it would seem, largely because we are now starting to see the limitations of the 'belief in unlimited material progress' that characterized that much-demonized century. But, if our present situation requires us to be 'busy in overhauling the values of the last three hundred years', this does not involve any repudiation of the proper work of reason: writing in 1943, Knights saw the dreadful consequences of *that* choice all around in Europe. Rather, the task, as he puts it, is 'simply to recognize that reason in the last three centuries has worked within a field that is not the whole of experience, that it has mistaken the part for the whole, and imposed arbitrary limits on its own working'.[63]

By this point, the discussion seems to have moved a long way from his opening reflections on those researches that had revealed 'a direct line of connection' between 'the commercial and industrial enterprise of Elizabethan and early Stuart times' and the Industrial Revolution. But to Knights (and by implication to all those embraced in his opening use of the first-person plural) the intimacy of the connections among the various elements covered in this retrospect had become progressively more obvious in the course of the previous couple of decades. The 'divorce of reason from the feelings' and the 'rise of industrial civilization' are now treated as related—indeed, at times barely distinguishable—parts of the same received view.

The central node, both conceptually and historically, is signalled by that reference to 'the conscious and unconscious utilitarianism of the nineteenth century'. This is alleged to be the dominant temper of the society created by the Industrial Revolution of the late eighteenth century, and hence indirectly by those social and economic changes in the previous two centuries that made it possible. 'Utilitarianism' does not appear to be being used here in any exact or historical sense, but rather to symbolize the alleged defining characteristics of modernity—calculation, expediency, individualism, and so on. The present, Knights implies, is now able to see the period stretching from the early seventeenth century to the early twentieth not just as a particular historical phase, but as a pathology, a sickness from which the possibility of recovery is now becoming visible. An implicit parallelism obtains between the notion of 'disassociated' reason, on the one hand, and the category of 'the economic', on the other. In this way, the 'revaluation of the seventeenth century' that took place in the inter-war period, centrally though not exclusively in the work of literary critics, ultimately rested on the attempt to find a locus of human value that would enable 'disassociated reason' and 'the economic' to be recognized as two sides of the same coin, something that could thereby be relativized and transcended.

The general tenor of Knights's remarks, about both the seventeenth and twentieth centuries, was echoed in a good deal of cultural commentary by literary critics in Britain from the 1930s through at least the 1950s, a time when, as I observed earlier, such critics occupied a more prominent place in the national culture than either before or since. The status of this interpretation *as* orthodoxy was illustrated in a series of articles by a young American Leavisite, Harold Wendell Smith, that appeared in *Scrutiny* in the journal's closing years.[64] With the zeal of the acolyte, Smith almost unnoticingly ran together the idioms of the 'dissociation of sensibility' and the 'rise of capitalism'. In the article in the series bearing the former phrase as its title, the modern source most frequently cited was not in fact Eliot's essay but *Religion and the Rise of Capitalism*. This, claimed Smith, exhibits how 'the schism of abstract and material' (itself perhaps a vulgarized version of Eliot's original formulation) leads to the establishment by the Restoration of a 'comfortable, but confident, even jubilant, materialism'. By the latter part of the seventeenth century, the 'world of the spirit' that had flourished in 'the agrarian days of the early Elizabethans' has disappeared, replaced by 'a material world, urban and mercantile'.[65] In the not fully controlled vocabulary of such workaday criticism we can observe a phrase that began life as a way of discriminating phases of poetry being put to work to explain the rise of a distinctively modern form of economy. But however well established this interpretation had become in literary circles, professional historians could still register their scepticism. Even Marjorie Cox, a seventeenth-century historian who was well disposed to *Scrutiny* in general (her husband, Gordon Cox, was one of its most frequent contributors), wrote in after the first of Smith's articles to complain that 'there seemed to be over-much reliance on a single work, Tawney's *Religion and the Rise of Capitalism*', and to object that 'Mr Smith's article shows a too easy acceptance of the equation of "puritan" and "bourgeois"'.[66]

One reason why the frameworks inherited from Eliot and from Tawney could be so readily subsumed into a single account is that the category of 'the economic' itself had come to be used in such a tendentious way, as a placeholder for anxieties and aversions provoked by contemplation of the contemporary world. The rhetorical excess which I noted in characterizations of 'purely economic' activity not only reveals the presence of larger moral or even aesthetic antipathies, but also underlines just how little these characterizations corresponded to actual features of contemporary economic life. For, in reality, such activity was shot through with social and legal considerations that clearly promoted concerns other than that of 'unrestrained pursuit of gain'. Some of these were what Durkheim had termed the 'non-contractual elements in contract'—that is, the shared practices and expectations that needed to be in place for a contractual agreement to be possible in the first place, to have meaning and possess binding force.[67] But, more generally, contemporary economic activity had, when viewed more closely and less hostilely, several of the features that these critics were prone to identify as belonging to some notional 'pre-economic' epoch such as the Middle Ages. For example, it could be said that, just as medieval guilds were celebrated for having a concern for their members' welfare that exceeded the narrow preoccupation with increasing their productivity, so companies, business associations, professional bodies, friendly societies, trade unions, and the myriad other organizations that made up the texture of nineteenth- and twentieth-century economic life all in various ways restrained, limited, or supplemented any notionally 'pure' extraction of profit. In this respect, the continuity with nineteenth-century critics of 'industrial society' and of its legitimation by 'the dismal science' is marked. In this tradition of criticism, the abstract model of human behaviour assumed for the purposes of economic theorizing has to be projected as the dominant characteristic of whatever form of society is deemed, within a binary structure, to constitute 'modernity'. This always tends to obscure both the actual nature of contemporary societies, in all their 'non-economic' complexity and diversity, and the important part played by narrowly 'economic' calculation in earlier societies. The functions that the contrast serves encourage a simpler story in which wholeness gives way to atomism, just as it does in the implied narrative of the 'dissociation of sensibility'.

Both Knights's book and Willey's turn up over and over again on recommended reading for university and adult education students not just in the 1940s and 1950s, but well into the 1960s and 1970s, including at the new higher-education institutions founded or expanded in those decades (where the study of 'literature in context' particularly flourished). It was surely extraordinary that two of the most widely used literary-critical works of the middle decades of the century should, implicitly, be pointing to a homology between 'the origins of modern science' and 'the origins of capitalism', the two forces that have allegedly made human beings spiritually homeless in the modern world. No less remarkably, these two sedate-looking works of literary scholarship carried, into the second half of the twentieth century, the message that salvation must be looked for in the properly intense reading of such literature as Jonson's plays and Wordsworth's poetry. In this way, both books illustrate just how much covert or unacknowledged historical work can be done under the auspices of the innocuous yet capacious category of 'background'.

4

Rationalism, Christianity, and Ambiguity

I

'Pure criticism': whatever that misleading phrase might mean, it is generally agreed that William Empson must be one of its best representatives. No other critic has been so consistently celebrated, or so impatiently dismissed, for the sheer virtuoso display of critical technique. The bravura, crossword-solving ingenuity of his readings finds more multiplicity of meaning in lines of poetry, in single words, than other critics ever do—more, it is sometimes alleged, than is really there. For some, his very fertility is, like that of the old woman who lived in a shoe, his downfall: the reader becomes lost in a showroom of dazzling exhibits that seem to have become ends in themselves, not contributing to any larger interpretation or appreciation. And so Empson—without question one of the two or three most significant English critics in the twentieth century—seems to present the greatest challenge to the enterprise of this book. Here, surely, is ahistorical criticism, a form of creative over-reading that takes its specimens from various sources while parading a showy insouciance about period or context. Professional historians have never had cause to attend to Empson, and nor, it would appear, did he much attend to them.

However, in this chapter I shall argue that the assumption that Empson's work is ahistorical and contains nothing to interest historians is a mistake, though I would concede at the outset that Empson is the most improbable, or at least most challenging, candidate for inclusion here. But I take comfort from the fact that when he mock-disparaged his own 1935 book *Some Versions of Pastoral* as not intended to be 'a solid piece of sociology', one of his most admiring and sympathetic readers, the American scholar Roger

Sale writing in the 1960s, responded by saying: 'It is in its way a hugely solid work on English history.'[1] This chapter will be devoted to trying to make sense of that surprising description in respect of Empson's work as a whole. My account of the historical assumptions in play in Empson's criticism will, nonetheless, reveal him to be the odd man out in a different way. Most of the figures I have discussed thus far encouraged, in one form or another, a declinist view and a self-conscious repudiation of the claims of Whig history. Empson, as we shall see, though he unquestionably belongs alongside the other critics I am discussing, does not share these attitudes, and that is not the least of the reasons for thinking that intellectual historians of the period need to take his measure.

It was not Empson's way to make a fuss about the business of criticism. Whenever he was driven to any meta-critical statement, it usually amounted to little more than a variant on the injunction to 'get on with it'. And so it is with the place of history in his criticism, starting with *Seven Types of Ambiguity*, published in 1930 when he was just 24.[2] His very first literary example in the first pages of the first chapter of his first book—'Bare ruined choirs, where late the sweet birds sang', from Shakespeare's Sonnet 73—is plonked rather matter-of-factly into what is assumed to be a familiar history. Taking the line to refer to, among other things, monastery choirs, he briskly mentions elements that contribute to its richness of meaning, including, as he puts it, 'various sociological and historical reasons (the protestant destruction of monasteries; fear of puritanism) which it would be hard now to trace out in their proportions'.[3] The itemized reasons may seem to be the small change of textbook history, though the choice of *'fear* of puritanism' as a way of gesturing towards the most relevant aspects of the 1590s setting may already indicate a characteristically Empsonian twist. But the very briskness suggests that these are to be taken as shared historical commonplaces, and that the need to assume or refer to such historical circumstances was so obvious and indisputable a feature of literary interpretation that it did not require comment. Finding his reading challenged by later critics, Empson fell back on the self-evidence of his point: the example 'was mainly meant to illustrate the familiar process of putting in a little historical background; a reader in Shakespeare's time could easily think of actual ruined choirs'.[4]

This air of cheerfully taking a lot for granted pervades the opening chapter of *Seven Types*. Its first section is taken up with a polemic against those who understand poetry as being 'pure sound' or 'all about atmosphere', independent of verbal meaning. For the most part, the level of the discussion tends towards abstraction without quite being theoretical. And then, suddenly, we are offered what seems to be intended as a historical explanation:

> Interest in 'atmospheres' is a critical attitude designed for, and particularly suited to, the poets of the nineteenth century; this may tell us something about them, and in part explain why they are so little ambiguous in the sense with which I am concerned. For a variety of reasons, they found themselves living in an intellectual framework with which it was very difficult to write poetry, in which poetry was rather improper, or was irrelevant to business, especially the business of becoming Fit to Survive, or was an indulgence of one's lower nature in beliefs the scientists knew were untrue. On the other hand, they had a large public which was as anxious to escape from this intellectual framework, on holiday, as they were themselves. Almost all of them, therefore, exploited a sort of tap-root into the world of their childhood, where they were able to conceive things poetically...[5]

We cannot help but wonder how seriously we are being asked to take this as an 'explanation'. It may be seen, at one level, as yet another sub-Eliotic denunciation of the 'romanticism' of the Victorians, a view that had great currency during Empson's student years in 1920s Cambridge. It sees nineteenth-century poetry as a form of escapism from a society assumed to be less congenial to poetry than those that had preceded it. Commerce, Social Darwinism, Science: these are the dark monsters that drive poor poets to scuttle back to the warmth of childhood, and these are understood to be the dominant, and distinctively modern, features of the Victorian period. But are these anything more than the truisms of textbook history? It all has a rather knockabout quality, and, as he goes on, the hint of Wildean *superbia* is frequently detectable ('as for Keats' desire for death and his mother, it has become a byword among the learned'). Having slain most of the leading nineteenth-century poets with a phrase each, he concludes: 'Browning and Meredith, who did write from the world they lived in, affect me as novel-writers of merit with no lyrical inspiration at all'—which surely recalls Wilde's epigram: 'Meredith is a prose Browning, and so is Browning.'[6]

In such a passage, it can be hard to separate the hint of playful excess in the descriptions from the summary despatch characteristic of a writer quickly running over familiar reference points. Yet the paragraph also has some of the forensic vigour associated with conducting a convincing argument, the rhythm of inference culminating in a 'therefore' designed to present the final, rather bizarre, claim as the natural, only-to-be-expected outcome of the conditions guyed in the previous sentences. This note is very characteristic of Empson, especially of his earliest work, and is part of what makes it difficult to know quite how to take—how much, as it were, to *credit*—the various off-hand historical assertions we encounter along the way. Nonetheless, I suggest there is a unifying narrative thread, even though it is only intermittently visible.

Much of what delights Empson about 'ambiguity' in poetry depends, in effect, upon the fast-developing nature of early modern English and the ubiquity of the conceit in everyday language at that time. As double meanings move, in later centuries, towards being deliberate or explicit, as in the pun, they lose most of their poetic force. Thus, he says of his third 'type' of ambiguity:

> its most definite examples are likely to be found, in increasing order of self-consciousness, among the seventeenth-century mystics who stress the conscious will, the eighteenth-century stylists who stress rationality, clarity, and satire, and the harmless nineteenth-century punsters who stress decent above-board fun.[7]

These summarizing remarks clearly presuppose a larger literary history, a fairly conventional one apart from his dismissive smirking at the nineteenth century. But they also hint at the ways in which a sequence can start to become a narrative.

Considered in this way, *Seven Types of Ambiguity* can be read as, implicitly, a history of increasing self-consciousness about multiplicity of meaning. For the Elizabethans, especially Shakespeare, ambiguity was a natural property of the language. The Metaphysicals deliberately cultivated it, but no great self-consciousness was required on the part of the reader for such conceits to succeed. In the eighteenth century these effects were more contrived, and part of their success lay in the reader's awareness of, and admiration for, the element of contrivance, which nonetheless contributed to the meaning. By the nineteenth century, the language had lost much of this natural richness, and anyway the prevailing poetic was against it, preferring sincerity, so double meanings tended to occur as deliberate puns, always a poor relation. In seeking to account for the nineteenth century's relative poverty in these respects, he says:

> it may spring from their respect for logical punctuation, from their admiration for simple ecstasies (it was no longer courtiers and administrators who wrote poetry), from their resulting admiration of smoothness of lyrical flow, and from the fact that the language had become less fluid, a less subtle mirror of

the mind (though a more precise mirror of the scientific world) since the clarifying labours of the eighteenth century.[8]

This curious sentence runs together very different types of 'explanation'— changes in the language, in aesthetic ideals, in the sociology of writers, in theories of the relation of language and reality, and so on. The suggested explanations also vary greatly in persuasiveness—it is not, for example, altogether clear why full-time poets should cultivate 'simple ecstasies' in their verse more than, say, 'courtiers' do. Insofar as there is a chronological focus here, it is a change located in the eighteenth century, seen in trad-itional terms as the rationalist product of the Scientific Revolution. It is worth remarking that, when locating a major turning-point in cultural and literary history in the transition from the eighteenth to the nineteenth centuries, Empson, unlike so many of his contemporaries, here makes no mention of the transformation allegedly effected by the Industrial Revolution.

Throughout the book, Empson implicitly relies on the fact that English is a largely uninflected language that depends on word order for meaning, so that the poets' disruption of 'normal' word order could be one fruitful source of 'ambiguity'. Reflecting on this in a more general and extended way in his final chapter, he acknowledges that 'people are accustomed to judge automatically the forces that hold together a variety of ideas' in expression, and that the communication of meaning relies upon this kind of tacit knowledge. He then gives this point a historical twist by observing how the English language has come to abandon many of its former gram-matical markers, with the result that 'it is growing liable to mean more things and less willing to stop and exclude the other possible meanings'. Communication is still effective because various speech communities each have their own form of the necessary tacit knowledge. 'English is becoming an aggregate of vocabularies only loosely in connection with one another, which yet have many words in common, so that there is much danger of accidental ambiguity, and you have to bear firmly in mind the small clique for whom the author is writing.'[9]

Empson is not dismayed by this development; he believes that the implied grammar of, say, the compacted noun sequences of newspaper headlines can yield a rich semantic field in themselves. 'It is possible that a clear analysis of the possible modes of statement, and a fluid use of grammar which sets out to combine them as sharply as possible into the effect intended, may yet give back something of the Elizabethan energy to what is at present a rather exhausted language.'[10] The hope expressed here prevents this ungainly sentence from falling into a familiar form of cultural pessimism, but it is nonetheless uncharacteristic of Empson to throw around such a slack, and unsustainable, cliché as 'a rather exhausted language', a description generated more by the contrast implied in the commonplace idea of Elizabethan English as a high point of fertility and creativity than by any systematic linguistic survey of contemporary usage. In any event, while this tacitly regulated Babel may be a peculiarly modern situation, the model underlying it—where 'meaning' is understood as 'intended uptake', how the author intended the relevant public to understand—is applied to all periods.

Thus far, the historical consciousness present in the opening chapters of *Seven Types* may not seem to provide much evidence of Empson's being, as Leavis had described him in his review, 'as alive as [Eliot and Richards] to the exciting strangeness of the present phase of human history'.[11] For Leavis, the marginal place of poetry in a world supposedly dominated by commercialism and machinery was one symptom of the strangeness of this phase. Leavis suggested that the importance of 'a mind that is fully alive in this age' was 'brought home particularly in the last chapter' of *Seven Types*, but perhaps here he was a little hasty in recruiting Empson to this familiar form of interwar cultural alarmism, for the final chapter of *Seven Types* is a curious performance, an offhand justification of the practice of close analysis. It is couched in very general, though hardly theoretical, terms, yet it, too, is implicitly historical in interesting ways. The circuit around which meaning has been mercilessly harried throughout the book passes from the critic through the poet and on to the reader. But the reader is, in effect, doubly represented, because the key regulator of the meanings that the critic and his readers may agree upon is the meaning that it is presumed the poet intended *his* immediate audience to apprehend. The critic could, in principle, identify all possible meanings and the mechanisms by which they operate, so the key question in practice, Empson suggests, is how far it is 'profitable' to attend to the possible ambiguities that such syntactical implicitness generates. His initial answer to this is less permissive than one might have expected. 'Clearly, the critical principles of the author and of the public he is writing for will decide this to a considerable degree', and he goes on to emphasize the different conventions of different periods in this respect. The meanings it will be 'profitable' to pursue, his elaborations suggest, seem to be those that the author could have intended his original audience to apprehend.

Empson did not, in the first half of his career, labour this historicist claim; he appears, rather, to take it (along with so much else) as almost self-evident. He recognizes that concentration on what the author could have intended may be 'very interesting to the biographer, but...have nothing to do with the enjoyment of the poem', but he counsels against taking this distinction too absolutely—'those who enjoy poems must in part be biographers'.[12] This is not an assertion one might expect to hear from an Eliot-inspired young critic in 1930, though it could perhaps find a warrant in some of Eliot's critical practice. The contemporary reader needs some appreciation of 'what was likely to happen in a reader's mind' in the poem's original setting, and Empson takes a purely pragmatic view of how extensive or how limited might be the steps that the critic needs to take to help prompt that appreciation.

In the course of the chapter, he moves on to the question of whether the reader needs to share the beliefs of the poet if he is to 'understand his sensibility', and again his answer is an implicitly historical one. Since 'we' obviously do not share all the beliefs of poets from previous centuries,

> it becomes puzzling that we should be able to enjoy so many poets. The explanation seems to be that in the last few generations literary people have been trained socially to pick up hints at once about people's opinions, and to accept them, while in the company of their owners, with as little fuss as possible....It is for reasons of this sort that the habit of reading a wide variety of different sorts of poetry, which has, after all, only recently been contracted by any public as a whole...[makes people less sure of their interpretations] and makes it necessary to be able to fall back on some intelligible process of interpretation.[13]

Whether the remarks about the social 'training' and being 'in the company' of the owners of the opinions should be taken literally as referring to ordinary social interactions, or more ironically as a description of an education in ways of reading, may not matter. What matters much more is Empson's sense that the general scheme of analysis that his book promotes meets a distinctively modern need. The relevant readers here are 'literary people', but, unlike literary people of centuries past, they have, presumably as a result of changes in both education and publishing, become used to reading and appreciating the poetry of various periods. In talking about 'any public as a whole', he seems to be gesturing towards the expansion of the terrain of reading, and the availability of cheap reprints of earlier work to meet that expanded market, that is commonly dated from the late nineteenth century.

Empson was, of course, aware that 'many people' would think his ingenious analyses were excessive, as indeed they did and do. His first move in self-defence was to insist that he was remedying a local lack: those objectors need to remember 'that English literary critics have been so unwilling to appear niggling and lacking in soul that upon these small technical points the obvious, even the accepted, has been said culpably seldom'. One way to read this is as a complaint against the belletrist tradition of criticism that held pretty undisputed sway in English literary culture until after the First World War. Empson here puts on his lab coat, or perhaps even his engineer's overalls: he is the man who knows which levers and which valves make the thing work, whereas 'English literary critics' have tended to write as admirers, making a bit of a display of their exquisite sensibilities. But then, repeating that dialectical rhythm that punctuates the whole chapter, he rounds on himself and puts the case for such appreciative criticism:

> the position of a literary critic is far more a social than a scientific one. There is no question of dealing finally with the matter, because, in so far as people are always reading an author, he is always being read differently. It is the business of the critic to extract for his public what it wants; to organise, what indeed he may create, the taste of his period.[14]

He is not entirely reneging on his more scientific enterprise, but this may at first seem to strike a largely concessive note. Those belletrist critics were—it would be a reasonable inference from the popularity and longevity of the type—giving their public what it wanted.

But does his historicism here work for him more than against him, perhaps? His terms acknowledge the temporal and located nature of criticism, the pragmatic and tactical character of its transactions. A point that Empson was to reiterate several times later in his career was that the critic, in order to decide what needs to be said to enhance his readership's understanding, has to have a good idea of its current level of apprehension. It may then be said that, in the climate of uncertainty and relativism about literary value allegedly current at the time, Empson's readership needs precisely the kind of 'scientific' demonstration of how meaning works that he provides. His own remark about the need 'to bear firmly in mind the small clique for whom the author is writing' has, *mutatis mutandis*, an application here. We may now feel that his target readership is assumed to be improbably well read in earlier English poetry and to have a notably scholarly cast of mind, with interests in past social conventions, the history of the language, and much else besides, as well as a very high tolerance for critical self-consciousness. It is hard not to think that this category was best represented in Empson's mind by that small circle of contemporaries whose company he had enjoyed at Cambridge. Certainly, in the first decade after the book's publication, it did not appear to find large numbers of other readers.

In any event, it is the needs of this distinctively modern category that provide the rationale for his book. In its closing pages he restates his historical premise:

> It is only recently that the public, as a whole, has come to admire a great variety of different styles of poetry, requiring a great variety of critical dogmas, simultaneously, so as to need not so much a single habit for the reading of poetry as a sort of understanding that enables one to jump neatly from one style to another.[15]

The contemporary reader needs, more than readers of previous generations, the general reassurance that poetry is susceptible of analysis. Without this, the confidence to take pleasure in any particular poem can be sapped, producing a generalized anxiety about possible failure of response and interpretation, which in turn leads to 'a sterility of emotion'. Demonstrating the power of analysis, as a general practice, is, therefore, not the enemy of a properly emotional response to poetry, but its necessary backdrop. And that is the chief justification for his book and what he concedes (or affects to concede) are its 'many niggling pages'.[16]

II

Seven Types of Ambiguity makes no reference to the work of historians, not even literary historians—but, then, it makes practically no reference to scholarly work of any kind. Such historical allusions as it offers are treated as nods to familiar, common possessions not in need of support. Empson's second book, *Some Versions of Pastoral* (published in 1935), maintains the offhand manner and the lack of scholarly apparatus, but it, I suggest, is making a more fundamentally historical case. The clue here is, once again, given by Sale when he says that the 'subject' of the book is not the individual works Empson discusses, but 'the history that can be made by considering the works in sequence'.[17]

Reading *Some Versions of Pastoral* can be a dizzying experience as one comes to realize that, while ostensibly discussing a limited, and indeed very dated, literary convention, Empson is uncovering something so fundamental in the relationship between writer and reader that he is identifying a dynamic that is at work in some form in *all* literature and *all* criticism. These larger claims are gestured to in the almost unintelligibly condensed opening chapter on 'Proletarian literature', which must rank as one of the most puzzling and unintroductory first chapters ever written. The situation is scarcely eased by the fact that the subsequent chapters, each devoted to a single work or single subgenre, are self-contained, with little by way of cross reference or cumulative argument. Nonetheless, Sale's comment points us in the right direction: the *sequence* of chapters gives us not just the larger argument of the book but its specific contribution as a kind of history.

Putting this part of my argument in its most provocative form, I suggest that *Some Versions of Pastoral* gives us an oblique history of class relations in England from the sixteenth to the nineteenth centuries. Part of what made the genre of pastoral workable in the sixteenth and seventeenth centuries, Empson implies, was the acceptance of the fixed gulf between the aristocrats and the shepherds. Classical pastoral depended on the pretence that, though the shepherds lived simpler uncluttered lives that enabled them to show up the vanities of their social superiors, they could put forward their philosophical reflections about existence in a form of highly elaborate educated speech without any attention being drawn to the incongruity of this procedure. Indeed, acceptance of the clash between their lowly social position and their elevated rhetorical style was part of what made the convention so powerful, creating the sense that the truths expressed applied to everyone. As Empson puts it: 'To make the clash work in the right way (not become funny) the writer must keep up a firm pretence that he was unconscious of it.'[18] Empson's reference to 'pretence' here raises some awkward questions. If 'the essential trick of the old pastoral' depended upon a kind of connivance by all parties not to find the artificiality 'risible', was even the old pastoral a form of mock-pastoral? For Empson the key seems to lie in whether the artificiality is in some way acknowledged in the literary genre itself: mock-pastoral trades on just this acknowledgement, whereas the old pastoral manages to exclude it.

In any event, 'pretence' is at the heart of the genre: the shepherds are and are not 'real' or 'ordinary' shepherds (the genre depends on the you-know-that-I-know-that-you-know relation). The shepherds can also have their representative function reinforced by comparing their ruling of sheep to monarchs or bishops ruling over men, so that in effect they become part of an extended metaphor. 'Such a pretence no doubt makes the characters unreal, but not the feelings expressed or even the situation described; the same pretence is often valuable in real life.' So the contrivance or artifice is not necessarily a drawback: what seems essential is that the reader should not find it jarring or ludicrous, and for this to be the case there has to be not merely acceptance of the genre but unembarrassed acceptance of the different mores of the various social ranks.

It is at this point that Empson casually introduces a very important historical claim (using, characteristically, a metaphor that knowingly evokes English class behaviour), when he writes: 'I should say that it was over this fence that pastoral came down in England after the Restoration.'[19] But what, exactly, is 'this fence'? It looks as though it has something to do with keeping up the pretence without feeling that something silly or comic is involved. After the mid-seventeenth century, he seems to suggest, people became less willing to connive in this fiction. Those philosophic swains came to seem pretentious as well as implausible. Puritanism was hostile to such antique affectations, 'and', he writes, 'Puritanism, suspicious of the arts, was only not strong among the aristocracy'. So the 'harsh and unreal' criticism of cultivation came to 'make the polite pretence of pastoral seem necessarily absurd'.

At one level, there is a kind of Fall built into his story, and, as so often in early Empson, Puritanism is one of the main villains of the piece (as his career goes on, this comes to be broadened into an aggressive attack on Christianity more generally). What changed, his account suggests, is not the actual position of social classes (their 'objective situation', as the comrades of the 1930s would call it): both pre- and post-seventeenth-century England were dramatically class divided—indeed, the stock characters of pastoral necessarily reflect these vast disparities in rank and social position. What changed was the increasing unwillingness to ignore the incongruity of the expression by ordinary people of lofty sentiments in high-flown language. 'Even so', he continues, 'there was a successful school of mock-pastoral for so long as the upper and lower classes were consciously less Puritan than the middle. When that goes the pastoral tricks of thought take refuge in child-cult.'[20] These two phases clearly correspond to the last two chapters of the book, on the Beggar's Opera and on the Alice books respectively, which seem to chart steps in a retreat from the world. Initially, therefore, the class basis of the mock-pastoral seems to have something to do with the unspoken bond between rogues and aristocrats: it is 'mock' because its knowingness puts it at one remove from the innocence of the true pastoral relation, but it is still a form of pastoral in that a mirror to life is held up by the lowest of the lower orders, on the margins of respectable society, where their life of vice is not unconnected to that of the aristocracy. And when even that model is no longer usable, the truths have to be put in the mouth of a child.

So this pastoral machinery always involves, as Empson puts it in a celebrated passage, a 'double attitude' of 'the complex man to the simple one ("I am in one way better, in another not so good"), and this may well recognize a permanent truth about the aesthetic situation'.[21] That's to say, the writer or artist belongs to a 'higher' social stratum and engages in a more sophisticated kind of labour; but the characters he or she creates, though lower in social station, are implied to be possessed of a greater native dignity or natural understanding of the human situation. And, since all characters in literature are in some sense 'representative', we may say that all literature has a pastoral dimension.

This line of thought enables Empson to return to his critique of 'proletarian literature', a category of writing much lauded on the left in the 1930s: 'To produce pure proletarian art', he writes, 'the artist must be at one with the worker; this is impossible, not for political reasons, but because the artist never is at one with any public'. In other words, proletarian literature is, above all, a form of *literature*: by the very fact that the author writes it, he or she cannot simply be one among the characters described in it. The writer has in some sense to stand apart from life to describe it. 'It is for reasons like these that the most valuable works of art so often have a political implication which can be pounced on and called bourgeois,' he writes, reflecting the endless discussions along these lines by 1930s Marxism, and then continues: 'My own difficulty about proletarian literature is that when it comes off I find I am taking it as pastoral literature; I read into it, or find that the author has secretly put into it, these more subtle, more far-reaching, and I think more permanent, ideas.'[22] Seen thus, Empson's chapter, indeed his whole book, becomes a brilliant demonstration of how the reach of literary analysis can undercut the assumed primacy of political categories.

Reading Empson in this way inevitably raises a further question: is *Some Versions of Pastoral* itself an example of the pastoral 'form'? Although I have not seen this suggestion developed anywhere, we may come close to it in an observation by the American critic Arthur Mizener, reviewing *Some Versions of Pastoral* (under its misleading American title *English Pastoral Poetry*) in *Partisan Review* in 1938. Mizener observed that Empson's style of criticism carried some of the same risks as are involved in having to explain a joke.

If he explains too much he appears to condescend foolishly to his readers, and if he explains too little, his tacit assumption that his special knowledge is commonplace has the effect of making him appear in the end, not humble, but supercilious. Mr Empson has, how consciously it is difficult to say, taken the latter course by adopting a sophisticated version of the very device he is analyzing: he presents himself to his readers by a pastoral device; he is the revolutionary critic in the guise of a correspondent of *The Times Literary Supplement*.[23]

I take Mizener to be suggesting that Empson treats his significant new insights as though they were the familiar coin of critical exchange. This could be considered a form of 'putting the complex in the simple', or (adapting one of Empson's own subtitles) 'the *TLS* critic as swain', the cultivation of a kind of faux innocence.

Pastoral, we might say—deliberately superimposing a modern on an ancient category—is a form of social criticism. The vanities, excesses, and corruptions endemic to the life of the well-born are exposed by contemplation of the simple goodness and satisfactions of the shepherds' existence. But is there, in turn, a sense in which all social criticism retains an ineliminable element of pastoral? In asking this, I am not referring to the largely rural or pre-industrial character of so many of the ideals looked back to by, say, nineteenth-century critics of industrialism. I have in mind the manner in which the social critic portrays the corruption or unnaturalness of the present from a standpoint that implicitly claims to be in touch with more fundamental, and perhaps more universal, human interests, as encountered in those from a lowly social position.

How far these are given any concrete instantiation varies according to the literary tactics of the critic, but it is certainly noticeable that many of the classics of twentieth-century English social criticism do find some such touchstone in the alleged simplicities of working-class life, suggesting that a kind of pastoral sensibility is at work. Something of this kind might be claimed about, say, Robert Tressell's *The Ragged-Trousered Philanthropists*, George Orwell's *The Road to Wigan Pier*, or Richard Hoggart's *The Uses of Literacy*. Such critiques do not, in any obvious sense, romanticize a bygone rural age. But in their celebrations of the solidarities of working-class life, their admiration for the hardiness and endurance of the poor, their respect for the directness of the human relations, and the simplicity of the pastimes characteristic (or allegedly characteristic) of working-class communities— indeed, in their very evocation of the idea of 'community' as opposed to the atomized selfishness of market society—these works, too, hold a mirror of simplicity up to the painted shows of the dominant social form. And in doing so, they cannot altogether escape the hovering idea that such simplicities represent the eternal verities of human existence.

Some Versions of Pastoral cannot, in any simple sense, be said to stand alongside these works: for one thing, it says nothing directly about the present, and, for another, its focus is almost wholly literary. But what it does offer is an oblique commentary on the genre of social criticism itself. For what it may be said to reveal is the extent to which such works share a formal structure with the literary genre recognized as pastoral. In this respect, Empson's book can be seen as a vindication of the claims of literary criticism. It is his response to the political challenge issued by his more straightforwardly 'committed' contemporaries in the 1930s. Where they hold up proletarian literature as the one politically acceptable form of literary production, he shows that it is, precisely, a *form*. When it works, it works as a form of pastoral. And pastoral is about the positioning of the author in relation to the reader and about degrees of knowingness shared by author and reader, matters that it takes the peculiar attentiveness of literary criticism to identify.

Returning to the phrase from Roger Sale with which I started—that *Some Versions of Pastoral* is 'a hugely solid work on English history'—it now seems worth calling attention to the preposition: a work *on*, not *of*, English history. It is certainly not a work *of* history in any conventional sense, but it surely is a kind of meditation *on* aspects of English history, as well as on the perspective on human existence that we cannot throw off even when attending to such historical matters. Empson is, as so often, the odd man out among the critics discussed here, but, however we might characterize his distinctiveness, it certainly cannot be by claiming that he ignored history.

III

To describe one of the major works by one of the twentieth century's most celebrated critics as a *terra incognita* may seem a particularly vulgar attempt to shill for trade, conjuring up promises of a radical revisionism that are not, in the nature of the case, likely to be redeemed. But Empson's third major work, *The Structure of Complex Words*, published in 1951, has become one of the great unvisited monuments of English literary criticism—or, at least, visited only rarely, perhaps by readers who have enjoyed other work by its architect, or occasionally by those who have heard rumours of untold riches piled in its deserted rooms. Even ardent admirers of Empson—of whom there were many in the middle decades of the twentieth century and a smaller but deeply devoted band from the 1970s onwards—have responded to what is much his longest book with a mixture of selective praise and puzzled respect.

And with some reason. At first meeting, the book can seem deliberately uninviting. One way to describe its structure would be to say that an outer ring of barbed wire surrounds an inner ring of ditches and ha-has, at the heart of which there is a labyrinth. It requires more than the usual readerly effort and commitment to come to terms with *The Structure of Complex Words*, but few works of criticism offer such rewards in return. I shall argue that among the many things to be got from this difficult, brilliant work are not only a general method that should be of interest to all intellectual and cultural historians, but also a series of substantive interpretations of phases of English, and indeed European, history. More provocatively, I want to suggest that Empson should be regarded as an idiosyncratic but unusually interesting historian of English ethical life.

At its most ambitious, *The Structure of Complex Words* is an enquiry into how meaning happens. Its focus is not on the grammar of sentences but on what Empson calls the 'grammar' of individual words, especially those 'vague, rich, intimate words' through which human relations are primarily negotiated. He contends that the co-presence of multiple senses *within* many words, at certain stages of their history, takes the form of a structure or an assertion of relation between the senses, which allows the word to carry what he calls, with his usual camp exaggeration, a 'doctrine'. The reader may miss or misinterpret the meaning and force of given statements unless the interaction of senses within such words at a particular period of their use can be identified.

As Empson brilliantly demonstrates, the *OED*, always the first resource, almost entirely fails to capture this essential component of meaning as a result of its rigid policy of identifying only what it regards as *distinct* 'senses' of a word and then tying its illustrative quotations to those separate senses. Empson's interest, by contrast, was in what he called his 'equations'—that is, the way in which the relation between senses buried in a complex word at a particular moment in its history carried an implicit assertion. When the Victorian matron says to the potential suitor: 'You can't take Amelia for long walks Mr Jones; she's *delicate*', Empson unpacks the work done by the adjective 'delicate' as carrying the equation 'refined girls are sickly', and its italicized compactness is intended to carry the further reproach 'as you ought to know'.[24] The structure of senses in a 'complex word', therefore, is not a pun or deliberate play on meanings by an artful individual, but part of the established verbal currency, the common possession of a community of language-users in a particular period.

Empson later described *The Structure of Complex Words* as a 'sandwich' in which chapters devoted to individual words within particular works of literature provide the filling between two outer layers of theoretical chapters.[25] What, in effect, the central chapters illustrate is that there can be no adequate recovery of meaning without the kind of attentiveness to tone and responsiveness to individual voice that characterizes the work of the literary critic. But, at the same time, they also show how any adequate interpretation of a passage in a literary text will necessarily be informed by a more extensive historical semantics, drawing on evidence of usage from *beyond* literary texts. Empson does not parade his own learning, or indeed provide any systematic record of his sources; his habit of quoting from memory scarcely conformed to MLA guidelines (Ian Parsons, his editor at Chatto, found that when the quotations in Empson's typescript were checked in-house, 'about 90% needed corrections—some of a major order').[26] But something of the ambition of his approach is conveyed by his characteristically offhand assertion that 'to give all the structures of all words would only mean writing the history of opinion in the most prolix possible manner'.[27] More appealing to Empson, in both its economy and its focus on rich literary texts, was what may look like the reverse of this laborious enterprise: 'I should think indeed', he writes, 'that a profound enough criticism could extract an entire cultural history from a simple lyric'.[28]

The playfully titled chapter on 'The English Dog' contains some memorable illustrations of the ways in which changes in the use of everyday terms encapsulate larger shifts in social and moral attitudes. One of the most telling is the passage discussing Dr Johnson's *commendation* of a young Scottish laird as a 'dog', as in the teasing-cum-admiring usage of calling a scampish friend 'You dog!'. It is striking, argues Empson, that a lot of the thought of a man like Dr Johnson was

> not carried on his official verbal machinery but on colloquial phrases like the one about dogs; phrases that he would have refused to analyse on grounds of dignity, even if he had been able to. No doubt you need to know a great many other things before you can understand the working of a society; but there is a claim to be made for the branch of study I am touching on here. You need to know, as well as the serious opinions of a man in the society, how much weight he would allow, when making a practical decision, to some odd little class of joke phrases, such as excite, he would feel, sentiments obvious to any

agreeable person, and yet such as carry doctrines more really complex than the whole structure of his official view of the world.[29]

Though the phrasing is concessive and ostensibly cautious, the actual claims made here are far from modest. The goal is nothing less than understanding 'the working of a society', and the yield from attending to such uses of language is 'doctrines more really complex than the whole structure of [a person's] official view of the world'. At the very least, this seems to propose a supplementary way of doing intellectual or cultural history. One of the small, but perhaps significant, changes between the essay and book versions comes where the passage refers to 'the branch of study I am touching on here'; in 1938 he had merely written 'this sort of essay'. The change may have felt called for simply by the place of the chapter in the larger context of the book, but it may also indicate that he now wished to press the academic or disciplinary implications of his approach a little more. The passage (and, indeed, the chapter as a whole) is also an expression of affinity on Empson's part, since his sympathy with the worldly, anti-Puritan uses he surveys is palpable.

The Structure of Complex Words does not endorse or even overtly engage with either Eliot's 'dissociation of sensibility' or Leavis's 'organic community'. But it does, I want to suggest, propose its own reading of English history in the form of an account of some of the main shifts in ethical attitudes from, roughly, the late sixteenth to the late eighteenth centuries. Empson's narrative of moral change has to be pieced together from hints and asides, but it is a story with two main turning points. First, beginning in the mid- to late sixteenth century, there was the displacement of the largely feudal code of honour by the earnest ethics of Protestant Christianity. And, second, beginning in the mid- to late seventeenth century, there was the challenge to Puritanism and its legacy by a more worldly code of self-assertion. The more obviously literary-critical chapters that make up the middle of the 'sandwich' are, simultaneously, brilliant essays on individual works such as *Lear* or *Othello*, or Pope's *Essay on Criticism*, and, through their discussion of terms such as 'wit' 'fool', 'dog', honest', and 'sense', an informal intellectual history of everyday attitudes to truth-telling between the mid-sixteenth and the mid-eighteenth centuries.

In a history written in terms of what he nicely called a 'shrubbery of smaller ideas'—those 'vague rich intimate words' that inform human relations so much more pervasively than the 'clear words of [the] official language'[30]— a central place is assigned to the Restoration and the 'Augustan settlement' that eventually followed from it. Empson's seventeenth century turns not on such conventional moments as 1603 or 1641 or 1688, but rather on the subterranean processes that allowed the phrase 'You dog!', used in commendation of a friend, to mean: 'That's a bit naughty, but you are openly displaying human appetites which, let's be frank, we do all share.' (Incidentally, this use of direct-speech paraphrase, which I have here parodied, is one of Empson's most characteristic critical strategies, one that has the effect of staging meaning as part of a communicative encounter.)

The notions expressed in such everyday terms functioned, Empson proposes, as 'a half-conscious protest against the formulae' of the official beliefs of a society, 'a means of keeping them at bay'. He then spells out this function for the present group of words in revealing terms:

> The web of European civilization seems to have been slung between the ideas of Christianity and those of a half-secret rival, centring perhaps (if you made it a system) round honour; one that stresses pride rather than humility, self-realization rather than self-denial, caste rather than either the communion of saints or the individual soul; while the words I want to look at here, whether in their hearty or their patronizing versions, come somewhat between the two, for they were used both to soften the assertion of class and to build a defence against Puritanism.[31]

Such passages as this offer, in effect, a manifesto for a kind of informal intellectual history, one which, instead of focusing on the doctrines announced in formal statements of belief, attends to the attitudes and appraisals embedded in the richness of everyday speech. But, in addition to this methodological commitment, the passage announces a historically substantive interpretation as well. It turns on European society of this period having kept alive a set of beliefs that implicitly held up a different set of ideals for human beings to aspire to than those endorsed by the established religious creeds. The subtlety of his identification of the range of senses of this group of words lies in his not turning them into a rival set of 'formulae' but recognizing the ways in which they only partially evoke or rely upon this alternative conception of life 'to soften the assertion of class and to build a defence against Puritanism'. It will already be obvious that Empson is implicitly endorsing the sympathy with ordinary human appetites expressed in these terms, suggesting, in effect, that we all live in the shrubbery much of the time.

Over and over again the Restoration turns out to be the key period in Empson's history of ethical attitudes. One reason for this is touched on early in the chapter on 'The English Dog'. Reflecting on the way 'roguish'

approval had installed itself in the Restoration libertine's use of 'You dog!',
he remarks that

> there were plenty of people under Victoria inventing slang phrases of this sort,
> but there was not a general political revolt against Puritanism to make it catch
> on. The point for the linguist is not that the Restoration gentry were unusually
> roguish, but that during the Restoration a fairly permanent way of feeling had
> enough influence to affect certain words.[32]

This is a reminder that Empson's linguistic reconstructions presupposed
and drew upon a conventional body of political and social history that he
nowhere spells out.

Critics, like other people, absorb a good deal of history without knowing
it. Often, what is absorbed earliest endures longest, lying dormant for decades, unobtrusively directing one's attention or shaping one's responses,
occasionally resurfacing, immune to correction by later scholarship, a bed-
rock of assumption, prejudice, and identity. In the decade after 1945, when
Empson's form of 'verbal analysis' attracted a growing volume of comment
both in Britain and the United States, the method's alleged ahistoricism was,
as I have already suggested, a frequent topic of reproach. One of Empson's
own later reflections on this matter runs as follows: 'When I returned to
England from [living in] Communist China in 1952, I was frequently told
that I obviously didn't know any history, so I have had to look into the evidence for the opinions I was taught at school, and I found every time that
they stand up like a rock.'[33] Empson, of course, always liked *épater les profes-
seurs*, and reducing the required level of historical learning to 'the opinions
I was taught at school' suited his teasing habits. Still, one is bound to wonder
just how much of the historical or chronological framework of Empson's
later thinking actually *had* been laid down by such teaching and reading of
history as came his way in the 1920s, first as a boy specializing in the science
side of a notably intellectual, Classics-dominated public school, and then as
a maths student at Cambridge dabbling in various other literary and cultural
activities.

Do we perhaps encounter an instance of the rocklike solidity of such
early opinions in this passage, written some thirty-five years later? It comes
from *Milton's God*, published in 1961, where Empson is reflecting on the possibility that his attitude to Christianity will seem out of date, and that such
hostility is no longer necessary. Insofar as that is the case, he maintains, it is
because 'Christians have been kept under a fair amount of restraint for about
two hundred years', thanks to a rise in scepticism from the late sixteenth

century onwards, which slowly led to a decline in their cherished practice of burning people alive for heretical beliefs. 'Buckle's *History of Civilization* (1857–61)', he affirms, 'contains so far as I know the best examination of how the change occurred', and then he goes on:

> I read the book as an undergraduate because it was praised by a character in a novel of Aldous Huxley, and was much impressed by the ample detail; it excites a sickened loathing for Christians when they are let loose which I have continued to feel. So I was interested recently to come across a scholarly re-edition by J. M. Robertson, who had checked the references of Buckle (1904). He scolds the author a good deal in footnotes for errors of theory, but decides the facts are correct, and he was well competent to check them. . . . It so happened that this bit of casual reading put me a month or two ahead of the Centenary of Buckle, which was celebrated by two Lives reviewed in all the weeklies. The reviewers were professional historians, quite certain that history teaches nothing whatever; they treated him with contempt for having any theories about history at all. It felt to me as if night had descended; only a hundred years, and the historians genuinely no longer had any idea even of what the question was that he had been discussing. And yet it is still a practical question.[34]

Milton's God itself, along with so much of Empson's writing in his last three decades, amply attests to the strength of his conviction that Buckle's was 'still a practical question'—essentially, the question of the harmful consequences of Christian doctrine and the continued desirability of free thought to liberate mankind from this pernicious system. But what is, I think, notable in this passage is not just the attitude Empson evinces towards professional historians, but the way in which he relates himself to a phase in history. Empson never shared Leavis's obsessive rage against the corruption of standards in 'the weeklies': he took them as an important index of current educated opinion. In this case, the reception of the biographies of Buckle by the reviewers, writing for this educated general readership in 1957, showed how professional historians had fallen into either a familiar form of Eliotic nostalgia or else a kind of neutered agnosticism about the lessons of the past, leading them to patronize Buckle for his demonstration of what was, Empson agreed with Buckle (in the face of contemporary professional historical opinion), a decisive progressive step in the increasing civilization of Europe. The sturdy Victorian rationalist had, Empson believed, grasped a truth that his scholarly descendants a century later had lost sight of.

In addition, the passage suggests a brief intellectual genealogy for part of Empson's own mind. The undergraduate of fashionably advanced opinions in the science-animated Cambridge of the 1920s reads Aldous Huxley, the very emblem of progressive thought among the young at the time (the importance of Empson's early reading of Huxley is attested at various points in his writing, ranging from his admiration for *Antic Hay* in 1928 to his championing of *The Perennial Philosophy* in the mid-1960s[35]). Huxley's character reads Buckle, a byword, even among Victorians inclined to optimistic readings of the universe, for having the most unrelentingly intellectualist (and thus anti-religious) theory of progress of them all. The older Empson then reads the edition by Robertson, himself a didactic popular historian (termed by Eliot—see Chapter 1—a Whig) who was a pillar of turn-of-the-century rationalism. These names bespeak an intellectual milieu confident in the powers of the human mind, especially as methodized by science, to make advances by identifying and eliminating error. And chief among these errors, a relic of an earlier and more benighted stage of European history, was belief in Christianity.

Insofar as a historical story can be intermittently glimpsed through the cannon-smoke of *Milton's God*, it bears no relation to 'the loss of the organic community' or 'the rise of capitalism', or any of the other meta-historical accounts familiar from the literary criticism of the mid-century. The premise of *Empson's* story is, as he puts it, the 'tragedy that Europe got saddled with such a very corrupting religion'. His assessment of Milton's *Paradise Lost* is set within this framework:

> The poem really does survey the Western half of civilization and express the conflict which arose from the introduction of Christianity into this great area.... The root of [Milton's] power is that he could accept and express a downright horrible conception of God and yet keep somehow alive, underneath it, all the breadth and generosity, the welcome to every noble pleasure, which had been prominent in European history just before his time.[36]

It is possible to hear an almost Nietzschean sentiment at work in this last sentence, an invocation of the larger, essentially aristocratic code of living that had its roots in ancient paganism, a more generous ethic that had not been altogether eliminated by the moralizing *ressentiment* at the core of Christianity. But the chronology hinted at here is a reminder that Empson always seems especially exercised by the appallingness of *Protestant* Christianity, for all his antipathy to the fanaticism and persecution endemic to the medieval Catholic form of the religion. After all, 'just before' Milton's time was hardly the heyday in Europe of a creed of Classical hedonism, though it may have been a period, in England at least, when aristocratic values were not yet wholly subordinated to the censoriousness of righteous Puritanism.

In pursuing the question of Empson's wider historical allegiances, I want
to return to the slightly tetchy response he wrote a few years later, in 1967,
to what had actually been a very appreciative and generous assessment of his
work by the American scholar Roger Sale, which I quoted earlier. Empson
complained that Sale treated him as 'not being such a fool as to believe in
history, but just cracking jokes about it', and he grumbled that such a dismissive attitude towards history was one of Eliot's unfortunate legacies.
Empson then went on (in the passage also cited earlier about the situation
he encountered on his return to England in 1952 after some years teaching
in China):

> A history of some sort had to be fubbed up to support [Eliot's] 'tradition', but
> was sure to fall down at a touch.... Of course a lot of professional historians
> became neo-historians to suit this fashion, but they are getting a bit ashamed
> of it. The Whig Interpretation of History is the correct one, and it is remark-
> able that the book given that title offers no single reason to think otherwise,
> being merely a fashion report of some High Table giggles. Anything I print
> about the past, ignorant as I know myself to be, is intended as real truth about
> the past which I think worth fighting over.[37]

One of Empson's own favoured terms of praise is 'sturdy', and we cannot
help but be struck by the sturdy liberalism of this passage. The movement of
his mind through these sentences says a lot about where he saw himself in
terms of contemporary cultural politics. Eliot's attempt to 'fub up' a history
to underwrite his poetics is what starts him off, with Empson moving on to
register his sense that on his return to England in 1952 he found this sort of
Eliotic history to be dominant, at least in Eng Lit circles. Counterposing
'the opinions I was taught at school' bears its own impish intent, but also has
the effect of suggesting that once upon a time an alternative historical story
was simply a common possession, 'what every schoolboy knew' (at least,
every precocious schoolboy who had been at Winchester in the early 1920s).
One would like to know more about the 'evidence' he had more recently
'looked into' to confirm the truth of these opinions: but, however sceptical
we may be on this point, we register that Empson wishes us to believe that
he has done a good deal of reading in the latest authorities.

Not that some of those authorities weren't guilty of falling in behind cultural fashion. A 'neo-historian', presumably, is someone who endorses the
meta-historical cultural declinism associated with Eliot, a phrase suggesting a
deliberate parallel to 'neo-Christian', one of Empson's favoured terms of abuse.
And then comes the ringingly sturdy assertion that 'the Whig Interpretation

of History is the correct one'. Since he goes on to refer, however dismissively, to Butterfield's book, we have to consider the sense in which he uses this phrase. The original 'Whig interpretation', of course, was a story, parliamentarian rather than royalist in its allegiances, about the continuity of English constitutional development from the Middle Ages through the seventeenth century, in which liberty, as the hallowed phrase had it, 'broadened down from precedent to precedent'. As I suggested in the Introduction, by the end of the nineteenth century this sense had undergone some expansion to become a story of political and moral progress more generally, albeit with English liberties still at its heart. In his book, Butterfield had extended this sense much further still to refer to *any* narrative in which the earlier stages of the story are understood in terms of their contribution to the later (desirable) outcome. It seems pretty clear that it was the moderately expanded historical sense, rather than either the narrower original sense or Butterfield's greatly-expanded figurative sense, that Empson was declaring allegiance to. His scorn for Butterfield's book, published a year after *Seven Types*, suggests he was unmoved by the larger methodological concern that animates that famous polemic, finding in its (admittedly skimpy) analysis no reason to change his mind about the traditional story of progress. And that story still had, for Empson, its militant purchase on the present: it was a story, as he puts it, 'worth fighting for'.

Another way to draw out Empson's distinctiveness when compared to his immediate critical peers is by observing the relative unimportance to him of Matthew Arnold's literary and cultural criticism. The mantle of Arnold sat heavily on the shoulders of Eliot, Richards, and Leavis and constrained their movements. Less burdened by anxieties about cultural decline, Empson was less drawn to the idea of literature's secular mission (of course, in time Eliot, Richards, and Leavis each distanced themselves from the Arnoldian conception, but even so the struggle had a formative influence on them all).[38] Indeed, Empson was not, at bottom, close to Arnold even on the topic on which they seemed at first sight to concur—namely, the enormous importance of Puritanism in English life. Where Arnold saw the legacies of Puritanism and Benthamism as the twin faces of English philistinism, both equally in need of the corrective power of culture, Empson took Benthamism to be the enemy of Puritanism, the properly rationalist antidote to the latter's malign mixture of moralism and superstition.

As I suggested earlier, it may be hard to recall now just how much literary discussion in mid-twentieth-century Britain took place within a framework derived from Eliot's throwaway remarks about the seventeenth century's 'dissociation of sensibility'. Empson, of course, was very much part of this milieu intellectually and socially, and Eliot is undoubtedly a brooding presence for him in his early work—or, as he put it: 'I do not know for certain how much of my own mind he invented, let alone how much of it is a reaction against him or indeed a consequence of misreading him.'[39] But, exceptionally, Empson did not structure his historical assumptions around the Eliotic scheme, and he became more overtly hostile to it as he grew older. As he put it, with characteristic downrightness, in a letter late in life: 'I don't believe, and never have believed, that a social and literary "dissociation of sensibility" ever occurred. I don't even believe that everything is getting worse and worse. . . . I think a great deal of progress has gone on since then, pretty steadily.'[40] Empson's sturdy rationalism may not appeal to all later readers, but it should at least be recognized as part of a consciously and pervasively historical understanding—one resting on a distinctive method of linguistic analysis to which, even now, historians might with profit pay closer attention.

5

The History of 'the Reading Public'

I

The charged topic of 'the reading public' appears to be ineliminably historical. Generalizations about this reified entity almost always have assumptions about either 'growth' or 'decline' built into them, and so presuppose, if only implicitly, larger historical stories. More specifically, accounts of the history of the reading public can often turn out to be indirect ways of writing the history of cultural elites and their relations with other social groups. In the middle decades of the twentieth century, one of the most influential channels through which literary critics disseminated wider historical understandings was through their treatment of this ever-elusive entity. Here the most detailed historical discussion was provided by Q. D. Leavis's 1932 book *Fiction and the Reading Public* (to avoid confusion, its author will be referred to as 'QDL' and her husband as 'Leavis').[1] While there are complexities to the relationship between the Leavises, and contrasts between their characteristic styles of writing, these may be set aside for the present, since the consilience of their views on this topic is not in doubt. Leavis and the *Scrutiny* circle always treated QDL's book as a founding document, one that provided the necessary historical and sociological evidence to underwrite their relentlessly bleak analysis of the contemporary cultural situation. The book has to be recognized as a major expression of the Leavises' engagement with history.

Not that History figures as the most salient contiguous discipline in the Leavises' early work. From the outset, *Scrutiny* described its approach as 'anthropological'. When Leavis had first referred to *Middletown* as early as his 1930 pamphlet, only a year after the book's publication, he had called it 'a remarkable work of anthropology'.[2] And, when QDL submitted her work for a Ph.D. in late 1931, it was subtitled 'A Study in Social Anthropology'.[3] Although she (wisely) dropped this for publication, the emphasis it signalled remained—namely, a commitment to exploring broad social patterns of taste that went beyond that small number of works a literary critic would have considered worth attention.[4] However, this most certainly did not signal the 'value-neutral' approach of the social scientist, since the book is frankly and unapologetically evaluative throughout.

The ostensible focus of *Fiction and the Reading Public* is the present: it contains a good deal of information about the current marketing and reviewing of different kinds of publication, chiefly novels, as well as other features of contemporary literary journalism. But the presentation of this material is underwritten by what is, in its condensed form, a relatively simple developmental sequence. Once upon a time, there was only one public, and so the taste of the cultivated set the standards of taste as a whole. Since then, there has been a vast expansion of cheap (= low-quality) publications for much bigger markets, so now the taste of the cultivated is confined to a small minority of the population. This means that standards have fallen catastrophically; an interest in serious literature is confined to an embattled minority, largely without influence on the broader publics.

This argument about the debased state of contemporary taste is presented as the outcome of the long historical evolution of the reading public and a relatively sudden decline in its standards and cohesiveness from the end of the nineteenth century. The 'first English reading public' is to be found, unsurprisingly, in the Elizabethan age. This period allegedly possessed a single culture, shared by all social classes: the groundlings had no choice but to go to *Hamlet*, and so on. There simply was no printed literature deliberately aimed at a lower level of readership (more recent scholars of the period might be inclined to cite chapbooks and the like as counter-evidence here). Then came the Puritan culture, as expressed in Milton, Defoe, and, above all, Bunyan, and the power of this culture is said to have lasted, in terms of reading habits, until almost the end of the nineteenth century. Indeed, in a retrospect written over thirty years later, QDL claimed that one source of her book's originality lay in its 'discovery' of 'the importance of the Puritan conscience in English literary history'.[5] Everyone's taste in reading was, apparently, elevated by the influence of this Puritan culture: 'It appears axiomatic', she writes in a particularly shaky proposition, 'that one cannot spend Sundays over the Bible and *Pilgrim's Progress* and read the *Windsor Magazine* happily in the week. But if for the Bible and *Pilgrim's Progress* are substituted the *News of the World* and the *Sunday Express*, it will be evident that popular taste is likely to be in some danger.'[6] As this suggests, scrupulous comparison of like with like is not really the book's forte, but we should not overlook the implicit acknowledgement here that in the second half of the seventeenth century the reading public was already stratified; it is '*popular* taste' that was formed by reading the Bible and Bunyan. This, however, does not mean that Bunyan was 'popular' in the pejorative sense in which she has used the term to refer to contemporary middle-brow literature: 'Bunyan's religious vocabulary has only to be translated into the more general language of conduct and sensibility for it to become evident that he is on the side of the highbrow.'[7] Clearly, the declinist case exacts a certain dextrousness from its proponents when handling such ambiguous evidence.

In the chapter entitled 'Growth of the Reading Public' we come to the age of the *Spectator* and the *Tatler*, and these journals, she claims, 'combined two hitherto separate reading publics (Aphra Behn's and Bunyan's)'. As a result, the eighteenth-century reading public is described as 'homogeneous', despite its considerable growth in size in the third quarter of the century. (This is one of the places where she is closest to Leslie Stephen's *English Literature and Society in the Eighteenth Century*, which was, as we have seen, an acknowledged inspiration for both the Leavises.) Even after that growth, there was, in a revealing phrase, no separate 'semi-literate public to interfere with the book market'—'interfere' suggesting that the natural state of the book market was one where serious books were provided for serious readers.[8]

For the same reasons, eighteenth-century fiction, up to and including Austen and Edgeworth, is said to exhibit an emotional decorum: 'It is essentially the critical temper that produced and maintained this code of good taste and good sense—a sense of standards even in the realm of emotion.' By comparison, 'the novels of Charlotte Brontë, for instance, exhibit a shameful self-abandonment to undisciplined emotion which makes these latter seem the productions of a schoolgirl of genius', and we find similar 'crudities of feeling' in Dickens or Thackeray or Kingsley. 'The decline and disappearance of the eighteenth-century code is part of the history of the reading public.'[9] Of course, what is presented here as a story of loss and decline could be redescribed as simply a change in sensibility, and one is already bound to wonder how this account could be squared with that given later by F. R. Leavis in *The Great Tradition* in which George Eliot, Henry James, and Joseph Conrad represented the great age of the novel.

In any event, the beginnings of what QDL terms 'the disintegration of the reading public' are dated to the first half of the nineteenth century, which sees the rise of sensation fiction, serial publication, cheap magazines, and the 'portent' of Dickens. 'The beginnings of a split between cultivated and popular taste in fiction is apparent.' But the chronology is not straight-forward, for, as she says, 'as late as George Eliot's day, the serious novel could be, and actually was, read with interest and pleasure by the general reading public'. Hardy, it appears, is 'the last' who could combine serious artistic ambition with popular success. But now, in 1932, 'the serious novel can no longer percolate through successive strata of the reading publics'.[10] In these respects, the great abyss became unbridgeable only in the 1890s, which were marked by a double whammy. First, the ending of the old, expensive three-decker novel in 1894 signalled the symbolic transition to the dominance of the bestseller in the fiction market; and, second, the founding of the *Daily Mail* in 1896 marked the beginnings of the 'yellow press', so that the twin devils who dance on the grave of serious standards are Marie Corelli and Lord Northcliffe. 'From the beginning of an organized reading public [which she had dated to around 1700] till the late nineteenth century,' she writes with one of her grander historical sweeps, 'tradition and authority were guarded by a consciously civilized press', and (rather remarkably, given her earlier evidence) 'there is no radical change to report in the tone of the Press' during almost two centuries. But, thereafter, the history is 'the history of the overthrow of authority'; the cultivated elite no longer set the tone. There had been what she later called a 'saddening disintegration' of the public that had sustained Dickens and George Eliot, and it was the Northcliffe press, above all, which had 'degraded popular taste', resulting in 'an unbridged and impassable gulf between Marie Corelli and Henry James'. As a result, she insisted in 1932, 'the reading capacity of the general public, it must be concluded, has never been so low as at the present time'.[11] Looking back from the mid-1960s QDL seemed to take some satisfaction from the way her thesis about a decline attributable to the exploitation of the new public created by the Education Act of 1870 had angered those on the left, such as Harold Laski, who wanted to tell a more positive story of cultural enfran-chisement. Laski 'was furious, I was told, if he saw a student of his reading my book. My offence was to have challenged the automatic optimism on which the attitudes of the fashionable left-wing intellectuals were based.'[12]

The Leavises' estrangement from, and later hostility to, I. A. Richards that developed in the early 1930s should not obscure how closely QDL followed her one-time supervisor's lead on the question of reading capacities. Richards was already identified with the claim that, as he phrased it later: 'The capacity to read intelligently seems undoubtedly to have been greater among educated men in Coleridge's time than it is today.... It was maintained—for modes of meaning close in structure to those in Wordsworth, Shelley, or Keats—until towards the end of the nineteenth century. Then came a sudden decline in performance.'[13] QDL believed that her detailed research on recent and contemporary literary culture bore out Richards's contention. 'The impartial assessor of the evidence brought together here [surely an improbable persona for QDL, of all people, to claim] can hardly avoid concluding that for the first time in the history of our literature the living forms of the novel have been side-tracked in favour of the *faux-bon*.'[14] It is not immediately clear how we should understand this assertion. As with most such claims, it involves being extremely selective about what is to count as a 'living form' of the novel in the present (so that any novel that sells well is more or less automatically excluded), and equally selective in ignoring all those publications in the past that were enormously popular at the time but that have subsequently dropped out of literary history (so that 'classics' can be made to seem to have dominated the market).

'We have now, apparently, several publics.' This declaration is not as much of a concession as it may at first appear. It is not simply that the adverbial pause in the statement implicitly raises a quizzical eyebrow at the reported development. It is, more significantly, that the subsequent analysis is not really informed by acceptance of the logic of this proposition: in her story there is a *single* set of standards from which successively more popular markets have fallen away. The circumstances that determined these various developments are only patchily covered; selected moments are idealized; inconvenient objections are glossed over. Thus, like many commentators on this topic, she is greatly impressed by the success of the *Edinburgh* and *Quarterly* reviews in the early nineteenth century, and she contrasts this with 'the insecurity of the acknowledged "highbrow" organ in the twentieth century', instancing Eliot's *Criterion*.[15] The contrast had some historical basis: for two or three decades, the great quarterlies did indeed command an impressive level of attention in society, one greater than circulations of 9,000 to 12,000 might suggest. But, before drawing any conclusions from a contrast between the 1800s and the 1920s, a more adequately historical account would need to explore relative levels of literacy, standards of living, disposable income, range of competing publications, other sources of analysis and criticism, and changes in the speed of the circulation of information and indeed of life in general. QDL underwrites her declinist case by claiming that the *Edinburgh* reached a far higher proportion of the population in 1810 than the *Adelphi* did in the 1920s, but, as with so many of her contrasts in this vein, the deployment of this 'fact' without any supporting analysis may seem simply to amount to a preference for a smaller, more homogeneous (and more unequal) society.

And this points to the main problem with her larger argument. She provides a moderately well-informed account of the development of new markets for different types of fiction in the early twentieth century, and she may have been one of the first to chronicle these developments in any detail. But her report is marred by her finger-jabbing insistence on seeing all this as evidence of an unambiguous decline in the quality of 'the culture' (always treated as a unity). There is now only a tiny handful of 'serious novelists'—Lawrence, Joyce, Woolf, and Forster, with special mention for T. F. Powys as the author of *Mr Weston's Good Wine* (a book much lauded by the Leavises for a while, though one that soon disappears from their pantheon)—but these authors are, it is alleged, either unknown to a wider public or, if known, sneered at as unreadably 'highbrow'.

This depressing contemporary situation calls, she announces, for 'resistance', and for a 'missionary spirit' in education. It is here that we encounter what may be the most remarkable sentence in a book full of remarkable sentences: 'As a minor instance of what may be done by conscious resistance, the case of British Honduras comes to mind.' She cites no reference, but the allusion would seem to be derived from Stuart Chase's then popular account of 'traditional' life in Mexico and related attempts in Latin America to resist 'American influence'. One cannot help thinking that setting literary critics to harvesting bananas by hand in the Central American jungle seems a rather high price to pay for escaping reminders of the success of J. B. Priestley. Looking closer to home, she concludes that hope can only be invested in the creation of 'an all-round critical organ'.[16] *Fiction and the Reading Public* was published in March 1932; the first issue of *Scrutiny* appeared on cue at the beginning of May.

One of the features of QDL's book that is characteristic of polemics about the decline of the reading public is the unsteadiness of its chronology and the tendency for the postulated condition of a flourishing reading public to turn into the ever-receding horizon of the argument. Another, no less characteristic, is the selectiveness of the literary history: when a period is to be celebrated, it tends to be defined in terms of its masterpieces, whose very existence clearly indicates a healthy state of affairs; but when signs of decline are required, the focus switches to publications aimed at a more popular market, obscuring the diversity and coexistence of actual readers in both cases. This became an acknowledged weakness of her work, as in a later criticism of David Holbrook for using 'Q. D. Leavis's trick of comparing today's average with yesterday's best'.[17]

From QDL's encompassing dismissals, it is difficult to extract much idea of what might count, now, as a desirable state of the reading public. The segmentation of the market according to social stratum having happened, there seemed no way back to the Edenic unity attributed to Elizabethan culture or even to any of those moments before the late nineteenth century when the standards of cultivated society dominated in literary as well as social terms. Yet there is clearly more than a hankering for a state of affairs in which the standards of the 'educated minority' might still dictate taste for the society as a whole—or, rather, in which such standards would be acknowledged and deferred to even by those whose personal preferences ran to something more vulgar. Sometimes it seems to be the sheer journalistic prominence of middlebrow opinions that most irks her; at other times it seems to be the enforced defensiveness of 'highbrow' culture, as though it half accepted the sneer implied in that label. But she tells such an overdetermined story of historical decline that it is hard to see how any of the deleterious trends she anatomizes could ever be reversed or withstood. The minority has no choice but to be embattled—though fortified, it would seem, by its understanding of just what a decline the present situation really represents.

It is correspondingly difficult to decode the signals in QDL's prose about the implied reader of her book. The most obvious analysis would be to say that she is simply preaching to the choir, providing historical or sociological chapter and verse for a select readership already broadly familiar with the outlines of the story. This was certainly Richards's view when acting in the role of her Ph.D. examiner: 'The candidate has provided documents for an argument about changes in the reading habits and abilities of the general public which many people would agree to without the evidence.'[18] But her prose does also hit other notes that make the book rather more interesting than this suggests. For example, there is a recurrent tone of belligerent impatience, as though reproaching a broader swathe of well-educated readers for their failure to realize how bad things have become. Alongside the characteristic Ph.D.

student's insistence on the novelty of her findings, there is a recurrent assertion that what she is saying is too evident to require demonstration: her readers, it is implied, can hardly fail to know these things, yet somehow they do not seem to have absorbed their significance. Certainly, there is no attempt to persuade or recruit the champions of 'popular' taste; they are assumed to be both beyond the pale and beyond redemption. Similarly, aesthetic judgements about individual writers are tossed off with careless confidence, the accepted currency of a small circle, so indisputably right that any attempt at justification would be otiose, even a little gauche. For the most part, these judgements are the recognizable staples of Eliot-inspired Cambridge English, with a few difficult modern writers attracting high praise and nearly all the more popular names of the late nineteenth and early twentieth centuries being dismissed as irretrievably mediocre.

II

The question of the implied reader of such indictments of contemporary taste turns out to involve a further range of historical assumptions that may best be explored by turning back to the work of F. R. Leavis. Reviewing his 1936 study *Revaluation: Tradition and Development in English Poetry*, John Hayward noted that Leavis 'assumes a degree of perversity or ignorance in his audience for which there is no justification', and he astutely observed that this assumption leads to 'a certain element of intellectual priggishness'.[19] Hayward was right in his conclusion here, though not quite right in his analysis. It is true that the audience explicitly *referred to* in the book is always assumed to be beyond redemption in this way; but the audience implicitly *appealed to* is assumed, by contrast, to recognize the locus of value in a literary work at a glance. And this same structure recurs in Leavis's broader jeremiads about the disappearance of the reading public, which always assert, simultaneously, (*a*) that things are so bad there is now no chance of getting a serious hearing for proper critical standards, and (*b*) that there exists nonetheless an audience capable of appreciating this diagnosis. The repeated pattern is one in which the slack or inattentive misreaders are said to possess all the cultural power, while those who can immediately recognize the truths to which Leavis is pointing are curiously powerless.

But how, we are entitled to ask, did things work in the past, when, according to his account, the true believers *were*, or at least should have been, the orthodoxy? When speaking about 'the reading public', Leavis always proposed a tight connection between the answering responsiveness of such a public and the possibility of sustaining true critical assessments. Such a public existed in earlier centuries—existed, perhaps, if in slightly less authoritative form, right up to the end of the nineteenth century. However, the false estimations of writers and works with which he does constant battle—the overvaluing of this writer, the mistaking of that writer for a serious artist, and so on—are nearly all errors with a long history. It was, after all, the periods that are supposed to have possessed an active and responsible reading public that over-rated Herrick or Gray or Shelley or Swinburne, or for that matter Fielding or Scott or Brontë or Thackeray. To take just the first of these as an example: Herrick, we are reminded in *Revaluation*, is 'still an overrated figure'—'still' signalling that this is not just a recent piece of foolishness. Yet, the 'triviality of Herrick's talent' (in Leavis's unforgiving phrase) means that 'beside him Carew looks like a major poet'.[20] The mere act of juxtaposition is sufficient to sustain the judgement. But in that case, must not the serious and respon-sible and (what is more) authoritative reading public that allegedly existed in earlier centuries have been asleep on the job?

For the most part, Leavis does not attempt any systematic analysis of the making and unmaking of literary reputations in the past. In his early criti-cism, he tends to take for granted the decisiveness of the Eliotic challenge to a supposed late-Romantic orthodoxy, without enquiring at all closely into how, say, the merits of the Metaphysicals had gone so long unrecog-nized or how Shelley had come to be so greatly admired by the Victorians in the first place. Later in his career, his attention is more focused on the effects of 'coterie flank-rubbing' in the present than on the sources of crit-ical error in the past. There is, of course, a shadowy meta-sociology hovering behind his more specific historical assumptions throughout, but the familiar laments about the rise of the machine and of 'mass civilization' can only underwrite a broad unilinear story of cultural decline; they cannot account for smaller-scale fluctuations in literary standing.

In the case of *Revaluation*, the ground for a certain kind of optimism is present in the implication of a recent change in critical opinion. After all, Shelley's great reputation, it is implied, may be starting to look out of date. It derived, we may say, from the years BE (Before Eliot). Much of the appeal of the book is that it offers to display the reorganized literary history that is the consequence of having accepted the terms of the Eliotic revolution. Indeed, as Leavis says of the altered understanding of the poetry of the seventeenth century: 'The work has been done, the re-orientation effected: the heresies of ten years ago are orthodoxy.'[21] Here, perhaps, was a case where the alert and responsive readers *had* successfully stormed the ramparts, driving out the misreaders, though it would have to be said, as Hayward's comment indicated, that Leavis still seemed to think it necessary to pour copious quantities of boiling oil on the latter's heads. But, as Leavis's career went on, even such recent and local victories seem to disappear from the account; no critic is ever subsequently allowed to have made such a difference.

It is only fair to acknowledge that Leavis was frequently taking issue with the standing certain writers had acquired in the previous fifty or one hundred years rather than, in the case of writers from earlier centuries, with their reputations during their lifetimes or immediately thereafter. Emphasizing this allows us partially to rescue his theory of the functioning of the reading public, at least for the more distant periods. But even here there is some unsteadiness about the effectiveness of earlier reading publics—why, to take just one example, was Milton revered for more or less the whole of the period between his death and Eliot's 'dislodging' criticism of him if his failings are so 'clear'? In addition, there is the problem, evident (as we have seen) in QDL's *Fiction and the Reading Public*, which provides much of the basic history, of deciding exactly when a serious responsible reading public ceased to exist. When contrasting the early Victorian popular taste for sensation fiction with the sober aesthetic consensus alleged to have formed around the *Spectator* and the *Tatler* in the early eighteenth century, the Leavises write as though the days of an authoritative reading public were already over before Dickens published a word. But, when contrasting the yellow-press-and-book-club world of the present with the cultural centrality of the much-admired 'great reviews' of the mid-Victorian period, they insisted that such a public had existed for George Eliot, even perhaps for Hardy. Yet this was the same public, presumably, that exalted Walter Scott above Jane Austen and admired Tennyson and Browning as great poets.

In an exchange in 1956 with the Oxford scholar Wallace Robson, Leavis illustrated once again (as he had repeatedly done in his disputes with F. W. Bateson over the years) his distinctive engagement with the question of 'literary history'. Robson was by this point only the most recent of those who had in one way or another accused Leavis of being insufficiently historical in his literary criticism and more particularly in his ideas about a literary education. Leavis countered the charge by insisting that he told his students 'they should be all the while asking themselves: "What *is* literary history?" (for literary history as we find it in Elton or Saintsbury is hardly what Mr Robson can be appealing to when he attributes such virtue to the "historical sense").' It would be interesting to know whether any students in the mid-1950s still turned to Elton or Saintsbury, though this choice of names may have indicated not only the site of a formative reaction in Leavis's own early days, but also the fact that such large-scale literary history had gone out of fashion in the previous thirty years. Leavis evidently saw his own work as having, in a sense, replaced these forms of old-fashioned literary history. 'When I frankly avow that I wrote my *Revaluation* in an effort to "define" or present, in this spirit, the idea of "literary history", I make it quite plain that my view of the relation between "history" and "criticism" *is* very different from Mr Robson's.'[22] Leavis was always quick to insist that there can be no adequate description of a work of literature that is not grounded in an intelligent, discriminating personal (and yet more than personal) reaction, and thus that literary history must be in some sense evaluative, embodying critical judgement. Still, it is interesting to see how this campaign to redefine literary history continues to seem to him a vital matter in the mid-1950s, and that he wishes *Revaluation* to be understood as, among other things, a work of history.

In his selective engagement with history, Leavis always speaks of the reading public in the singular. For earlier periods, what his analysis actually reflected, though this was not his preferred way of putting it, was essentially a matter of class domination: only a tiny fraction of the population possessed the education and leisure required to participate in the reading and criticism of literature, and they therefore enjoyed an unchallenged monopoly of public judgement. Leavis's sociology of decline identifies, above all else, the growth of mass literacy following the late-nineteenth-century education acts that culturally enfranchised new social groups, who, empowered by the increasing commercialization of the cultural sphere, break up the old cultural monopoly of the educated class.

What is crucial about Leavis's response to these developments is that he is, in effect, unwilling to accept that there can, even now, be a plurality of so-called reading publics. He continues to operate with the concept in the singular even in the present, and, no less important, he identifies this essentially notional or abstract entity with one specific indicator. As I mentioned earlier, in his idealizing of the relatively recent past, Leavis looks to the example of the great Victorian reviews, which, in his formulation, addressed 'the diverse intellectual interests of a cultivated mind in its non-specialist capacity'.[23] In calling for 'a real contemporary performance of the critical function', he looked in precisely the same social space, that space that is at once 'cultivated' and 'non-specialist'; or, translated into a mid-twentieth-century idiom, between the popular on the one side and the academic on the other. This, surely, helps to explain his obsessive concern with that sphere of cultural opinion that was, for him, marked out by that familiar litany of the dwelling-places of Sin and Error, 'the Third Programme, the intellectual weeklies, and the smart Sundays'. This is where the contemporary expression of an effective reading public would have to be found. Leavis does not expect the literary critic to find an 'answering responsiveness' in, say, the *Daily Mirror* or the *News of the World* any more than in, say, *Notes and Queries* or the *Review of English Studies*. 'The diverse intellectual interests of a cultivated mind in its non-specialist capacity' can be properly addressed only in the space imagined to lie between these cultural extremes.

But (and this is where his critical practice and his implicit sociology of the reading public reinforce each other with insidious effect) the implied addressees of his criticism are never imagined as actually taking control of that space. His own critical voice is self-consciously positioned as antagonistic to two rival voices: that of the belletristic impressionism of the metropolitan man of letters, and that of the historical and philological scholarship of the cloistered academic. (Something like this, it should be remarked, is the identity recurrently claimed throughout the twentieth century by university-based figures who aspired to play the role of the intellectual.[24]) But this self-positioning complements the feature of his analysis that I have just pointed to—namely, that his categories of imagined misreaders represent actual social groups, whereas the implied addressees of his criticism are not defined by any such sociological or institutional markers, but simply by an individual ability to see the self-evident. So, once again, these alert and responsive readers can be endowed with no effective agency, though effective agency is, for Leavis, a defining mark of 'a serious and responsible reading public'. In the present as in the recent past, therefore, the misreaders seem to have a near-monopoly on cultural power.

In the decades following 1945, there is a curious disjunction between Leavis's increasing cultural pessimism and his increasing publishing success. Of course, the closure of *Scrutiny* could be presented as a vindication of the pessimism: there was no longer a sufficient public even to sustain one properly critical journal. But, actually, these were the years that saw the public reached by his books increase quite rapidly, as we know from the Chatto and Penguin records.[25] This growth in the sales of his books coincided with, and was partly due to, the expansion of the universities in the 1950s and 1960s; the pattern of regular reprinting of relatively modest print runs of his books surely indicates a largely academic rather than trade market. We may be tempted to wonder how, in the face of such success, he could still maintain that the public necessary to sustain the critical function had all but disappeared. But he could, of course, not be satisfied until any putative public had demonstrably become *the* reading public, and for him this meant controlling the commanding heights of the cultural economy as represented, it hardly needs saying, by the Third Programme, the intellectual weeklies, and the smart Sundays. Moreover, not all those readers could be relied upon to recognize and respond to the true message of his books. His fierce repudiation of that 'orthodoxy of enlightenment' he saw triumphing in the Lady Chatterley case arose in part from the way in which his own high claims for Lawrence were conscripted into the defence of a novel 'to which I (explicitly) did not apply them, and to which they do not apply'.[26] As ever, the slack misreaders still possessed all the cultural power. An effective and properly critical reading public remained a regulatory ideal, not an empirical reality.

III

Any examination of mid-twentieth-century literary critics' historical assumptions when discussing the question of the reading public needs to take the measure of the early work of Richard Hoggart. He was a generation younger than the Leavises, and, as we shall see, his relation to their legacy was not straightforward. Hoggart is not usually accorded any place in histories of literary criticism, but in an analysis of what will, beyond all question, always be thought his most significant publication, *The Uses of Literacy*,[27] the question of disciplinary identity cannot altogether be ignored. The book had, I suggest, an intimate relationship to the practice of literary criticism in the decade or so after the end of the Second World War, and there turn out to be some complex and unobvious connections between that practice and claims about cultural decline.[28]

In his later reflections, Hoggart always insisted that he did not share the cultural pessimism of those commentators who wrote in the style of Eliot and Leavis, and it is certainly true that, once he was given, from the end of the 1950s onwards, a prominent public platform from which to pronounce on such matters, his was a valuable voice arguing for a more discriminating assessment of contemporary social change than, as he put it in 1965, either 'a self-indulgent nostalgia or a brash band-wagonning'.[29] But the focus of my enquiry here is at a double remove from these explicit pronouncements: first, because it returns to the actual idiom and strategy of the second half of *The Uses of Literacy* itself, rather than to its author's subsequent, self-conscious affirmations of its affinities and purposes; and, second, because here I am reconsidering the cultural logic of a whole style of critical prac-tice, one that I believe Hoggart shared more fully when writing his classic work than either his later self or other scholars have always registered.

In his explicitly autobiographical writings, Hoggart on several occasions acknowledged a general debt to the work of the Leavises while recording the expected reservations. Speaking of the early years of the Birmingham Centre for Contemporary Cultural Studies, for example, he declared: 'We had learned a lot from F. R. and Q. D. Leavis, but could not accept much in their position, literary and social.'[30] In another passage he spelled out a little more fully the reservations he claimed always to have had about the work of QDL 'as well as similar material in *Scrutiny* and associated publications', pointing particularly to 'a distancing from the material in her, too wholesale a rejection of it and all it might imply'. He, by contrast, urged that 'one had to know very much more about how people used much of the stuff which to us might seem merely dismissible trash, before one could speak confi-dently about the effects it might have'.[31] Perhaps we should not attach too much significance to this use of the first-person plural, but it does suggest that 'we' are the educated literary-critical readers who already know what this material is worth, and thus we are far removed from its actual working-class consumers. Here, the author of the celebrated discussion of 'Them and Us' may seem to be implicitly acknowledging he writes as one of the edu-cated 'Them'.

The connection or possible indebtedness to which Hoggart mostly attended in these later statements concerns *Fiction and the Reading Public*. *The Uses of Literacy*, he declared in a retrospect, 'pays tribute to the work of Mrs Leavis and it is a genuine tribute'.[32] But in fact it is not at all clear that his book pays any such 'tribute'. Neither QDL nor *Fiction and the Reading Public* appears in the index; nor, for that matter, does the name of F. R. Leavis or of *Scrutiny*. Of course, indexes can be patchy or merely mechanical indi-cators of a book's contents, but I can find no direct reference to QDL or her work in the body of the text itself. The title of her book appears once in an endnote, attached to a paragraph about sincerity and cynicism in popular romance writers; the note in its entirety reads: 'See the statements by some popular novelists in Mrs Q. D. Leavis's *Fiction and the Reading Public*.'[33] Her book, it is true, is listed in the Bibliography, but so are approximately 100 other titles. No doubt Hoggart did feel some sense of indebtedness to QDL's work, and he certainly attempted to acknowledge this in the various later reflections, but her book is if anything more noticeable by its absence in *The Uses of Literacy* itself. This contrast is strikingly legible in the 1992 Penguin edition of the book, since in the interview by John Corner (conducted in 1990) Hoggart went to some lengths to emphasize that he was 'a great admirer of *Fiction and the Reading Public*' despite his reservations.[34]

Something similar might be said of his more general indebtedness to Leavis's whole critical idiom and approach. I do not mean that in his early work Hoggart deliberately suppressed acknowledgement of these affinities; it may rather have been that they were so deep, so constitutive of his intellectual identity at this point, and so widely shared in the relevant critical milieu that any such acknowledgement might have seemed both unnecessary and too specific. His direct contact with Leavis himself was minimal, but a few letters between them survive, and in one of these dating from 1953, when the writing of *The Uses of Literacy* was in full spate, Hoggart concluded an otherwise business-like brief note by saying: 'Meanwhile, I'd like to take this opportunity to say, in complete sincerity, that I have learned more from you and from <u>Scrutiny</u>—far more—than from anyone else.'[35]

So, although Hoggart did not see himself as endorsing the Leavises' embattled and disdainful attitude towards contemporary social changes, and although in the 1960s he elaborated his own distinctive approach to the study of such changes, accompanied by several position statements that emphasized his distance from Leavisite condescension, matters look somewhat different if we return to *The Uses of Literacy* itself. That book, we should recall, was largely drafted between 1952 and 1954 (it was first sent to the publisher in the early summer of 1955): although it came to have almost iconic standing in the 1960s, it grew out of the decade after 1945. And here the central questions are, first, how far Hoggart's book shared in what was the, or at least a, dominant critical practice of the period; and, second, how far there was an intrinsic rather than merely contingent connection between this critical idiom and a pessimistic or alarmist interpretation of the direction of contemporary cultural change.

Although no one way of writing about literature had a monopoly on critical practice in Britain in the first ten or fifteen years after the end of the war, there was one highly visible strain within the greater variety that in some sense made the running during this period. It was very much a critical *practice*, only patchily formulated into an explicit set of methodological protocols. Its practitioners increasingly tended to be based in universities though at least as actively concerned with the world outside the walls as with conventional scholarly preoccupations; it also had a strong presence in adult education and in sixth-form teaching. In so far as the practice had institutional connections, it tended to be with certain journals rather than particular university departments: *Scrutiny* was its primary natural habitat, until its closure in 1953, and thereafter *Essays in Criticism* (founded in 1951) and, in its early years, *Critical Quarterly* (founded in 1959), but also publications associated with adult education (such as *Highway*) and with the teaching of English in schools (especially *The Use of English*, founded in 1949).

As a critical style, it was marked by close attention to the verbal texture of literary works; it had learned from Eliot, Richards, and Empson, as well as from the beginnings of the New Criticism in the USA, though it tended to scant the value of detailed textual explication for its own sake and scorned mere critical showiness. It was of its time in its intolerance of the kind of belletristic connoisseurship that had survived into the interwar period, but it was equally disdainful of the type of detailed historical scholarship *about* literature that abstained from personal and evaluative engagement with the work—the practice associated with a different type of journal such as *Review of English Studies*. Above all, it was a critical practice that aspired to be diagnostic of the quality of human living 'embodied' or 'enacted' in particular uses of language. Literary language was taken to be distinctively 'exploratory of experience' in ways that favoured 'authenticity' and 'concreteness'. 'Great' literature was assumed to furnish the most powerful illustrations of how such use of language operated at its most creative and hence provided a yardstick against which lesser, shallower, more flawed or inauthentic uses of language could be measured. In this mode, the 'energy' and 'tautness' of a piece of writing revealed the 'healthiness' and 'maturity' of the attitudes to 'life' that it embodied. All the key terms involved this kind of ethical as well as formal appraisal. The quality most admired in literature and criticism alike was—in a conjunction of terms that served as the signature of this practice—'seriousness' about 'life'. As one of Hoggart's fellow Adult Education Tutors put it in the late 1940s: 'The culture of a society in its broadest meaning is the index of the quality of living within the society. Its assessment is the social function of the literary critic.'[36]

It would be too easy to label this critical practice as 'Leavisite', even though it clearly owed more to Leavis and *Scrutiny* than to any other single source. Many of its practitioners were ambivalent about the minority emphasis and the intransigent cultural pessimism associated with *Scrutiny*; their own styles tended to be less dismissive and more catholic than that of *pur et dur* Leavisites, though no less strenuous. They endorsed the broadening of literary criticism's remit to include what Leavis had called 'culture and environment', while remaining sceptical of some of the more belligerent forms of anti-modernism or celebrations of 'the organic community'. They returned with almost incantatory frequency to a similarly restricted range of literary touchstones: Shakespeare or Bunyan, for the 'vitality' of a language that had roots in both polite and popular culture; George Eliot, for her combination of imaginative sympathy and 'ethical seriousness'; and, above all, Lawrence, for his hold on 'finer human living'. But they ranged more widely than this, being more appreciative of the diversity of eighteenth- and nineteenth-century writing than had been common among the *Scrutiny* faithful, and notably more responsive to contemporary work since Eliot and Lawrence—to Auden and Orwell, for example.

Hoggart fully shared the romance of this ideal of criticism in the late 1940s and early 1950s: indeed, it provided his principal intellectual identity. Its presence is already evident in his early study of Auden, not an author admitted to the *Scrutiny* canon. As he put it in the introduction to that book: 'This essay is addressed to people with no special literary training, but with an interest in the quality of our lives today, and a readiness to examine whether the reading of poetry has an important relation to that interest.'[37] Though the book gives an admiringly sympathetic account of Auden's best poetry up to that point (and Auden was to remain one of Hoggart's most cherished modern authors), the terms in which he itemized some of the poet's failings bore the stamp of the diffused Leavisism of these years, something implicitly confirmed by the manner in which the reviewer of the book in *Scrutiny* could endorse Hoggart's criticisms and then go on to wonder why, given these failings, Hoggart had nonetheless thought Auden worthy of an extended critical study.[38] The same affirmations and affinities are evident in Hoggart's contributions in the late 1940s to *Adult Education* and *Highway*, the journals written and largely read by adult education tutors, though also in an essay on Graham Greene for *Essays in Criticism*, a journal that attracted some of the same contributors. One of these was Raymond Williams, who wrote, among other things, a response to a piece on the teaching of literature by Hoggart in *Adult Education* in 1948, and who was closely involved with F. W. Bateson in the early years of *Essays in Criticism*.[39]

Once the success of *The Uses of Literacy* had catapulted Hoggart into a position where he was frequently asked to pronounce for a wider audience on the justification for his chosen approach, he attempted to generalize the principles informing this common practice. Literature, he declared in one such manifesto, 'explores, re-creates and orders human experience in a *unique* way.... Its peculiarity is its special relationship with, its special form of engagement with, language...a relationship which is intellectual and emotional at the same time and is almost always a relationship by values.'[40] Though it is not altogether clear what is meant by the syntactically curious phrase 'a relationship by values', readers of Leavis will recognize the echoes of a familiar idiom and rhythm here, including the insistence on the unique power of literature to educate the intellect and the emotions simultaneously. (For example: 'The essential discipline of an English School is the literary-critical; it is a true discipline, only in an English School if anywhere will it be fostered, and it is irreplaceable. It trains, in a way no other discipline can, intelligence and sensibility together...'.[41]) And it is even harder not to hear such echoes later in the same essay when he declares: 'I do not think a trivial outlook will produce great literature.... Overall, a shallow view of life will produce a shallow penetration into experience.'[42] (Again, one might recall Leavis defending the 'puritan' values of George Eliot against Lord David Cecil's presumed condescension: '[These values] seem to me favourable to the production of great literature. I will add (exposing myself completely) that the enlightenment or aestheticism that feels an amused superiority to them leads, in my view, to triviality and boredom, and that out of triviality comes evil.'[43]) It is a question, of course, whether 'a shallow view of life' and 'a shallow penetration into experience' are not fundamentally the same thing. In so far as they are not, a 'trivial outlook' seems to mean any elaborated position that does not acknowledge the primacy of 'values' grounded in 'felt experience', and so another kind of circularity threatens. 'The bodilessly aesthetic production which tries to treat words and forms as ends in themselves' is cited as an indisputable example of such triviality, though it is not difficult to think of a number of writers for whom what it can mean for 'words and forms' to be, or not to be, 'ends in themselves' is the (far from trivial) animating preoccupation of their work.

It is surely possible to make statements in a confident, undefensive way about 'a belief in the power of language itself as the most important indicator of a hold on values' only if experience has habituated one to expect a considerable level of agreement from the relevant community of readers.[44] Similarly, when Hoggart praises a passage or work for being 'an exploration of felt experience', as opposed, say, to being 'formulaic' or 'shallow' or 'overdirected' (to cite terms that occur frequently in his writing), critic and ideal reader are implicitly agreeing on what counts as 'exploring' and even more on what counts as 'felt experience'. If they do not, the critical observation can have no toehold: what is being dismissed as 'formulaic', for example, may be judged by a different reader as an interesting formal experiment, perhaps a playing with or subverting of artistic conventions by means of deliberate repetition (much postmodern polemic against realism has taken this form). In the critical idiom that Hoggart inhabited, there was no relativism about what might count as 'felt experience' any more than there was about 'a hold on values'.

As I have already indicated, this style of criticism was always prone to fall into pastoral in the extended sense so brilliantly analysed by Empson. The combination of its ethically strenuous idiom with the confident presumption of agreement made it fatally easy to project the *ethical* contrast between, on the one hand, what is 'genuine', 'grounded', and 'humanly representative', and, on the other, what is 'shallow', 'inauthentic', and 'commercially driven' onto a *temporal* contrast between a past simplicity and a present corruption. Considered abstractly, ethically diagnostic literary criticism of this kind ought in principle to seem equally available to support a story of progress, in which the narrow, limiting values exhibited in past literature give way to the liberating and expressively rich abundance of contemporary culture. And yet that bald statement of possibility pulls us up short, immediately aware of how incongruous, even slightly scandalous, that version would have sounded during this period. This may have something to do with the critic's education in the acknowledged masterpieces of the past, and something more with the way in which the ethical idiom appeared to favour values that were seen as 'grounded' in a stable way of life, emphasizing community, sense of place, 'normal' sexuality and family life, and so on. This encouraged a tendency to associate the results of accelerated change with ways of life that were 'ungrounded', lacking the vitality of deeply felt shared experience.

IV

Although it has nearly always been overlooked in subsequent accounts, there is a loosely historical narrative at the heart of *The Uses of Literacy*, one that operates at two levels. There is, first, a lightly sketched history of the formation and transformation of the urban working class from the early nineteenth century onwards. But, second, there is also what might be termed a historical logic to the book's main arguments, a trajectory that, I shall suggest, shapes but also depends upon the kind of literary-critical engagement with popular publications to be found in the second half of the book.

The long-term account of the formation and re-formation of the working class on which Hoggart relies was familiar from the standard narratives to be found in the work of a range of progressive or radical social historians writing in the first half of the twentieth century. Its longest perspectives stretch back to the urbanization consequent upon the Industrial Revolution, and to the formation of a relatively self-enclosed working-class life from about the 1870s or 1880s onwards, especially in the northern industrial cities and towns. As internal evidence suggests and the book's bibliography confirms, the Hammonds and G. D. H. Cole were among the chief sources, and we know from the acknowledgements and the notes that H. L. Beales and Asa Briggs were his chief historical advisers.[45] Within this larger narrative nestles one about the gains achieved by working-class organizations and by state action from the late nineteenth century onwards: political self-expression, opportunities for cultural self-improvement, better conditions of work, basic gains in health and welfare. Notoriously, *The Uses of Literacy* has little to say about political action and the world of organized labour, but a few of the key moments in this familiar story of social and political progress are nodded to in passing.[46] And then, nestling within this in its turn, there is clearly an awareness (that had not yet taken the form of an established historiographical narrative) of the initial effects of full employment and rising prosperity from the late 1930s onwards. The hardship of working-class life in the 1920s and during the early years of the Depression receives frequent mention, but the material gains of the past ten or fifteen years are also registered, developments that were soon to be discussed in contemporary social science under the headings of 'the affluent worker' and 'the embourgeoisement thesis'. Later historians have substantiated the impressionistic judgements about changes in patterns of employment, rises in real wages, and so on, along with associated changes in social attitudes that Hoggart had in fact also touched upon, such as the unwillingness of working-class young women to go into domestic service after the Second World War.[47]

What I am terming the historical logic of the book's main arguments is stretched across this basic chronological frame without being closely tied to it. That logic suggests that the moral qualities displayed by the older working-class life were born out of the difficult circumstances dwelled upon in the radical histories; given such conditions, dignity, resilience, and mutual support were adaptive responses. In addition, this was a world that produced its own amusements and forms of self-expression; its culture was endogenous, not subject to the pressures of 'commercial' media from 'outside'. Indeed, it was a world that most members of the middle and upper classes knew very little about at first hand. This was the world so fondly and movingly evoked in the first half of the book. Quite when 'the newer order' of publications and entertainments started to impinge on this older culture is left a little vague, but several references to 'the last ten or fifteen years' suggest it does not predate the late 1930s and is largely a post-war phenomenon. The book contains numerous qualifying asides about how it is not idealizing the older world or undervaluing the benefits of the more recent prosperity. But, as so often in Hoggart's writing, these qualifying statements do not in practice modify the thrust of the overall treatment. As I shall illustrate in more detail, the positive terms are practically all attached to the older order, the negative terms thickly clustered around the new.

Of course, it is famously part of his strategy in the book to argue that the working class are not passive and endlessly malleable recipients of the messages put across by the newer media, but that they have resources of discrimination and resistance. Yet, in so far as they do—and once again his general statement that this is the case is in practice rather overborne by the weight of examples illustrating the corrupting power of the newer publications—it is only because the values of the older order have not yet entirely disappeared. In other words, this does not really qualify the pessimistic reading of the central clash; it just says it takes longer than alarmist jeremiads may at first suggest. As with all accounts of a Fall into a world governed by commercial forces, there is no real grasp of the part played by economic imperatives in shaping the old world. In this respect, the contrast Hoggart makes is structurally similar to that emphasized by historians such as the Hammonds in their account of the Industrial Revolution, in which an older order ruled by settled ethical and religious ideals gives way to a new world powered by the pursuit of economic gain.[48] In Hoggart's account, the self-contained working-class districts in the large northern industrial centres have some of the features that early anthropologists were prone to attribute to 'primitive' communities, most notably a freedom from 'outside' commercial forces.

As my insistence on this informing historical logic may not meet with immediate acceptance from those used to thinking of Hoggart as both more even-handed and open-minded than the well-known proponents of decline among his contemporaries, it may be as well to come at the issue slowly and somewhat obliquely. Let me begin, therefore, by spelling out the extent to which the second, prosecutorial half of the book is pervaded by, and its case dependent on, a traditional moral vocabulary that assumes agreement. It is a vocabulary in which the residues of the nineteenth century's secularized Protestantism are prominent, though adapted for the purposes of that quasi-Existentialist strenuousness that particularly flourished in the first couple of decades after the war. At its core is the contrast between, on the one side, effort, self-control, and social purpose, and, on the other, passivity, indulgence, and selfishness. Hardship is held to encourage the first set, prosperity the second.

This provides the framework for considering the impact of the 'newer publications' and the social changes they portend. In brief, the older virtues give way to 'a soft mass-hedonism', 'an arrogant and slick conformity', and 'a destroying self-flattery'. That the changes tell in only one moral direction is taken to be self-evident: 'The enquiry, it will be seen, is mainly concerned with what may be called invitations to self-indulgence.' There has been economic improvement for the working class, but it threatens to leave them with 'a largely material outlook'. 'The temptations... are towards a gratification of the self and towards what may be called a "hedonistic-group-individualism".' The moral lesson is enforced in general terms: 'These forces would not have their success were it not that we are all inclined to prefer the easy to the hard road, and the levelling half-reason which justifies weakness to the hard fact which shocks and insults before it braces.' The working class are especially vulnerable to this: they now have more money and freedom, 'but they also have the freedom of a vast Vanity Fair of shouting indulgences'.[49] To say that the cadences of the Protestant preacher are audible in such passages is to make a cultural, not a reductively biographical, observation.

Since it is the pervasiveness of this vocabulary in the second half of the book that I am drawing attention to, simple listing may be rhetorically the most effective form of illustration. So, in quick succession we get 'shiny barbarism', 'the new callowness', 'barbarians in wonderland'; 'a slick and hollow puppet-world','a passive visual taking-on of bad mass-art geared to a very low mental age'; 'we are a democracy whose working people are exchanging their birth-right for a mass of pin-ups', though there can sometimes still be 'the remnant of a healthier quality'. The old songs, for example, were 'strong and healthy in idiom', had 'fibre' and 'vitality'; the new are 'un-vital', displaying 'hollow brightness'. The newer publications have 'a cheap gum-chewing pert glibness'; these publications 'weaken the moral code they evoke'. There are constant warnings of 'the spread of self-indulgence', 'the dangers of spiritual deterioration', and 'the hypnosis of immature emotional satisfactions'. 'Integrity and devotion to a craft' are praised, and a single page celebrates 'energy' and 'vitality', 'moral resources', 'a valuable ethical rudder','a moral appeal', a 'stock of moral capital'.[50]

Throughout, the moral confidence and the cultural pessimism reinforce each other. For example, the enthusiasm for cycling 'is valuable evidence that urban working-class people can still react positively to both the challenge of their environments and the useful possibilities of cheap mass-production'. Hoggart feels no need to argue for the assumption that going cycling is a 'positive' reaction but going to the cinema is not. And why 'can still', unless we are all supposed to be taking for granted that working people used to respond more positively before technology and prosperity combined to weaken their fibre? It has often been observed that Hoggart was writing just before the widespread ownership of television sets, and therefore did not include this medium in his analysis, but his few asides make the likely drift of any commentary all too plain, as in his references to 'an undiscriminating looking in, night after night, at TV', in which 'the eyes would register but not connect to the nerves, the heart, and the brain'. By this point it is hardly surprising that, when he wants an emblematic figure who is 'of his time', he begins by considering 'a rootless minor technician, trained by a technical institute to serve a technocratic age; some of his attitudes are in part the product of a special form of not-belonging to any traditional social order'.[51] Here is one of the several places in Hoggart's writing of this period when we are reminded of Orwell in grumpily conservative vein, as in his distaste for

the new townships that have developed as a result of cheap motor cars and the southward shift of industry....In those vast new wildernesses of glass and brick the sharp distinctions of the older kind of town, with its slums and man-sions, or of the country, with its manor-houses and squalid cottages, no longer exist.... It is a rather restless, cultureless life, centring round tinned food, *Picture Post*, the radio and the internal combustion engine. It is a civilisation in which children grow up with an intimate knowledge of magnetoes [*sic*] and in complete ignorance of the Bible. To that civilization belong the people who are most at home in and most definitely *of* the modern world...[52]

To bring out the relation between Hoggart's diagnosis of moral decline and the literary-critical practice discussed earlier, consider, first, the note he strikes when discussing the current prevalence of a form of cynicism: 'It may be that this attitude is stronger among those under thirty than among older people, since most older people have memories of the thirties and the war, of sacrifice and co-operation and neighbourliness: the later forties and the fifties have not given such scope for the rediscovery of these virtues.'[53] Adverse circumstances are, it seems, conducive to morality: virtue develops out of effort in the face of difficulty. 'Re-discovery' suggests each generation needs to refind these values for themselves, but the current ease is not propitious to this kind of moral education. Hence the decline from 'cooperation' and related values to 'cynicism'. However, he strikes a slightly different note in his remark made about those serious but uprooted souls whom, following Arnold, he calls the 'aliens':

> Many of them have resisted the worst drugs; they stand for something. And as society comes nearer to the danger of reducing the larger part of the population to a condition of obediently receptive passsivity, their eyes glued to television sets, pin-ups, and cinema screens, these few, because they are asking important questions, have a special value.[54]

The countervailing resistance of the 'older' values is not much in evidence here; instead, we do not seem far away from Leavis's 'mass civilization and minority culture' argument.

Or, for an example of his obliquely invoking the values of the older order as a way of criticizing the present, take this sentence from his celebrated philippic against 'milk-bar culture':

> The milk bars indicate at once, in the nastiness of their modernistic knick-knacks, their glaring showiness, an aesthetic breakdown so complete that, in comparison with them, the layout of the living-rooms in some of the poor homes from which the customers come seems to speak of a tradition as balanced and civilized as an eighteenth-century town house.... Compared even with the pub around the corner, this is all a peculiarly thin and pallid form of dissipation, a sort of spiritual dry-rot amid the odour of boiled milk.[55]

There is a fine eloquence in the service of outrage here, but it again laments a kind of Fall: those 'modernist' knick-knacks represent the 'breakdown' of an older aesthetic order, a 'balanced and civilized *tradition*' to be found in those 'older' working-class homes. Even working-class pubs start to acquire the authenticity of 'vitality' here.

Placing *The Uses of Literacy* within the literary-critical practice I described earlier helps alert us to the ways in which several of the commonplaces of that practice structure Hoggart's account of cultural decline, as in this passage from late in the book where he is discussing the contemporary popular press:

> The new-style publications fail not because they are poor substitutes for *The Times* but because they are only bloodless imitations of what they purport to be, because they are pallid but slicked-up extensions even of nineteenth-century sensationalism, and a considerable decline from the sinewy sensationalism of Elizabethan vernacular writers.[56]

This strikes me as one of the most revealing sentences in the book, and an encapsulation of so much of the informing rhythm of its argument. First, there is the disowning of an anyway improbable requirement: that the benchmark for measuring the worth of any popular paper is provided by *The Times*. This same gambit is repeated at several points in the book. Thus, when deploring a crudity of character portrayal in popular fiction that makes readers less willing to engage with any subtler analysis, he writes: 'This is not to regret that they are unwilling to tease out the situation of Strether in Henry James's *The Ambassador* [*sic*].' Or again in disclaiming any wish for all lowbrows to be highbrows he writes: 'The ability to read the decent weeklies is not a *sine qua non* of the good life.'[57] In all three cases, he is making things easier for himself by contrasting his position with such patently unrealistic notions: he can then go on to say that he is asking only that publications, whatever social class or level of 'brow' they are addressed to, should have a seriousness or authenticity of their own. Hoggart may appear to anticipate an unsympathetic response from those readers who entertain the monocultural standard represented by *The Times*, Henry James, and 'the decent weeklies'; in practice, his prose assumes a ready assent to his waving aside of such unrealistic expectations.

The second characteristic of the quoted passage, one representative of the book as a whole, is the surely bizarre intrusion of Elizabethan pamphleteers into an account of mid-twentieth-century popular newspapers. Part of the conventional wisdom of the English critical tradition from Eliot, if not from Arnold, onwards included the belief that the last truly common culture in which both educated and popular speech and writing shared similar creative energies was to be found in the Elizabethan and early Jacobean period. (Those familiar with Leavis's critical idiom would also have recognized that 'sinewy' was one of the master's favoured terms for good prose, a quality he held to be conspicuously lacking in most modern writing.) The casualness of the allusion, the very lack of a justification for this improbably remote comparison, is what is most eloquent in this passage. Any reader of *Scrutiny* or *Essays in Criticism* could immediately feel at home despite elements of foreignness in the surrounding material from contemporary popular culture.

The third thing to remark is the submerged presence of a two-stage version of decline. Here again, many of his first readers would have recognized a classic Leavisian rhythm: there had been a long decline from the Elizabethan period to the nineteenth century, but even then elements of a common culture survived; their final destruction had taken place in more recent decades. Marked by pauses and unevennesses of pace though it may have been, the process was emphatically unidirectional: within this critical idiom there seemed to be no question of proposing that contemporary popular fiction marked an *advance* on Victorian sensationalism, still less on 'Elizabethan vernacular writers'. No like-for-like comparison is seriously proposed: the latter citation has totemic force.

The question of Hoggart's implied readers intrudes in a different way in the following passage, where, having quoted several working-class phrases about enjoying oneself when possible ('a little of what y'fancy does y'good', and so on), he continues:

> In all these, still much used today, there is a note which has never been silent in English working-class life since the Wife of Bath, which sounds in Shakespeare's clowns, Mistress Quickly and Juliet's nurse, in Moll Flanders and in the nineteenth-century music halls. It has lost some of its old quality now, but more of its raucous and earthy flavour remains than is usually thought.[58]

'English working-class life since the Wife of Bath': this is a remarkable conflation of the historical and the literary. The whole sequence—Chaucer, Shakespeare, Defoe—bespeaks the literary canon, a world of reference having little to do with the contemporary working-class attitudes he is ostensibly characterizing. The move into 'the nineteenth-century music halls' reveals the attempt to see this as a single tradition of popular culture, though it should hardly need saying that the representation of a certain type of character by the highly educated Chaucer in a work addressed to a tiny minority of the population had precious little in common with the demotic entertainments of the music halls over four centuries later. And then the movement of that final sentence, which epitomizes so much of the argument of the book: some of the 'old quality' has been lost, but not as much as 'is usually thought'. Thought by whom? is one question: perhaps by those who habitually talk about Chaucer and Shakespeare and Defoe? And is this in practice a repudiation of declinism or a refinement of it? So often this part of the book claims to be disowning a prevalent nostalgia while simultaneously using the literary motifs associated with that nostalgia to reinforce an attachment to the 'older order' now on the brink of extinction.

What I am calling the historical logic of his argument becomes so insistent as the book moves towards its conclusion that almost any page might furnish illustrations. Thus, he introduces an additional example by calling it 'a further instance of a possible interplay between material improvement and cultural loss': the possibility of cultural *gain* seems excluded in advance. He then goes on: 'At present the older, the more narrow but also more genuine class culture is being eroded in favour of the mass opinion, the mass recreational product, and the generalised emotional response.'[59] Such sentences would have been entirely at home in the pages of I. A. Richards's warnings of the perils of 'mass' culture in the 1920s.

A final example brings several of these notes together. The passage serves as, in effect, the peroration to Hoggart's celebrated description of the listless youths he observes in the milk bar; he allows that they are not wholly typical of working-class people, not yet at least, but he insists that nonetheless they are the kinds of reader implied by the 'newer working-class entertainment literature':

> These are the figures some important contemporary forces are tending to create, the directionless and tamed helots of a machine-minding age.... The hedonistic but passive barbarian who rides in a fifty-horsepower bus for threepence, to see a five-million-dollar film for one-and-eightpence, is not simply a social oddity; he is a portent.[60]

There are hints of a Huxleyean dystopia present here, but the louder reverberations surely come from a central strand of the English critical tradition. It is not fanciful to hear distant echoes of Matthew Arnold, not merely in the transposed class ascription of 'barbarian', but also of Arnold's inveighing against 'your middle-class man' who 'thinks it the highest pitch of development and civilization when his letters are carried twelve times a day from Islington to Camberwell, and from Camberwell to Islington, and railway trains run to and fro between them every quarter of an hour'.[61] There are even closer affinities with one of T. S. Eliot's most unlovely rants against the 'possessors of the inner voice' who 'ride ten in a compartment to a football match at Swansea, listening to the inner voice, which breathes the eternal message of vanity, fear, and lust'.[62] Audible, too, is the familiar Leavisian cadence, above all in that favoured word 'portent'—for example, Leavis described Edmund Gosse as 'a portent' of low critical standards early in the century, and C. P. Snow as 'a portent' of a similar shallow relativism almost thirty years later.[63] In passages such as this, assumptions about cultural decline seem intrinsic to the critical practice, not merely contingently associated with it.

V

In re-creating something of the original and, as it seems to me, most illuminating context of this part of Hoggart's early work, I am not intending to belittle his achievement. *The Uses of Literacy*, the first half above all, remains a brave and important book to have written at any point. But almost all discussion of that work is now coloured by a kind of double retrospective teleology. The more obvious of these is conventionally dated back to 1964 and the founding of the Centre for Contemporary Cultural Studies at Birmingham: the book's role as a founding text for 'Cultural Studies' has undoubtedly shaped much interpretation of it. The less obvious perspective dates from 1958 and the appearance of Williams's *Culture and Society*: the timing of the two books and the partially similar class backgrounds and class concerns of the two authors led to their being bracketed together in subsequent discussion, and encouraged the interpretation of Hoggart's book as a late contribution to what it soon became common to call 'the culture-and-society tradition'. By the mid-1960s this emphasis was given a kind of official endorsement by the in-house account of the Birmingham centre's history (largely written by Stuart Hall), which saw Hoggart's book as part of 'the response to industrialism', 'the prolonged engagement of the literary imagination with industrial society', that had been charted by Williams.[64]

There was clearly some point to seeing the relationship between the two works in these terms, but it also fostered an enduring misperception of the kind of book Hoggart had written. His work was not driven, as Williams's was, by the political desire to relativize individualism, as the expression of a form of economic life that dated only from the end of the eighteenth century, and to supplant it by a systematic ordering of society on the principles of equality and solidarity. In the dominant left story, which Williams extended and redirected, the focus was on the structural injustice introduced into English society by the unchecked dominance of the competitive principle at the end of the eighteenth and beginning of the nineteenth centuries. In *The Uses of Literacy*, by contrast, an ethic of effort and self-restraint had been built up in precisely the circumstances created by the settled industrialism of the late nineteenth and early twentieth centuries, only then to be undermined by the arrival of a combination of populist egalitarianism and material prosperity. Forces vaguely designated as 'commercialism' were assumed to be adept at preying upon those whose moral fibre was ripe for weakening, but there is no very clear story of what enabled these forces to be more insidiously effective in the present than they had been in the past, other than an undeveloped sense that the lack of material prosperity in the pre-war working class meant that there had not been sufficient financial incentive for 'outside' forces to cultivate a working-class market.

In several ways, *The Uses of Literacy* belongs to the extended tradition of 'condition of England' writing that stretched from the nineteenth century deep into the twentieth, not least in its combination of a personal voice, an attention to emblematic aspects of contemporary culture, and a marked moral passion. But Hoggart, despite obvious affinities, did not altogether belong with those 'happy peasants' who took some pre-capitalist, rural order as their benchmark, nor did he line up with those who advocated the supersession of capitalism by some social order founded upon an alternative economic principle.[65] The values his book endorsed were recognized to have grown up *within* the conditions of industrial capitalism. By contrast with the positions to which his work was assimilated in the 1960s and 1970s, Hoggart's was a less political and less theorized account, one that was more personal, more moral, and above all more literary in its inspiration and focus. It was preoccupied above all with *ethical* decline, with the loss of meaning and value that are alleged to come with mobility and prosperity. Rather than belonging with *Culture and Society*, *The Uses of Literacy* is better seen as a non-fiction version of *Sons and Lovers* interwoven with an updating of *Fiction and the Reading*

Public. The moral urgency that gave the book so much of its force was articulated through the literary-critical idiom that flourished at the time, particularly in the milieu in which Hoggart was writing. It has often been remarked that the book was fortunate in its timing, indeed that it could only have been written as a particular set of changes in working-class life, associated with the first wave of post-war prosperity, were taking place. But the book could also not have been written had Hoggart not been able to presume a large measure of agreement from his readers that the proper aim of literary criticism is to identify indications of 'moral health' in *King Lear* or 'maturity' in Lawrence, and then to deploy such insights in an inescapably declinist critique of contemporary culture.

6

The Long Industrial
Revolution

I

An understanding of the transformative effect of the Industrial Revolution has long been at the heart of conceptions of the distinctiveness of modern British history. This chapter addresses a particularly influential reworking of that understanding that emerged from the forms of literary criticism I have been discussing and that has continued to have a shaping presence in subsequent interpretations of the intellectual and cultural history of nineteenth- and twentieth-century Britain. The story begins, improbably enough, in the basement of the Seaford public library in Sussex. As Raymond Williams recalled the episode in the introduction to *Keywords*, published in 1976, he had in the late 1940s been thinking about the notion of 'culture' and the ways it was deployed in contemporary debate, especially after the publication of T. S. Eliot's *Notes towards the Definition of Culture* in 1948. He had also been pondering its relations with other terms such as 'art' and 'industry'.

> Then one day in the basement of the Public Library at Seaford, where we had gone to live, I looked up *culture*, almost casually, in one of the thirteen volumes of what we now usually call the OED: the Oxford *New English Dictionary on Historical Principles*. It was like a shock of recognition. The changes of sense I had been trying to understand had begun in English, it seemed, in the early nineteenth century.[1]

As anyone familiar with Williams's various historical retrospects will be aware, such reconstructions of earlier episodes are not always to be trusted, and certainly not taken literally. This is especially true of some of the accounts he gave of his earlier thinking in the interviews published in 1979 as *Politics and Letters*, interviews largely conducted in the year following the publication of *Keywords*. The apparent specificity of the passage I have quoted is thus no guarantee of its reliability, though it presumably signals both an actual memory of some kind and a claim that was important to Williams and that it pleased him, during his period of later fame, to recount in this way. As it happens, we also have, from the records of his teaching during the relevant years, some contemporary evidence of his thinking about this topic, to which I shall return.

In narrative form, the little vignette I have quoted conforms to the classic 'eureka' moments celebrated in various branches of scientific or intellectual discovery, including the earlier unsuccessful or frustrated enquiries into the topic, the casual or accidental nature of the key moment, and the inauspicious banality of the location. One rather surprising feature of the quoted recollection is that if, as Williams emphasized, he had been thinking about the concept for some years, and had already taught adult education Tutorial Classes on the subject, it seems curious that he had not consulted this most obvious of sources before, and to say that he now did so 'almost casually' is an odd way to describe looking up a word in those large volumes. Then there is that resonant sentence: 'It was like a shock of recognition.' This seems to imply that in some sense he already knew what he claimed to have discovered there, or at least half-knew or was prepared for. And what, it could be said, he 'recognized' was that the relevant sense of a term he had been brooding over dated from a specific period, the early nineteenth century. Since he was writing almost twenty years after the publication and great success of the book that issued from this moment, he knew that his readers would appreciate the structuring centrality of this 'discovery' to his eventual argument. After all, the very first sentence of that book, *Culture and Society*, published in 1958, is: 'The organizing principle of this book is the *discovery* that the idea of culture, and the word itself in its general modern uses, came into English thinking in the period which we commonly describe as that of the Industrial Revolution.'[2] By making the issue of this 'discovery' so salient and so central, Williams was laying claim to a kind of originality, for which the episode in the library basement was the light-bulb moment.

When reading Raymond Williams's writings, we get a much stronger sense than with most critics of the *contemporary* presence of the various pasts that engage his interest. Ostensibly, his work is pervasively and assertively historical, a series of arguments about change, usually about what he terms

'growth' and 'development'. Yet there is a sense in which the *pastness* of
the past can seem to be only an incidental characteristic of it for Williams:
whatever is significant or interesting about it is experienced as active within
the present, a collective present in which a capacious 'we' embraces all relevant predecessors in a community that, at least in his earlier work, is now
and England—where, for all his later insistence on being a 'Welsh European',
Williams, like so many of his contemporaries, allowed 'England' to stand
unselfconsciously for the larger political unit of which it has been only
a part. Of course, there is a lot of Williams's writing, even in the books
that exhibit these characteristics, that is historical in a more conventionally
chronological sense, but even then there is a constant undertow, a pull
towards the omnivorous present of Williams's determined, all-encompassing
argument.

The two books that made Williams famous and that, by his own testimony, completed the programme of work he had embarked upon in the
post-war years—*Culture and Society 1780–1950*, published in 1958, and *The
Long Revolution* published in 1961—presented themselves as accounts of
change over long periods of time. Yet they were in their form and their
manner of argument very distant from the work of contemporary professional historians, who in turn largely ignored them. This disciplinary gulf
has had curious consequences. Few books did as much to shape the wider
public understanding of modern British intellectual history as *Culture and
Society*, an understanding that particularly flourished in the world of literary
and related cultural studies, yet that barely registered on the thinking of
modern British historians at the time. The book's reach has been immense,
yet for long it remained unintegrated into the established historical narratives of the period it deals with. So what kind of historical story does that
book tell? This chapter will explore the presence, at once ghostly and
all-pervading, of a conception of the Industrial Revolution as defining
modern British history and culture, and it dares to suggest that we may, even
now, still not quite have taken the measure of this idiosyncratic classic.[3]

Given Williams's emphasis on that moment in the Seaford public library,
it is worth asking what he would have found when he looked up the entry
on 'culture' in the *OED* round about 1950. That edition of the dictionary
identified four main senses of the noun, and it provided no illustrative
quotations later than 1891 (the relevant fascicle of the dictionary having
originally been completed in 1893). The first two main senses have to do
with agricultural or animal husbandry. The third sense, marked 'figurative',

is defined as: 'The cultivating or development (of the mind, faculties, manners etc.): improvement or refinement by education and training.' This is clearly a familiar extension of the agricultural senses—a movement from, as it were, 'the culture of the vine' to 'the culture of the mind'—and refers to a *process*; the illustrative quotations range from the early sixteenth to the mid-nineteenth centuries. And then the fourth or abstract sense is: 'The training, development, and refinement of mind, tastes, and manners; the condition of being thus trained and refined; the intellectual side of civilization', to which are appended four illustrative quotations, one dated 1805 and three from between 1860 and 1889. Although the third sense emphasizes a process while the fourth focuses on a condition or outcome, the distinction is obviously going to be hard to sustain in interpreting many concrete uses. 'Culture' as 'development or refinement of mind' could refer to either process or outcome.

It seems, therefore, that a consultation of the *OED* entry could (with the exception of the 1805 quotation) only confirm what any passably well-informed student of the topic of culture around 1950 would have known already. The term had a long-established agricultural sense; from some point in the seventeenth or eighteenth centuries it became common in a figurative sense as describing the process of cultivating the intellect or sensibility; from the 1860s onwards it was well established in the familiar modern sense of 'the condition of being thus trained' or 'the intellectual side of civilization'. In fact, the more closely one looks at the *OED* entry, the less clear it becomes just what Williams believed he had discovered. Perhaps the fact that the earliest quotation for the fourth sense is dated to 1805 could be read as indicating that the sense of 'culture' as some kind of achieved or embodied values came into use at the beginning of the nineteenth century. But, as with most 'discoveries', one would have to be primed to think this in order to reach such a conclusion from the dictionary's entries, since, taken alone, they tell no such simple story, and, most important of all for my argument, they certainly suggest no connection with the Industrial Revolution.

Williams, however, treated the entries as though they did demonstrate such a connection, as is evident in the earliest published version of his interpretation, his 1953 article in *Essays in Criticism* entitled 'The Idea of Culture', in which he clearly follows and depends upon the trail of illustrative quotations given in the dictionary, and asserts: 'The decisive change came in the first half of the nineteenth century.'[4] He had by this point tracked down the '1805' quotation to a passage in Wordsworth's *Prelude*, which he reproduces in full in his article (the *OED* quoted from the 1850 *Prelude*, though, following Wordsworth's account of the composition of the poem, it dated the passage to 1805; Williams, writing subsequent to Ernest de Selincourt's 1926 edition of the 1805 *Prelude*, gives both the 1805 and 1850 versions). But first he gives a quotation from *The Excursion*, which, he claims, shows that Wordsworth is 'still conscious of the figurative use of the word'. '*Still* conscious' is intended to suggest that it was now rather outmoded and that Wordsworth elsewhere tended to follow the more up-to-date usage, though actually the lexicographic evidence suggests otherwise. Certainly, Wordsworth's use of 'culture' in *The Excursion* (a poem that may have been written after *The Prelude*) exhibits the 'process' sense:

> that none
> However destitute, be left to droop
> By timely culture unsustained . . .

The use of 'droop' reinforces the horticultural association here: the 'timely culture' involves the process of tending or cultivating. Williams then gives the passage from *The Prelude* in which, he suggests, Wordsworth is 'combatting the argument that "love" depends on "leisure" and its advantages':

> True is it, where oppression worse than death
> Salutes the Being at his birth, where grace
> Of culture hath been utterly unknown,
> And labour in excess and poverty
> From day to day preoccupy. . . .

Williams immediately comments:

> This use of *culture*, it seems to me, is genuinely transitional. It has elements of the old sense of *process*, but it can be read also in the developed nineteenth-century sense of an *absolute*. However this may be (and I think myself that it is the first significantly modern use), the development of *culture* as a concept, the *idea* of culture, was thereafter rapid.[5]

It is indeed hard to say how the word should be construed in Wordsworth's line: it looks more like a genuinely Empsonian ambiguity than a straightforward case of one sense or the other. Williams's rather breezy 'however this may be' indicates that his mind is made up: this is where the 'modern' sense dates from. And one would certainly have to put a lot of weight on this single, ambiguous illustration in order to conclude that the abstract sense emerged at the beginning of the nineteenth century and then developed rapidly, since that edition of the *OED* gave no other example for this sense earlier than the 1860s, starting then from that most predictable of sources, Matthew Arnold.[6] In other words, the whole case for the claim that the modern sense of 'culture' becomes established at the beginning of the nineteenth century thus far seems to rest on a highly contestable reading of one line of poetry, and that from a source which, though probably written in or prior to 1805, was not actually published until 1850. Interestingly, the relevant section of *Culture and Society*, which does not follow the 1953 article in attending so closely to the *OED* entry, also does not reproduce the passage from the *Prelude* and the related commentary, though Williams's later claim would seem to make it the essential stimulus for that book.

I have dwelt on this short passage of autobiographical retrospect because Williams himself made it so central to the story of his most famous work: the emphasis on the appearance of the *term*, and hence on the role of the dictionary, is his, something partially borne out by his reproduction of its examples in his 1953 article. There is, as I have suggested, something a little odd about it, and we can perhaps get closer to the heart of this oddity by returning to the opening sentence of *Culture and Society*, which announces, as already quoted, that the central theme of the book is 'the discovery that the idea of culture, and the word itself in its general modern uses, came into English thinking in the period which we commonly describe as that of the Industrial Revolution'. I do not want here to get entangled with the extensive literature about what might or might not count as an 'Industrial Revolution' in British history of this period, but let us simply accept that, for most readers in the 1950s, this phrase would point to the period from about 1760 to about 1830. Williams begins his book in 1780 with Burke and Cobbett, taken to represent contrasting aspects of what he calls 'the mood of England in the Industrial Revolution'.[7]

Now, given the enormous authority that Williams's book has achieved, the taken-for-grantedness that his account of the development has for some time possessed, it may seem almost perverse to begin by asking whether his book *does* in fact show that 'the word itself in its general modern uses, came into English thinking' in this period. This question can be made sharper still by asking whether his book does in fact show that the word is used in this way *at all* before the 1860s. Of course, the concerns that he argues were condensed into the later uses of the word are indeed there, as are some closely related terms such as 'cultivation'. But I want to suggest, heretically, that a close scrutiny of the book's first five chapters demonstrates that 'the

word itself in its general modern uses' *never* occurs in the works he discusses
by Burke and Cobbett, Southey and Owen, Blake and Wordworth, or even
Coleridge and Carlyle. The earliest unambiguous example of this sense of
the term comes in the chapter on Arnold, precisely where students of the
topic (as well as casual users of the *OED*) would, before Williams's book,
have expected to find it. In his 1953 article Williams claims there is no need
to wait for Arnold: 'But already, before Arnold, the word was commonly
used in this sense,' he writes, though his examples there do not in fact support this claim. For instance, he quotes a famous passage from Coleridge's
Idea of Church and State on 'civilization': 'a nation so distinguished [is] more
fitly to be called a varnished than a polished people, where this civilization
is not grounded in cultivation, in the harmonious development of those
qualities and faculties that characterize our humanity.' Williams then declares:
'This analysis of Coleridge's is the first Idea of Culture, in its modern sense.'[8]
Well, that is debatable, to say the least, and it is manifestly not an illustration
of the relevant modern use of the *word*, since the word Coleridge uses there
is 'cultivation'.

Culture and Society greatly extended the range of writers who are now
said to make up 'the tradition' of talking about culture in this way, taking it
back to Burke and Cobbett, but the more closely we examine the earlier
chapters, the more we find a certain slipperiness in Williams's assertions
about the appearance of this sense of the term. In several places he comes
close to speaking *as though* the term appeared in his chosen writers, even
when the textual evidence he cites does not support this. Take, as an example,
his discussion of Wordsworth's disdain for the clamour of the 'public': 'Towards
the Public, the Writer hopes that he feels as much deference as it is entitled
to; but to the People, philosophically characterized, and to the embodied
spirit of their knowledge . . . his devout respect, his reverence, is due.' In his
first pass at commentary on this passage, Williams very slightly adjusts the
quotation, seeing in it a final appeal to 'the embodied spirit . . . of the People',
which is not actually how the phrase is used by Wordsworth. He continues:
'The "embodied spirit", naturally enough, was a very welcome alternative
to the market,' which, though arguably close to Wordsworth's sentiment, is
not quite what he wrote. This, Williams is then able to say, 'is one of the
primary sources of the idea of Culture. Culture, the "embodied spirit of a
People", the true standard of excellence, became available, in the progress of
the century, as the court of appeal in which real values were determined.'[9]
Notice, first, the slight shift from 'the' People to 'a' People; then, second, how

the 'embodied spirit of a People' is now treated as a quotation, though that phrase does not appear in Wordsworth; and then, third, how this is equated (by Williams) with the term 'culture' that 'became available' in the course of the century. It may be thought that no great violence is done to Wordsworth's thinking in the course of this slightly high-handed procedure, but it requires an effort to remember that the passage contributes nothing to support the main claim about how 'the word itself in its general modern uses' appeared in this period.

Perhaps the most remarkable instance of Williams's rough handling of the textual evidence comes with his quotation of a long passage from Newman's *Idea of a University* of 1852. Newman begins: 'It were well if the English, like the Greek language, possessed some definite word to express simply and generally…' the values he then goes on to enumerate, but, Newman concludes sorrowfully, 'I am not able to find such a term'. Williams's first comment after quoting this long passage is: 'The most surprising fact about this paragraph is that Newman does not meet the want of "some definite word" with the word "culture".'[10] But wait a minute: who should be surprised by what here? If, in this passage, Newman specifies so fully the elements of what Williams maintains are the core of the 'tradition' of contrasting 'culture' and 'society', and if Newman then explicitly looks for a single term to refer to those elements, finally concluding that none is to hand in the resources of contemporary usage, does that not rather suggest, *contra* Williams, that the term 'culture' was *not* current in this sense by 1852? (This is, incidentally, another of the places where there is a significant difference of emphasis between the 1953 article and the 1958 book. In the article he finds it strange that Newman did not meet the need with the word 'culture' as 'a generation later… he would have seemed certain to do'.[11] Quite so; by the 1870s the term 'in its general modern sense' had achieved currency: in 1852 it had not. The quoted phrase does not appear in the discussion of the passage in *Culture and Society* itself.) So, a careful rereading of his 1953 article and of the first five chapters of *Culture and Society* suggests that Williams did *not* in fact demonstrate that this sense was present in his chosen writers before the middle of the nineteenth century. On his own evidence, that does not come until the 1860s: it is, as he himself observes, Arnold's use 'which at last gives the tradition a single watchword and a name'.[12] 'At last' surely makes its own commentary on what had gone before.

Of course, the book does not present itself as a purely lexicographical enquiry and nor should it, but, since the history of the word 'culture' does not in fact hold it together as neatly as Williams sometimes suggests, we have to recognize that the structure of the book, and the criteria for the inclusion of certain writers and not others, depend on less explicit premises. We can start to uncover these by recognizing the function Williams ascribes to the concept of 'culture'. He argues, in a functionalist manner, that the word, and therefore the associated concept, emerges when it is needed, and it becomes needed as a counterweight or court of appeal against the dominant logic of the allegedly new form of society introduced by the Industrial Revolution. So, even if the writers he discusses do not contribute to the history of the *word* in its dominant modern meanings, they do, it might be claimed, contribute to a history of thinking about the defects of industrial society that Williams argues was condensed into those meanings. Before moving on to an examination of how this argument is worked out in *Culture and Society*, we should return to the young man who consulted the *OED* in the basement of Seaford public library in the late 1940s to consider the development of his historical thinking from another perspective.

II

In his late twenties at that point, Raymond Williams, originally from a working-class home just inside the Welsh border, had gone up to Cambridge to read English in 1939. After two years, his studies were interrupted by war service, so he returned for his final year in autumn 1945, when he was strongly engaged by Leavis's work. Upon graduating in summer 1946, he immediately found a post as an extra-mural Tutor for the Oxford Delegacy, and he began to run classes in literature in small towns across east Sussex. At this point he had practically no formal training in history or engagement with the work of contemporary professional historians. 'The absence of history from your adolescent intellectual interests seems very striking,' observed his *New Left Review* interrogators in 1979. Williams acknowledged the lack, claiming that, when he went on to write the books that made him famous, 'I later had to reconstruct for myself the main lines of the history'. The Williams of the later 1940s and 1950s could be regarded as something of an autodidact where history was concerned: 'Even my cultural research', he recalled, 'taxed me with learning English history as I went along, for the autobiographical reasons that I have explained'.[13]

At this stage of his career, the quasi-historical perspective with which he operated, in lieu of any more systematic account, was largely derived from *Scrutiny*. This allegiance was evident in his earliest writings, especially for the short-lived radical journal *Politics and Letters*, which Williams edited from 1947 to 1948 with two friends from Cambridge.[14] For example, in one of his first contributions he insisted that D. H. Lawrence was vital to 'the work which *Politics and Letters* will undertake on culture and environment', and he still took a favourable view of the contribution of Matthew Arnold: *Culture and Anarchy* and 'The function of criticism', he asserted, 'were the beginnings of the study of Culture and Environment, and still serve as models for it'.[15] In an article on 'The Soviet Literary Controversy in Retrospect', also published in 1947, Williams stated his belief plainly:

> We must, then, retain the right to judge a civilization by its culture. For culture is the embodiment of the quality of living of a society; it is this 'standard of living' [note: As insisted upon by F. R. Leavis and Denys Thompson in *Culture and Environment*] with which the critic is concerned. Assessment of it is the social function of the critic and the creative writer.

And he concluded:

> We must attempt, however often we fail, to ensure that in our own inevitable development towards a planned, rational, society, the distinctive values of living embodied in our literary tradition are preserved, re-created, expanded, so that ultimately with material may grow human richness.[16]

The 'minority culture' argument enjoyed a considerable resonance in the years immediately after 1945, notably as a response to the supposed 'collectivism' of the Labour government. Clive Bell had earlier stated the argument in its purest form; Leavis had given it a more strenuous and in some ways appealing twist, though without altogether shaking off its conservative affinities; and the publication of Eliot's *Notes towards the Definition of Culture* in 1948 had brought the issue into fresh prominence, posing theoretical difficulties for those like Williams (and Richard Hoggart) who wanted somehow to rescue a critical notion of 'culture' from this anti-progressive embrace. However, the historical framework within which these matters were discussed in *Scrutiny* was not so easily sloughed off.

Two unpublished (and undated) typescripts in the Williams papers at Swansea throw light on the structure of his historical thinking at this stage of his career. The first is a substantial typescript, probably written around

1948, as part of a proposal for a film, to be directed by his friend Michael Orrom, commissioned by the Central Office of Information on the history and achievements of British agriculture. Entitled 'Effect of the Machine on the Countryman's Work, Life, and Community', this ran from in-depth accounts of the enclosure movement to depictions of the rural depression of the late nineteenth century and on to the interwar years. Williams's script compares, in its own words, 'the old peasant community, with its settled, integrated system', with the contemporary form of the village. 'The general conclusion', wrote Williams, 'is that there has been no settled organic community life in the villages since they were radically altered by the various phases of industrial expansion'.[17] The film would show, it was claimed, 'how and why late eighteenth-century industrialization altered everything'. (Compare Timothy Boon's claim, based on an analysis of films by, among others, Paul Rotha, for whom Williams wrote another script, that the 'catastrophic' view of the Industrial Revolution was how 'people historicized their lived experience' in the 1930s and 1940s, though this perspective started to lose its hold from the late 1940s.[18]) Although, as his biographer emphasizes, Williams was contesting a certain kind of fashionable cultural pessimism that romanticized the early twentieth-century village as the heart of an organic way of life now under threat from current changes in communication and travel, underlying his account was a deeper, structural contrast between life before and after the Industrial Revolution. Leaving aside the question of whether he was right to argue that this changed the lives of the countryman as well as of the town dweller, the framework once again suggested that a kind of pathology had been introduced in the late eighteenth century as a result of which all subsequent history was to be contrasted with what had gone before.

The second, shorter, piece, headed 'The Isolation of Culture' and probably written around 1950, begins: 'The Industrial Revolution is a myth: that is why it is important.'[19] Williams's purpose in describing it in these terms is, as he makes plain, to *emphasize* its importance, not to diminish it. By 'myth' he means a powerful conception by which a people understands itself. He recognizes that economic historians have challenged the traditional account of an 'Industrial Revolution', and so 'there are those who will say that because wage levels rose throughout the period the whole affair is a device of simplification or propaganda'. He is here evidently referring to the early phases of what economic and social historians came to know as 'the standard of living debate'. To this he immediately responds with a comment that is revealing both of the genesis of his famous work and of his relation to professional history:

These are matters, fit and serious matters, to be settled by historians, and we shall watch what they conclude. But the present importance of the Industrial Revolution is that it is a concept, a significant myth, in terms of which we have come to understand our origins as an industrial people. It is our own construct, the basis of our immediate tradition. It is in terms of the Industrial Revolution that we are interested in culture.

Three things stand out here. First, the enduring significance of the Industrial Revolution as a 'myth' is seen as unlikely to be changed or ended by the researches of professional historians. Whatever the truth about wage rates, the fundamental self-definition in terms of the Industrial Revolution will not be displaced. Second, this insistent use of the first-person plural signals membership both by the author and by the implied reader of a social entity that is unproblematic or taken for granted. Elsewhere in this typescript he speaks of 'the land and people of England' and again he declares that 'a particular consciousness of origins which we associate with the Industrial Revolution has impressed itself upon the English mind'. This was not an identification he would have been at all happy with later in his career, but at this point it accurately reflects his strong sense of an argument internal to a society he is securely part of. And, third, the interest in culture ('our' interest suggesting both his and his 'people's') is determined in advance by its relation to the Industrial Revolution. This is not a link he 'discovered' in the *OED* or anywhere else: it was the frame of understanding he brought to considering the question of 'culture'. There grew up a 'tradition', as he terms it, of protesting against the deforming effects of the Industrial Revolution. It did not matter that these protests took many forms: 'All that is really common is the myth, the myth of the Industrial Revolution. All that is really important is the response to the myth, a response that is scattered and diverse.'[20] The argument of *Culture and Society* is already dimly discernible in these few sentences.

A similar framework is prominent in the first full-length book that Williams wrote (though because of delays it was the second to be published), *Drama from Ibsen to Eliot* in 1952. In the introduction he set out some of his governing assumptions about drama and society. The historical scheme implicit in this argument was, by this date, familiar to readers of Leavis and of *Scrutiny*. He begins with the inadequacy of contemporary speech to the purposes of the naturalist drama:

> For many reasons—and perhaps primarily under the pressure of that complex of forces which we call industrialism—contemporary *spoken* English is rarely capable of exact expression of anything in any degree complex... The medium

of naturalism—the representation of everyday speech—is immeasurably less satisfying in the twentieth century than in the sixteenth.

This is simply asserted: Williams would presumably have felt that its truth had been amply demonstrated in countless *Scrutiny* discussions of the verbal richness of Elizabethan drama and its close relationship to the common speech of the time. That relationship had, in any case, made possible a kind of theatre that could not succeed under the conditions of contemporary speech. 'In a rich, vital, and intensely personal language such as the Elizabethan, the limitations of naturalism, if they do not disappear, are at least disguised.' He then moves out from this assertion to address the larger claim about the relation between drama and shared beliefs in a society. 'Very powerful arguments can be advanced in support of the idea that a fully serious drama is impossible in a society where there is no common system of belief.' Williams sounds pretty indulgent towards this Eliotic doxa, but he returns the question to language by insisting that what is really at issue is the question of a common sensibility, expressed through language and thus bearing shared ethical commitments.

> There is no such common sensibility today. The pressure of a mechanical environment has dictated mechanical ways of thought, feeling, and conjunction, which artists, and a few of like temper, reject only by conscious resistance and great labour. That is why all serious literature, in our own period, tends to become minority literature (although the minority is capable of extension and in my view has no social correlative).

So, serious drama, in these circumstances, can only be minority drama. However, Williams was not willing to accept resigned pessimism as the conclusion to this analysis, the pessimism that, in their different ways, Eliot and Leavis had made so fashionable in literary-critical circles around the middle of the century, and so he went on: 'But its communication may be extended, and its writing made more possible, if developments in society (the sum of individual developments) make possible the re-creation of certain modes of living and of language against which such complexes as industrialism have militated.'[21] The passing use of 're-creation' is telling. It was with good reason that twenty-five years later his *New Left Review* questioners remarked the book's 'categorical, unqualified fidelity to Leavis's meta-historical conceptions'.[22]

Perhaps too much weight should not be attached to the fashionable formulas through which young critics announce their allegiances, but these affirmations were deeply felt in Williams's case, and I would argue that they expressed a feature of his historical sensibility that, though much modified over time, is fundamental to *Culture and Society*. We may begin with that inelegant final clause about 'the re-creation of certain modes of living and of language against which such complexes as industrialism have militated'. It is not clear quite how the noun 'complexes' is being used here; it certainly hides, or displays, a considerable vagueness about the actual historical changes in question. But '*re*-creation' is plain enough: these more desirable modes of living once existed, they were destroyed or fatally damaged by industrialism, and now they could be reinstated in modern form. History would then show an interregnum, a kind of aberration, stretching from the Industrial Revolution to the present, before and after which uniquely desperate period there flourished or could flourish fuller, perhaps normal, human living. *Culture and Society 1780–1950*—the dates in the title are a crucial part of the argument: the book was to be the record of responses to that aberrant episode.

The main medium through which, in the late 1940s and early 1950s, Williams explored the question of culture was, of course, his adult education Tutorial Classes. Not surprisingly, given the suddenness of his transformation from student to teacher, the young tutor fell back on the intellectual resources he had already acquired, especially during his final year at Cambridge. The first short course he offered in Maresfield in 1946–7 was called 'Culture and Environment', and he used the book of that name by Leavis and Denys Thompson as his main text, with the opening class being devoted to 'the cultural tradition' (Arnold, Clive Bell, Eliot, Leavis).[23] The Leavis and Thompson primer *Culture and Environment* had been prepared with the practical demands of such teaching in mind, and Williams clearly followed its lead, analysing the constraining power of commerce on contemporary 'cultural' phenomena (cinema, newspapers, advertising, and so on), from which material was taken for exercises in practical criticism. The first course entitled 'Culture and Society' was given in 1948/9, and in 1949/50 he gave a course entitled 'What is Culture?', the outline for which addressed themes that were to receive more extended treatment in his later work, such as 'what is a highbrow?', 'who are the masses?', and so on.[24] At this point, the courses seem to have had, at best, a very sketchy historical dimension.

A one-page outline for a projected book on 'Culture and Work' (in the Williams papers), dated by Dai Smith to 1949, similarly focused on newspapers, radio, propaganda, advertisements, and so on, but was accompanied by a section headed 'The Theories', which listed an interestingly eclectic range of names: 'Marx; W. Morris; Arnold; Eliot; Dawson; Leavis; Social Democratic; Mumford; D. H. Lawrence; Caudwell'.[25] The presence of names such as Christopher Dawson and Lewis Mumford in this list suggests that the focus was still on the contemporary debate, which the publication of Eliot's book had done much to stimulate, about the conditions necessary to the flourishing of cultures (religious, economic, and so on). An article entitled 'Books for Teaching "Culture and Environment"', which Williams published in the adult education journal in 1950–1 (but which was probably first written in 1949), displays a wider range of reading, but even here the books that deal with the theme of 'culture and civilization' practically all date from the previous two or three decades. Only the mention of works by the Hammonds and Tawney starts to provide some historical background, though even here he cites the latter's *Acquisitive Society* not *Religion and the Rise of Capitalism*. At this point, there was no long list of nineteenth-century advocates of 'culture' and no explicit link to 'responses to the Industrial Revolution'.

In 1950/1 he taught another Tutorial Class (at Hastings) under the title 'Culture and Society'. Although this, too, was still recognizably in the 'Culture and Environment' mould, focusing on the 'mechanical' 'commercial' forces at work in contemporary culture, with topics on advertising, cinema, radio, and so on, Williams was now beginning to give these classes a more historical dimension, too, with a section entitled 'Theory and Practice in English Culture since the Industrial Revolution', for which he had been pursuing a somewhat haphazard course of reading in such nineteenth-century authors as Coleridge and Carlyle. As Williams later recalled, perhaps accurately: 'By then [1951] I was clear that since the term had emerged in the course of the industrial revolution, it was a very key moment in the interpretation of that experience and indeed in all the social thought that had accompanied it.'[26]

The intellectual framework of Williams's analysis of 'culture' in these years is most fully illustrated by the reading list for this class, which contained sixty-nine titles. The outline of the course expresses its Leavisite inheritance unmistakably, promising close attention to the development of advertising and the media—for example, fiction is treated as a business focusing on bestsellers, while the first gloss given for the section on radio is 'the problem of response to a mechanical institution', and so on. It followed from this focus that several of the books were contemporary works of analysis on these current cultural activities. But the course was explicitly premised on a historical development 'since the Industrial Revolution', while individual sections had their own historical dimension, such as 'development of the modern press (since 1881)'. This makes it all the more remarkable that, of the sixty-nine titles, only three are works of history by authors who would have been recognized as professional historians: Eileen Power's *Mediaeval People*, R. H. Tawney's *Religion and the Rise of Capitalism*, and Elie Halévy's *History of the English People*. These choices are themselves striking: Power's book deals with nothing later than the fifteenth century; Tawney's, though it had a legible contemporary moral, discusses developments in the sixteenth and seventeenth centuries. On the face of things, such books sit oddly with a course focused on the very late nineteenth and early twentieth centuries, though it is not hard to imagine the part they may have played. Only Halévy's work may seem directly addressed to this period, though even here the reference was most probably to the cheap reprint of the first volume of Halévy's six-volume set; this was marketed under the title of the whole series, *The History of the English People in the Nineteenth Century*, although the title of that particular volume was, strictly speaking, *England in 1815*, so even it did not bear directly on the relevant period. This was the volume in which Halévy argued that Methodism had made a crucial contribution to the avoidance of revolution in England at the beginning of the nineteenth century, an argument that could be congenial to those drawn to the moral critique of unrestrained individualism.[27]

The bulk of the list, and all of the asterisked 'essential' reading, comprises works in literary and cultural criticism, especially by Eliot, Leavis, Denys Thompson, and some of the studies that they drew upon, such as George Sturt, the Lynds, Stuart Chase, and so on. (Fourteen of the titles are asterisked as constituting 'the essential books', and these mostly comprise the works of Leavis, Thompson and their sources.) Although in these years Williams was known as something of a zealot for the methods of Leavisian practical criticism, he was far from unusual in drawing on this body of work for his classes. What this underlines is the extent to which there was a well-established interpretation of what might be loosely called cultural history, which depended scarcely at all on the work of professional historians.

Williams's understanding of how such work might be pursued is suggested by a review he wrote of Empson's *The Structure of Complex Words*, published the following year, a review whose existence appears to have been overlooked by all bibliographies and discussions of Williams's work.[28] There, Williams notes that Empson's 'historical comments, though always interesting, are often vague', and he linked this to the gentlemanly discursive manner of Empson's own prose. In Williams's view, this manner arose from a defensiveness on Empson's part about his larger theoretical claims (as in his apologies for his use of symbols). This defensiveness, it is suggested, indicates 'the public situation of which he is a victim'. Williams does not elaborate on this point, but in context it seems to suggest that an analytical form of criticism that is proposing a new theory of how language operates is unwelcome to the current climate and so Empson has to sweeten the pill with more readable literary explications and jokey asides. More substantively, Williams announces that Empson's book 'is an example of that kind of literary criticism which, beginning from analysis of language, proceeds not only to specific judgements on works, but also to generalizing judgements in the history of language and of society'. 'Generalizing judgements in the history . . . of society' might again seem to be part of the province of History, but for Williams (though not Williams alone) Empson's delicate unravellings of semantic change provided a form of historical illumination that was a good deal brighter than that obtainable from what Williams termed dismissively 'the study of dates and treaties and constitutions'.[29] From as early as 1948 Williams had been insisting that literature is central to any 'coherent record of human experience'. The study of literature, thus conceived, becomes one way to provide the missing social history.

Of course, by the 1950s other disciplines were also offering to undertake not dissimilar work in the service of social criticism. Williams published an essay on Eliot's idea of culture in *Essays in Criticism* in 1956,[30] but when he republished it as a chapter of *Culture and Society* two years later he made one significant interpolation. While still insisting that the modern sense of 'culture' derived from the literary tradition's 'general experience of industrialism', he now observed that this sense was being most fully elaborated in 'twentieth-century anthropology and sociology'. However, one consequence of the impact of these newer social sciences on 'ordinary thinking' he found to be of 'doubtful value', namely that

> we have been given new illustrations of an alternative way of life. In common thinking, the medieval town and the eighteenth-century village have been replaced, as examples, by various kinds of recent simple societies. These can reassure us that the version of life which industrialism has forced on us is neither universal nor permanent, but can also become a kind of weakening luxury, if they lead us to suppose that we have the 'whole arc' of human possibilities to choose from, in life as in the documents. The alternatives and variations

which matter are those which can become practical in our own culture; the discipline, rightly emphasized, drives us back to look at these within our own complex, rather than outwards to other places and other times.[31]

Here we see a striking instance of what I earlier termed 'the omnivorous present' of Williams's thinking. He is made uneasy by the way that fashionable invocations of, say, the Trobriand islanders get used to illustrate an alternative way of life to that of contemporary capitalism without being constrained to focus on what is practicable, starting from our modern capitalist present. But he apparently had not felt this unease with the long-established tradition of invoking 'the medieval town and the eighteenth-century village' for the same purpose. These, too, 'can reassure us that the version of life which industrialism has forced on us is neither universal nor permanent', but they are still somehow 'ours', and thinking about them is central to 'the English tradition of social thinking'. This suggests the need for a closer analysis of the way these claims contribute to the argument of *Culture and Society*.

III

Culture and Society aims to chart what it calls a 'structure of response'; not every element of the structure has to be present in each 'contribution'. Culture is presented as the form taken by the response to a new world. Although in a couple of places in the book Williams suggests that he is dealing with the response not to industrialism alone, but also to democracy, it is fair to say that the former overwhelmingly preponderates in his selection and, more tendentiously in some cases, his characterization of his quotations, as his later reflections again confirm. One question provoked by the very structure of the book concerns the issue of alleged novelty: in what sense did the kind of 'proto-cultural' concerns with the moral and spiritual health of society only begin, or take a decisively new form, at the end of the eighteenth century? Surely there had been a long tradition of recognizing that (to quote Williams's phrase) 'certain moral and intellectual activities' were practically separate from the 'driven impetus' of their society?

Even if we leave aside entirely, as Williams largely does, the role of religion, we could still point to the various forms of revived or adapted humanism in early modern Europe, including England. These were constantly proposing that the literary and intellectual inheritance of antiquity, in which the ideal of the whole man was enduringly embodied, furnished both a critique of, and a remedy for, the short-sighted, practical, and passion-powered activities that were the 'driven impetus' of their societies. 'Humane learning' and its cognates were recognized as, in this sense, standing apart from society and providing a kind of court of appeal in just the way that Williams claims 'culture' emerged to do.

This relates, in turn, to the implicit idealization in Williams's account of earlier periods of history. He writes at one point, collusively invoking a notion of the appallingness of social conditions introduced by industrialism and the accompanying political repression, especially in the years after Waterloo: 'Over the England of 1821 there had, after all, to be some higher Court of Appeal.'[32] But arguably this point could be made with equal moral or rhetorical force about the England of 1721 or 1621 or any other year, even if the scale of direct political repression may have fluctuated. Williams asserts that the 'new society' embodied 'primarily economic relationships', but, without any analysis of the sense in which this was not true for earlier periods, this amounts to little more than a rehearsal of the Lake Poets' complaints about how political economy encouraged the treatment of human beings as machines. The concept of 'culture' had not then been needed, the argument claims, because the values it invokes had previously been integrated with the lived fabric of life. This is the central, though often only implicit, premise of the argument. Despite all Williams's later disclaimers (and despite his own subsequent intellectual development away from such thinking), it is hard not to see a kind of nostalgic organicism informing the argument from the start.

Needless to say, an author has to be allowed to begin his book somewhere, and any beginning necessarily interrupts what, from another perspective, could be presented as a continuity. But it is important to notice that Williams's chosen starting point has the effect of making his claim about the emergence of 'culture' as a response to industrialism seem *necessarily* true. It must be allowed that the figures he chooses, at least from Southey and Owen onwards, do sometimes identify industrialism as a new and destructive force—though actually most of the figures discussed in the first two chapters do not do this—and so, when they invoke some ideal of human wholeness or level of moral and imaginative functioning, they will, inevitably, *seem* to be doing so as a response to these new circumstances. But one can see how they do not *have* to be represented like this if one conducts a little thought experiment and imagines a learned intellectual historian writing a book called, let us say,

From Humanism to Bildung: The Ideal of Human Wholeness in European Thought from the Renaissance to the End of the Nineteenth Century. This imaginary historian might well quote the same passages as Williams from the figures discussed in the first half of his book, but, instead of their seeming to articulate a new and distinctive response to the novel conditions of industrialism, they would merely seem to be late English examples of a much wider and more long-standing European pattern.

Once we have reoriented ourselves in this way, we can see how several of the passages that Williams quotes in his first few chapters do not really seem to be referring to 'culture' as a body of imaginative or intellectual activities set over against the logic of industrialism: they seem much more concerned with ancient issues such as the humanly damaging consequences of an individual overdeveloping a single skill or specialism. For instance, Coleridge's celebrated contrast between 'civilization' and 'cultivation', and his gloss on the latter as 'the harmonious development of those qualities and faculties that characterize our humanity',[33] ought to be immediately recognizable as a rendering of the German Romantic conception of *Bildung*, which is part of the larger German legacy of Neo-Hellenism. Or, to take an equally striking instance, having quoted John Stuart Mill's attempted balance sheet of the gains and losses of what Mill, in the essay of that title, calls 'Civilization', Williams says that Mill's essay is about what 'might better be called Industrialism'.[34] But this is a highly prejudicial move. In the relevant passage, Mill is evidently addressing the case—mounted in the eighteenth century by writers such as Ferguson or Rousseau—about the loss of the virtues of 'independence' in social relations (Mill even refers to the trope of 'the man in the woods'), an argument that finds its place in a long tradition of European moral thought, going back well before the arrival of industrialism, about the relations between virtue, opulence, corruption, and so on. Williams might be excused for failing to recognize parts of this vocabulary as that of a Civic Humanism whose centrality in early modern thought has been fully established only by the scholarship of the last generation or two, but in the essay in question Mill himself makes perfectly clear that the case against the independence-sapping effects of civilization long predated, and could in no way be seen as a response to, the specific economic arrangements of late-eighteenth-century Britain.

Williams's high-handed way with the evidence also came out in the kinds of small slip that would have particularly roused the ire of professional historians. Approaching his discussion of Arnold's classic contribution on 'culture',

Williams observes that there was by this date a more general response to the agitation of the industrial working class: 'One stock reaction to this agitation', he writes, 'is well known in Macaulay's phrase "we must educate our masters"'. Macaulay, characteristically, argued that the "ignorance" of the "common people" was a danger to property, and that therefore their education was necessary.'[35] The relevance of introducing the theme at this point was obvious: Arnold's reflections had notoriously been partly stimulated by the behaviour of working-class crowds at the time of the debates on the 1867 Reform Bill. The phrase 'we must educate our masters' was a later popular rendering of the observation made in the House of Commons on the passing of that Reform Bill: 'I believe it will be absolutely necessary that you should prevail on our future masters to learn their letters.' However, the remark was made, as any competent history textbook would have revealed, not by Macaulay but by the Liberal minister Robert Lowe; indeed, Macaulay could hardly have commented on the significance of the 1867 act in these terms, having died eight years earlier.[36] Williams's knowing use of 'characteristically' could perhaps be justified by reference to some of Macaulay's views expressed in earlier decades, but in this paragraph it risked turning an already bad mistake into a more general tendentiousness.[37]

If the passages from which Williams quotes so copiously were put together in an anthology, without any directing commentary, they would appear to be about a cluster of recurring themes: the whole against the fragmented, the general against the specialized, the common against the individual, and so on. Industrialism would, of course, be a significant presence, as how could it not be in this period, but largely insofar as it embodied or corresponded to the latter terms in these pairings. Conversely, the positive terms would all be linked to what is, in fact, one of the remarkable absences in Williams's work—namely, the huge presence of an idealized Hellenism in Victorian thought and beyond. The question of the book's range might also be raised from a different angle. The 'we' of Williams's prose, as I have said, is most often a national community of reflective persons stretching over time: Cobbett and Morris are living presences in Williams's sense of who 'we' are, whereas actually living foreign commentators such as, say, Sartre, Adorno, and Trilling are emphatically not. It is perhaps not surprising that such a book written in England in the 1950s should contain no mention of, say, Nietzsche, but it may seem more striking that a book on this theme at that time should not make any reference at all to, say, Spengler. In his 1982 introduction to a reissue of the book, Williams referred, in somewhat defensive

tones, to its exclusively English orientation, but he was essentially unrepent-
ant: 'I am still sure that the book could only be formed, in its particular
method, around this particular experience and tradition.' And his elaboration of this point only underscores the centrality of the response to the
Industrial Revolution: 'The fundamentally new social and cultural relationships and issues which were part of that historically decisive transition were
therefore first felt, in their intense and unprecedented immediacy, within
this culture.' He conceded that there may later have been comparable
responses to industrialism elsewhere, but 'it is nevertheless of some permanent general importance to see what happened where it happened first'.[38]
The organizing force of the response to industrialism in constituting 'the
tradition' is very evident here. I am making these points not, I hope, in the
spirit of that type of reviewer who berates the author for failing to have
written a different kind of book, but to indicate that Williams's chosen
chronological and national limits impose a kind of false unity of purpose or
concern among the figures he includes, and that it is only insofar as they can
be presented as addressing the same 'problem'—essentially the response to
industrialism—that they can be seen as constituting a single 'tradition'.

It is not until we get to the forty-five-page concluding chapter in which
Williams described himself as 'attempt[ing] to extend [the tradition] in the
direction of certain meanings and values' that the rationale for, and significance of, his interpretation of the book's selection of writers becomes fully
apparent. It is here that he introduces what he calls 'the crucial distinguish-
ing element in English life since the Industrial Revolution... [that] between
alternative ideas of the nature of social relationship'. On the one hand, we
have individualism, self-seeking, the middle-class notion of meritocracy; on
the other hand, the working-class ethic of collective action, communal loy-
alties, and, in a phrase redolent of the earlier phases of the Labour movement,
what he calls 'the general and controlled advance of all'. So 'working-class
culture' should not be understood in the narrow sense as 'proletarian' art
and literature, but, rather, as the solidaristic institutions produced by the
ethos of that class, such as 'the trade unions, the cooperative movement or a
political party'.[39]

But then we get what is in some ways the key move in the whole argument. Having sketched these two contrasting models of society, he writes:
'The development of the idea of culture has, throughout, been a criticism
of what has been called the bourgeois idea of society.'[40] Culture, it is suddenly revealed, really lines up with the working-class idea of community.

Culture, once its history has been properly excavated, should no longer be seen as the property of the elitists and the pessimists, as something that is of its very nature threatened by the progressive advance of the Labour movement, as Eliot and others had claimed in the late 1940s. On the contrary, the informing ideal of this whole 'tradition of English social thinking', as Williams calls it, has precisely been, when understood as a series of attempts to articulate the notion of a 'whole way of life', to posit an alternative to 'the bourgeois idea of society' of the kind that 'working-class culture', properly understood, now offers in the present.

It is important to recognize how this same decisive argumentative move has the effect of introducing a sharp binary division into British intellectual history of the period. The book is essentially structured around what, until the concluding chapter, has been a largely implicit contrast between 'the culture and society tradition' and 'the bourgeois idea of society'. But the scholarship of recent decades has persuasively demonstrated that this reductive contrast has a distorting effect on our understanding of British intellectual life in the nineteenth century. Where, in terms of this binary opposition, do we put, for example, a political moralist like Malthus or a social critic like Bagehot or a proponent of 'national purpose' like Seeley or a theorist of the evolutionary role of altruism like Kidd? On which side of the divide would we place a social and literary critic like Leslie Stephen, a disciple of Mill in politics and economics who, at the same time, makes notions of human wholeness and moral health central to his social and literary criticism? Or, again, Arnold obviously has to be at the centre of Williams's 'tradition', and that would seem to place his opponents in the 'bourgeois idea of society' or individualist camp. But is this really the place for, say, one of Arnold's most persistent antagonists such as Frederic Harrison, a Comtist, an upholder of the values of cooperation and altruism, and a proponent of the idea of a spiritual caste—all values that are the antithesis of the supposed 'bourgeois idea of society'? And what about all those historians and social theorists who explored the role of custom, of national character, and of the critical function of reconstructing earlier or other forms of society—precisely the kinds of consideration that are supposed to be on the 'culture and society' side of the divide from Burke to Morris?

Probably no one figure exerted greater influence over the whole discourse of 'character' that was constitutive of the supposedly individualist core of Victorian social and political thought than Carlyle, yet he is precisely the figure Williams recalled as being absolutely central to his 'discovery' of 'the tradition'—that is, the 'culture-and-society' side of the divide.[41] This is not just a scholarly quibble about the interpretation of Carlyle, or indeed of any other single figure, but rather a point about how the major figures and traditions of discourse in the nineteenth century cannot in fact be squeezed into these two categories. The danger in trying to impose this division on nineteenth-century thought is that in the end the only people left to represent the alternative to his 'tradition of English social thinking'—that is, the 'culture and society tradition'—would seem to be a few strictly orthodox political economists, a travesty of Victorian social thinking we have met before but that has now long outlived its day. It is worth mentioning here that, although the *New Left Review* interviewers for the *Politics and Letters* volume probed much else, they accepted this etiolated contrast unblinkingly when they themselves contrasted the 'culture and society tradition' with what they called at one point 'the opposite side—that of political economy'.[42]

To get the logic of Williams's book clear, we need to recognize that what his chosen figures had in common, therefore, was that they adumbrated ideas that were in some ways critical of, or suggested alternatives to, what he called 'the bourgeois idea of society'. Since they were essentially selected in terms of this *negative* criterion, such ideas were inevitably fairly diverse: they included ideas of the moral health of the nation, of human wholeness, of the distinctiveness of human spiritual or imaginative activities, of the precious inheritance of intellectual and artistic achievements, of the inappropriateness of quantitative or mechanical measures of human welfare, and so on. A selection of the figures who expressed some of these ideas in especially influential or interesting ways then become 'the tradition of English social thinking', and this tradition is, in turn, defined in terms of its criticism of the consequences of the Industrial Revolution.

This logic can be exhibited in another way by considering three books that someone might have considered writing in the mid-1950s:

1. A critique of the reactionary and anti-democratic uses of the notion of 'culture' in recent English thinking.

2. A history of arguments which could now be seen to have contributed to the contemporary concept or concepts of 'culture'.

3. A literary-critical analysis of some of the main statements in that history.

In writing *Culture and Society*, Raymond Williams could be seen as undertaking something of each of these three projects. The critique of the reactionary uses provided his starting point and much of his initial motivation; the history of contributing arguments partly defined the scope of his book; and the literary-critical analysis of some of the main statements provided the method and the greater part of the substance or texture of his book.

To this could be joined a fourth possible book:

4. An argument about the need to get beyond individualist premises in thinking about the proper relations between culture and community in contemporary Britain.

This, summarizing briskly, is more or less what Williams was doing in the conclusion to his book. But, even if we assume the successful integration of these four projects, we are still left some way short of the actual book that Williams wrote. For that, I want to argue, involved aspects of three other possible books:

5. A history of the development of the modern sense of the word 'culture'.

6. A history of responses to 'industrialism'.

7. A history of criticisms of laissez-faire individualism.

It is constitutive of the argument of Williams's book that the period he discusses saw the development of the modern meanings of the word 'culture'. But no less constitutive of it is the claim that this development expressed 'our' response to industrialism. And, more central still, what holds together the various ideas discussed in the book is that they are all repudiations of the bourgeois individualist ideal. Without any one of these themes, the book would not have been what it is, nor, we can reasonably assume, would it have been so influential. The upshot is that the book rests on a structuring polarity between what Williams calls 'the tradition of English social thinking' and what he calls 'the defenders of the existing system'. That binary polarity constitutes the chief and defining weakness of the book, despite its obvious and manifold strengths, and that in turn accounts for its questionable impact on much subsequent understanding of modern British literary and intellectual history.

IV

The question of where to place the book on the contemporary map of academic disciplines was one that exercised both publishers and reviewers at the time. Penguin editor Dieter Pevsner attempted to answer the question for his colleagues when recommending that they publish a paperback edition of *Culture and Society*:

> It is a notable example of the best work of the inter-discipline [*sic*] kind that is probably the most important and original contribution of the present generation of humanist academics.... Finally, this is very much a book of its time. Its approach, which takes it for granted that there is and can be no sharp dividing line between literature, politics, sociology, and linguistic analysis, is one which is producing some of the best results in contemporary social and literary studies.[43]

To a later eye there is one very striking absentee from this brisk assemblage of disciplines: Pevsner makes no mention of History, an omission that, at the time, would have seemed entirely justified when characterizing Williams's book. But, although the book was largely ignored by professional historians when first published, its problematic historical features did not altogether escape notice. In a review in the *New Reasoner*, V. G. Kiernan, writing both as an ally on the Left and as a historian, shrewdly identified a major structural weakness: Williams, he complained, does not

> draw any outline of the social order, the 'way of life', he thinks of as flourishing in England before 1780.... Mr Williams indeed leaves far too much room for supposing that he himself takes 'the good old days' at their face value.... [In this way, Williams] allows his traditionalists to go on one after the other, without any contradiction from him, founding their case on the assumption that what the Industrial Revolution brought to England was something essentially new, and essentially bad.

Kiernan was keen to insist that many of the relevant social and economic changes had been under way long before the late eighteenth century. For example, taking issue with Williams's treatment of Cobbett, he pointed out that 'what most moved his indignation was the oppressive agrarian capitalism of the age, long in train though intensified by the Napoleonic wars, and scarcely to be brought under the black flag of "industrialism"'. Similarly, he argued that it was far too simplistic of Williams to allow his subjects to imply that ugliness came in only with industrialism, just as in their concentration on the wretched condition of factory workers they entirely overlook the conditions of domestic servants who were in fact far more numerous. Moreover, once Williams has identified the late eighteenth century as the key moment of supposed qualitative transformation, Kiernan pointed out, he largely ignores historical change thereafter: 'as the book proceeds from decade to decade, there is very little reference to the rapidly altering condition of England.'[44] Although subsequent commentary seems to have lost sight of these features of the book, Kiernan was surely right to insist on the historical untenability of this 'before-and-after' view. In effect, the Industrial Revolution functions as the Fall, and the need for the modern sense of the word 'culture' is taken to be the index of man's fallen state.

In all these ways, Kiernan was suggesting, the book rested on an untenably simplistic historical or quasi-historical narrative. 'The prime requisite for any study of cultural history', he pronounced, 'is a firm framework of historical fact—economic, social, political; and . . . the one great deficiency of the book is the lack of just this'.[45] Perhaps it was partly for such reasons that Richard Johnson, writing twenty years later, could remark that, although Williams valuably expanded the sense of 'culture' beyond the narrow category with which earlier progressive historians had worked, 'Williams's concerns have none the less often remained too literary to deliver the full implications of such a profound re-ordering; his "cultural materialism" remains, centrally, a form of literary criticism'.[46] Here, yet again, is the question of the nature of the 'cultural history' that is being propounded: did it 'remain, centrally, a form of literary criticism'?

7

Literary History as Cultural History

I

In the introduction to *The Long Revolution*, published in 1961, Raymond Williams made, almost in passing, a striking claim. 'There is', he declared, 'no academic subject within which the questions I am interested in can be followed through; I hope one day there might be'. In context, his claim was both apologetic and reproachful. He was acknowledging that he had drawn upon work from several fields, fields in which his own expertise was necessarily limited, and that in so doing he had gone, as he put it, 'well beyond the limits of any kind of academic prudence'. But the questions he was addressing were important; he maintained that the response to his earlier book, *Culture and Society*, demonstrated that 'the pressure of these questions was not only personal but general'.[1] By implication, therefore, the real failing lay in the current state of academic disciplines: *anyone* attempting to 'follow through' the questions Williams was raising about the nature and development of culture would, it is suggested, encounter an absence or gap. In that earlier book, Williams had famously focused on culture as 'a whole way of life', and in *The Long Revolution* he expanded this remit to take in what he now described as 'cultural history', defined as the study of 'relationships between elements in a whole way of life'. Williams proposed this as a new synthesizing enterprise, constituting 'more than a department, a special area of change', embracing the interaction of the main 'systems' that compose the 'general organization' of society.

A recurring feature of the writings by literary critics examined in the previous chapters is their frequent invocation of something they tend to call 'cultural history'. This most often seems to refer to an aspiration, a desire for a kind of understanding of the lived experience of the past that, it was claimed, was not provided by professional historians. We have already encountered other examples, beginning with a passage quoted in Chapter 2 where, in 1933, Leavis and Thompson were recommending how the theme of 'Culture and Environment' might be taught and how pupils' awareness of change could be educated. The principal authorities they cited were not works of history but Bunyan and Sturt, and then they added this disconcerting rider, quoted in that chapter: 'Obviously, too, in the teaching of cultural history a historian would be able to co-operate, though he would have to be energetic as well as intelligent, for his formal historical training would not have helped him much, and there are few useful books.'[2] As I observed earlier, it is revealing that, although the subject to be taught is 'cultural history', the most 'a historian' is expected, perhaps allowed, to do is to 'cooperate'; literary critics are clearly to be the principal practitioners of this subject.

A couple of years later, writing about English poetry in the seventeenth century, Leavis observed: 'A serious attempt to account for the "dissociation of sensibility" would turn into a discussion of the great change that came over English civilization in the seventeenth century...'. This attempt would embrace 'intellectual and cultural history in general—a great and complex variety of considerations would be involved'.[3] As I remarked in my earlier discussion, his sustained use of the conditional here sufficiently indicates Leavis's conviction that no mere historians had thus far attempted this task. 'Intellectual and cultural history in general': that is what 'would' be involved, though it seems that it is literary critics who are most likely to provide it. L. C. Knights, writing two years later about 'Shakespeare and profit-inflations', reiterated a similar plea: 'Cultural history of the kind desiderated', he announced, 'still remains to be written. It will not be—need I say?—a "literary" history, and the literary critic who undertakes it will need to submit to a strenuous extra-literary discipline—including the discipline of grappling with "the materialist interpretation of history".'[4] Here, some twenty-five years before Williams's comparable remark, 'cultural history' is again projected into the future as a discipline that is yet to be constituted. Moreover, Knights clearly specifies that, although this will not be mere 'literary history', it will be written by 'literary critics', albeit critics also schooled in 'a strenuous extra-literary discipline'.

When, a few years later still, Knights addressed the question of 'the university teaching of English and History' under the heading of 'A Plea for

Correlation', his twin premises were, first, that a university education ought to prepare people to think about 'the quality of life' in society, particularly whether it was improving or declining; and, second, that literary criticism deals with questions of 'value' in a way that history does not. His conclusion is that, as he put it, 'some degree of *critical* ability is indispensable to the historian of culture'. The evaluative role of 'the historian of culture' appears unproblematic here, and, although it may at first sound like a role for historians, the clear implication, again, is that it will at present be filled only by a certain kind of literary critic. Moreover, Knights's illustration of what might be achieved by such an approach revealed some rather more specific historical assumptions. Proposing that the critic can illuminate a period by attending to 'the evidence of style and language', he itemizes: 'the vivid, idiomatic raciness of Elizabethan English, the "polite reasonableness" of Augustan prose, the increasingly "literary" language of most nineteenth-century poetry, the debased idiom of the modern newspaper'.[5] Not only is the trajectory unmistakably downhill, but these are oddly incommensurable units—why compare great literature of the past to the modern *newspaper*, why represent the nineteenth century exclusively by *poetry*, and so on? These four (ostensibly historical) characterizations make sense only as touchstones of the post-Eliotic, Leavis-inflected version of cultural decline. They certainly do not permit the telling of a story of, say, increasing diversity and sophistication of language use over these centuries.

William Empson, as we have seen, did not share the *Scrutiny* circle's declinist assumptions, but he, too, writing subjunctively in 1951, imagined (in a sentence quoted earlier) a similar discipline or subdiscipline into being through the agency of the literary critic: 'I should think indeed', he wrote, 'that a profound enough criticism could extract an entire cultural history from a simple lyric'.[6] Characteristically, Empson does not sound too exercised by this possibility, though for all its off-hand tone the remark indicates a confidence that the right kind of literary criticism could achieve something beyond the reach of mere historians—namely, to generate 'an entire cultural history'. Although Williams's version of these claims was, characteristically, more programmatic, it was certainly not new.

A pattern of this kind, once detected, calls for general or structural rather than merely individual explanations. Lurking in and behind these declarations was an aspiration to arrive at an understanding of the lived experience of the past, something it was felt that conventional professional history did not do, perhaps even *could* not do. At the time, the term 'cultural history' was used rather sparingly by academic historians in Britain, who tended to see it as an alien import—perhaps as part of the brilliant but unsound impressionism of the likes of Burckhardt or Huizinga or the *Kulturgeschichte* of theory-inebriated Germans. But a wider reading public, unconcerned by matters of classification or academic turf wars, eagerly sought pattern and significance in accounts of the past, and in decades during which, as I have indicated, literary criticism enjoyed an unprecedented intellectual prominence, the various historical schemas assumed or implied by works of criticism came to be influential.

II

One framework within which to address this theme is provided by the wider narrative of disciplinary formation in the late nineteenth and early twentieth centuries. I have already alluded more than once to the well-documented story of how the partial and uneven professionalization of history in the second half of the nineteenth century, largely but not entirely within the universities, brought together elements of German historicism, ideals of scientific accuracy and disinterestedness, and an inherited focus on the political, administrative, diplomatic, and legal machinery of the state. Late-nineteenth-century literary history may have focused on different material, but similar methodological protocols applied. Judgements about the 'quality of life' in a society were not part of serious scholarship. What historians of criticism sometimes call 'the critical revolution' of the 1920s and 1930s introduced a different note into what became the most fashionable style in academic criticism—more urgent and intense, more discriminating and evaluative, and, most relevantly here, more imperial and more comprehensive. When literature is approached as the most distilled or intense expression of life, it easily comes to serve as an index of human flourishing in whole societies. This encouraged what we might call a *qualitative* history of experience. If literature provided the most intense expression of lived experience, then the critic became the accredited assessor of the quality of life revealed by different moments in literary history.

This intimacy between literary criticism and 'experience', and the consequent attempt to compare and evaluate forms of experience across the generations and centuries, was bound to incite a certain level of disciplinary conflict, and we can see this playing itself out in various episodes of mid-twentieth-century intellectual history that are well known in themselves but that tend not to be analysed in these terms. But let me begin with an obscure, indeed almost entirely neglected, episode in which the tensions came to the surface. A special summer course on 'Literature in Relation to History' was held for Oxford Delegacy extra-mural tutors in literature and history in Hertford College in July 1950, with Raymond Williams as Director of Studies. The course was focused on the years 1850–75, and distinguished figures from both disciplines lectured for it, including, from the history side, Asa Briggs, Raymond Postgate, G. M. Young, and, less predictably, F. M. Powicke. But, as Williams's somewhat pained report on the course makes clear, the attempt at conjoining the two disciplines was far from successful. Williams took exception, in particular, to the way in which the historians appeared to treat literature simply as an inferior or unreliable kind of historical evidence, and this led him to voice a more general complaint about the practice of professional historians:

> I had thought that the study of dates and treaties and constitutions was now more widely recognized as only a part...of the general study of human actions in time. I had assumed that historians would be naturally interested in an account of the nature and quality, at any given time, of specific, though unpolitical, human experience; or of the particular workings of social institutions; or of the effect of economic change upon differentiated individual persons, as well as upon a class....The fact that experience, including social experience, had been shaped and assessed by the workings of an imaginative consciousness did not seem to me to make it any less important than experience which had passed through the statistical or generalizing process of the historical record.

This is at once an expression of disappointment, a rebuke to professional narrowness, and a manifesto for the kind of historical illumination that might be derived from literature. Williams went on to restate the by-then familiar case for reading literature *as* literature, the imaginative realization of human experience expressed in a unique sequence of words, and not as a piece of substandard documentary evidence. And, in a way that clearly signalled the direction of much of his future work, Williams emphasized the importance of studying changes in language:

> The change and continuity of a language, often seen most clearly in its use in literature, forms a record of vitally important changes and developments in human personality. It is as much the record of the history of a people as political institutions and religions and philosophical modes. Of all the evidence which

literature can contribute to the study of human affairs, this evidence of language is perhaps most important.[7]

Williams's report sparked a small debate in adult education circles that made clear he was not alone in his sense of the asymmetry between the disciplines of History and English in terms of their openness and their ambition.

He and his literary colleagues clearly had their own axes to grind, but in the early 1950s their strictures may not have been wholly groundless. To take a minor but relevantly local example, Jose Harris, writing in the large multi-volume history of Oxford University, made a not dissimilar point about a kind of narrowness in the Modern History school at this time: 'The review section of the *Oxford Magazine* in 1954 welcomed a monograph on the late Lancastrian receipt of the Exchequer as a "major event", but dismissed current interest in American history as a "fashionable craze".' Broadening the point, she observed: 'Most Oxford historians at the start of the period [sc. 1939] laid great emphasis on impartiality and precise archival accuracy.' These attitudes 'were not infrequently the complement of parochialism and philistinism—and lack of interest in philosophic, intellectual and aesthetic history, and of indifference or resistance to the relationship of history to archaeology, anthropology, psychology and the new social sciences'.[8]

Where such attitudes dominated—they were not universal, needless to say—there was clearly some room for more wide-ranging enquiries into the history of human experience, especially, it might be said, enquiries that addressed the concerns of non-specialist readers. In 1939 one observer could casually refer, without apparent fear of contradiction, to 'the fact that during the past fifty years historians have written primarily for specialists rather than for the general public', and he regretted 'the scarcity of good historical writing'. He went on: 'The ideal of scientific objectivity . . . and the consequent retreat by historians into the laboratory left a vacuum which has been filled by journalists, propagandists, and charlatans.'[9] Literary critics, too, were prominent among the miscellaneous types who came forward to fill the void, though perhaps it is hardly surprising, given that he was writing in *Scrutiny*, that he did not choose to add 'literary critics' to a list containing 'propagandists and charlatans'.

One can see somewhat similar disciplinary tensions working themselves out in the response by a literary critic to the publication in 1951 by C. V. Wedgwood, one of the few undeniably popular historians in the middle decades of the century, of a volume in the Home University Library series entitled *Seventeenth-Century English Literature*. Leavis, writing to one of his regular reviewing lieutenants, R. G. Cox, asked: 'Have you noticed what a portent the Wedgwood creature has become on the strength of being established by Bloomsbury? She's now an authority, not merely on seventeenth-century, but on contemporary literature: she holds forth on air, and recommends *Good-Houskeeping*-like jejune stuff as subtle and profound art...Clearly a firm and astringent note is wanted.'[10] Cox duly complied. In his review of Wedgwood that appeared in *Scrutiny* later that year, he tartly upbraided the author for failing to take the opportunity provided by a contribution to the Home University Library series 'to bring to the notice of a wider audience of students and general readers the remarkable interest and enthusiasm this literature has commanded during the last thirty years, to make available the results of something like a revolution in taste, and to exemplify the new critical principles and methods which have accompanied it'. Wedgwood's failure to have adequately imbibed the milk of the Eliotic word, as pasteurized by Leavis and *Scrutiny*, is then demonstrated at some length. Wedgwood, it is conceded, knows a lot about the history of the period, but she lacks 'the critic's power to distinguish sharply between the living and the dead and to enforce his judgements by convincing analysis'. (The use of 'enforce' in such a context is one of the minor tics of the Leavisian style; the use of the awkward masculine possessive might now be seen as part of a wider cultural deformation.) Cox ends, again in characteristic *Scrutiny* manner, by taking Wedgwood's volume as an indication of a larger problem:

> In healthier cultural epochs it is probable that things were different, but today the fluent expression of the opinions of an average cultivated reader, whatever specialist knowledge may be super-added, is just not sufficient for a task of this kind. One cannot help wondering how the academic historians would have received a work in this series on a historical subject by a writer who was primarily a literary critic.[11]

Scrutiny may have criticized unsparingly the 'academicism' of orthodox literary scholarship, but it was not about to allow the fashionable amateur to supplant those trained in the 'discipline' of literary criticism. However, the irony surely is that the clinching reversal of roles that Cox hypothesizes in his final sentence was precisely what had become common in the years covered here. Works on 'historical subjects' by those who were primarily literary critics were far from rare, and the response of the 'academic historians' was, by and large, to ignore them entirely.

One emblematic way to indicate the traditional version of the division of labour between general history and literary history would be to compare the character and remit of the most authoritative or influential series of such histories produced in this period. The *Cambridge Modern History* and the *Cambridge History of English Literature*, both originally products of the two decades before 1914, were strongly marked by a confident positivism, even though the material covered in their respective volumes revealed remarkably little substantive overlap. A comparison of the fourteen volumes in the original *Oxford History of England* series that appeared between 1934 and 1961 with the rather more ragged *Oxford History of English Literature*, conceived in 1935 and of which fifteen volumes were published between 1945 and, somewhat embarrassingly, 1997, would reveal some diminution in the confident evolutionary form of positivism that had governed the Cambridge volumes, but the division of the territory was relatively little changed. In the history volumes, literature, where it is treated at all, tends to appear in a rather dutiful final chapter, either on its own account or as part of a larger survey of the arts and cultural life, whereas in the literary volumes general history, in so far as it makes any separate appearance, is assumed to provide the relevant setting or context. An example of the former, dealing with the period at the heart of the developments I have been discussing, is provided by Godfrey Davies's volume in the history of England, *The Early Stuarts 1603–1660*, published in 1937. (Despite the patina of official neutrality attaching to such series, the seventeenth century seems to have retained its power to divide historical opinion. As late as 1956, Christopher Hill declared: 'It is noteworthy that in the *Oxford* and the *Penguin Histories of England* the volumes dealing with this period are among the least satisfactory in the series.'[12]) Davies's volume has a final chapter on 'Literature', though here the term is still used in the older sense, which embraces political thought, historiography, and so on. Perhaps not surprisingly, the chapter seems entirely innocent of the work and ideas of Eliot, Leavis, or Knights. The traditional division of territory partly expressed the demands of different professional communities, partly publishers' views of the needs of particular readerships, but clearly the two kinds of 'additional' chapters also represented different assumptions about the causal or explanatory role of their respective subject matters. There were, however, signs that the limitations of the assumptions governing the original *CMH* were coming to be acknowledged by the middle of the century. In the prospectus for the *New Cambridge Modern History*, G. N. Clark and Herbert Butterfield declared in 1945:

'The accepted idea of general history has changed. In the first place some branches of the subject will require fuller and more continuous treatment, especially economic and social matters and the history of literature, thought and religion.'[13] (Although Clark had made a similar plea in his inaugural lecture as Regius Professor at Cambridge the previous year, it had not been something he emphasized when planning the *Oxford History of England* volumes in 1929.[14])

By the 1950s it was similarly coming to be recognized that the conventional literary histories were old-fashioned—they tended, as was said of George Saintsbury's *Short History of English Literature*, to 'resemble a well-tended graveyard of noble monuments'[15]—and that they needed to be replaced by an enterprise that reflected the newer critical practices that had come to the fore since the 1920s and 1930s. One of the less bright ideas briefly entertained by Allen Lane, the founder of Penguin, in the early 1950s was that of reprinting the *Concise Cambridge History of English Literature*, compiled by George Sampson in 1941. This had attempted to condense the original fifteen volumes of the Cambridge history published between 1907 and 1916 into a thousand pages, and it represented all that was characteristic of traditional literary history as well as all that was alien to the Penguin ideal—it was comprehensive, dull, not easily portable, and almost unreadable. Fortunately, Lane's chief adviser, W. E. Williams, steered him away from this idea towards a specially commissioned series.[16] *The Pelican Guide to English Literature*, published in seven volumes between 1954 and 1961, became one of Penguin's minor commercial successes, although it is worth remarking that it sold poorly in the United States. However, it has not been recognized, I think, how far the *Pelican Guide* provided, for a very wide audience in Britain in the 1950s and 1960s and beyond, what amounted to almost a covert interpretation of English social, cultural, and intellectual history—and my use of 'Britain' to designate the market for the volumes but 'England' to refer to their historical interpretation reflects the realities. The volumes' historical function was touched on in the proposal for the series that its general editor, Boris Ford, wrote for Penguin, where he asserted that the *Guide* would not be

> another History of English Literature. Yet at the same time it must be an historical work and not simply a series of introductions to great writers. The critical sorting and placing is intended to establish a pattern of significances, to elucidate the nature of the literary tradition, and to suggest the relations of literature to social forms and the more inclusive intellectual traditions of this country.[17]

The series was certainly 'an historical work', but of a peculiar kind.

One can detect early signs of the eventual character of the *Guide* in a review that Ford wrote in 1941 of Sampson's one-volume condensation of the old *Cambridge History*. Ford made some predictable points about the datedness of the *CHEL* and the need for a more fashionably 'critical' approach. But in the final paragraph he called for something rather different: 'And finally the time has come for a history of English society at its margin of contact with English literature.'[18] Quite what this would mean is not immediately apparent. A 'history of English society' sounds familiar enough, suggesting some kind of systematic social history or history of social structure rather than the kinds of political and constitutional history to which professional historians had mostly devoted their energies for the previous half century. But 'at its margin of contact with English literature' suggests that the criteria for selection of what might be included in such a social history, and perhaps the sequence and manner of its presentation, would be determined by focusing initially on the literary works that were to be interpreted in the light of such history.

This construal is encouraged by his examples, as in the following interesting list:

> What one needs is a history which could supply one with the material necessary to an understanding of, for instance, [Ben] Jonson's satire, of the emergence of modern English prose, of Jane Austen's assurance—in short the kind of information that is lacking so patently when Mr Sampson describes George Sturt as a 'faithful interpreter of southern English village life'.[19]

The three illustrations of what is needed conjure up three rather different enterprises: a relatively straightforward history of the social types and social debates of early Jacobean England might assist the understanding of Jonson's satires, but what would similarly illuminate 'the emergence of modern English prose'? That the phrase could be used as though it referred to a known and accepted moment in the history of English writing may just indicate the standing of a post-Eliotic orthodoxy about the Royal Society-influenced prose style of the Restoration, but, even so, the history involved here would be of a radically different type—perhaps an intellectual history of philosophical presuppositions or religious ideals as much as a history of the development of science and of the rise and decline of Puritanism.

And what kind of history might contribute to an understanding of 'Jane Austen's assurance'? One suspects that Ford is here not simply implying that an elaboration of the social and economic position of the class to which Austen's family belonged would help account for her social confidence and her opportunities as a writer, but, rather, that the right kind of delineation of late-Augustan moral attitudes would give insight into the working of a widely shared socio-ethical code, which Austen could presume without having to defend. The implied criticism of Sampson's reference to Sturt involved not just the reclaiming of a *Scrutiny* touchstone, but an insistence that the critic or historian must be alive to questions about the *quality* of experience in any given setting. Sampson's phrase, Ford implies, fails to grasp the diagnostic or elegiac character of Sturt's writing and correspondingly fails to understand the significance of the changes in social experience that he is describing. Sampson is thus charged with treating Sturt as a celebrant of rural life when he was, according to Ford (drawing, of course, on a Leavisian orthodoxy by this date), writing about changes in English society rather more in the style in which the Lynds had written about 'Middletown'. It is hard to see what kind of history would 'correct' such a misreading unless it were one already infused with a belief in the decline of the quality of living in the contemporary world.

Attempting to illustrate further what is needed, Ford invokes 'something of the kind supplied by L. C. Knights in relation to Jonson or (if it had a more specifically literary reference) by Basil Willey in his two books', though even these two exemplars are notably different, as we saw in Chapter 3. But was there an existing example of the kind of historical work that would contribute to an understanding of 'Jane Austen's assurance'? It sounds rather like a version of Leslie Stephen's Ford Lectures but rewritten by Queenie Leavis. In any event, Boris Ford's clear implication was that none of the types of history he was calling for—forms of cultural-intellectual-social history directed to illuminating the literature of a period—seemed likely to be forthcoming from professional historians at the time, or even recognized by them as 'history'.

What may at first not be obvious when one encounters the familiar blue-liveried volumes of the *Pelican Guide*, now so plentiful on the shelves of second-hand bookshops, is how the very conception of the series depended on a contrast with orthodox literary history. As Ford wrote in his general introduction, reproduced in each volume: 'the *Guide* does not set out to compete with the standard Histories of Literature. . . . This is not a *Bradshaw* or a *Whitaker's Almanac* of English Literature. Nor is it a digest or potted-version, nor again a portrait-gallery of the Great. Works such as these already

abound and there is no need to add to their number.'[20] Even if we allow Ford
an element of dismissive hyperbole here, this does capture an important aspect
of orthodox literary history when viewed critically: the enumeration of facts
about literature could all too easily subside into a compendium resembling a
reference book or timetable. And yet the contemporary reader was in need
of some guide to what Ford had called 'the living tradition' of English literature, an elusive entity that inevitably came to function as a kind of ersatz
cultural history.

At the same time, there was the obligation to characterize and account
for the specificity of each period, so every volume would begin with two
more general historical chapters. These chapters, as Ford explained in his
introduction, would provide 'an account of the social context of literature
in each period', offering, in a phrase that echoed his own prescription from
thirteen years earlier, 'an account of contemporary society at its points of
contact with literature'. Once again, we are plunged into the ambiguities
of 'context', 'background', 'setting', and so on, a diverse series of attempts to
write a form of selective history that could stretch out a welcoming hand
to the analysis of writers and texts that is advancing to meet it. These chapters,
Ford continued, would address such questions as 'Why did the literature of
this period deal with this rather than that kind of problem?' 'What factors
tended to encourage the play rather than the novel, prose rather than verse,
in this period?' 'What was the relationship between writer and public?'
'What was the reading public like in its tastes and make-up?'[21] One, perhaps
rather oblique, thing to be said about this is that these are not questions that
appear to grow principally out of an engagement with a Marxist interpretation (in the way that was clearly true of some comparable preoccupations
in Leavis and Knights and others in the 1930s). The first question suggests
a rather low-level form of 'context': simply identifying certain themes
as expressive of contemporary society (for example, that literature in the
Jacobean period engages with the question of Puritanism in a way that
literature in the early eighteenth century did not have to, and so on). The
second is a more probing kind of context: at its lowest it is to do with the
market and the means of reaching it; more ambitiously, it might be trying to
identify some homology between literary genres and forms of social life (as,
say, Lukacs was doing at roughly the same time but in a totally different
idiom). The last two questions are about the reading public, and this is clearly
the central thematic concern. The two opening chapters of each volume
were, therefore, attempting to serve several purposes simultaneously, with

the result that they exhibit a curious unsteadiness—they do not read like chapters from a history textbook yet they do offer a general if partial interpretation of the period in question. Moreover, as Ford's introduction goes on, it makes almost embarrassingly clear that the whole venture had a kind of cultural criticism built into it: he presents the series as an antidote to what L. H. Myers is quoted as calling 'the deep-seated spiritual vulgarity that lies at the heart of our civilization'.[22] Literature, at least literature of the right kind or read in the right way, is once again being prescribed as an antidote to the failings of 'modernity'.

Both the historical unsteadiness of these introductory chapters and their inherently polemical character emerges most strikingly in G. H. Bantock's contribution on 'The Social and Intellectual Background' in the final volume of the series, *The Modern Age*, published in 1961. Bantock was by this point recognized as one of the most uncompromising champions of the anti-progressive strain in *Scrutiny*'s cultural criticism, and it is revealing to see how the neutral category of 'background' could be aligned with the expression of this perspective. 'Rarely, indeed, can there have been a time when "background" more readily obtrudes as an essential part of foreground', he remarked, gesturing towards both the seismic events of the twentieth century up to that date and the heightened capacity of society to shape individual experience. In practice, the elements Bantock treated as 'background' were heterogeneous: discussion of patterns of employment, the decline of agriculture, and the shifting alignment of political parties are juxtaposed to brisk accounts of the work of influential writers, philosophers, and social critics. It cannot even be said that 'background' signifies everything that is not literature, since figures such as Lawrence, Forster, and Woolf are among the most frequently cited witnesses, importing an element of circularity into his diagnosis of 'the writer's predicament'. Bantock acknowledges that 'the complexities of assessing the relative movements of a whole civilization' are 'immense', but he proceeds on the premise that this is nonetheless what an introductory chapter in such a 'guide' should be doing. And his indictment of contemporary popular culture is premised on some familiar historical assumptions. Having inveighed against 'the inane triviality' of the programmes most people now enjoyed on radio and television, he hectored his readers about the standard of comparison: 'And these, it is necessary to remind ourselves, are the "educated" and literate descendants of the people who produced the folk song and the folk tale, who built the parish churches and nourished Bunyan.' There is a somewhat promiscuous quality to his historical allusions, which are united only by the reproach they are supposed to offer to the present, as when he goes on to say: 'Today there is none of that interpenetration of artistic, social, and political life that characterized the Augustan age.' In concluding, he explicitly endorses Eliot's diagnosis of 'the dissociation of sensibility', and he insists that 'the role of the greatest writers, where intellect is suffused with emotion and emotion controlled by intelligence, points a way to "unity of being"'.[23] There may now seem to have been a dying fall to this analysis, as though its historical allusions must have seemed stale and its critical energies spent, yet its appearance in such a widely used volume meant that it was given a new lease of life for a readership in the 1960s unfamiliar with the originals of the ideas now embalmed in these phrases.

Inevitably, the introductory chapters in the volumes of the *Pelican Guide* are often representative of the understandings of history current among scholars of English literature, who, if they were of sufficient standing to be asked to write for these volumes in the mid- or late 1950s, mostly received their intellectual formation and early professional development in the 1930s and 1940s. This meant, as the chapters' footnotes reveal, extending the life of certain works of history that had been important thirty or forty years earlier. Several of Trevelyan's books are hardy perennials; Tawney's *Religion and the Rise of Capitalism* from 1926 makes frequent appearances; and a further boost was given to the already remarkable longevity of Beljame's book, now translated as *The Public and Men of Letters*, though first published as long ago as 1881. In this way, the *Guide* became one of the main conduits for transmitting the ideas I have discussed in previous chapters to a new generation of readers, including—for they were a notable element of the series's readership— students in the expanding higher-education system of the 1960s and 1970s. Individual volumes were selling over 20,000 copies a year in the UK in the late 1960s, and were mostly reprinted annually through the 1970s. By contrast, in-house reports showed each volume to be selling no more than 3,000–4,000 a year in the USA by the mid-1960s. As one of Penguin's New York staff reported, 'the reps tell me that the books are not well thought of in most departments of English, that the critical point of view is badly out of date'. A report commissioned from an American academic condemned the series as not professional enough to appeal to academics and graduate students: 'The whole tone is that of the facile amateur.'[24]

As Chris Hilliard has recently pointed out, some of the views originally associated with *Scrutiny* are reproduced in the volumes of the *Guide* but without what he calls the 'performative force' of the originals.[25] But this point can also be reversed to emphasize how such interpretations were represented as no longer being insurgent or sectarian but, rather, the accepted coin of literary studies—indeed, as the established fruits of critical-historical scholarship, a curious outcome given that these interpretations had initially been defined by their repudiation of all existing forms of historical scholarship. For example, the opening chapter to the volume on 'The Age of Shakespeare' by the Cambridge critic Leo Salingar distilled a good deal of social and intellectual history, but subordinated this to its overall contention that by the end of the period a damaging divorce between polite and popular culture had taken place. In other ways, too, the *Guide* often communicates a sense of decline, sometimes because of a nostalgia for the allegedly more settled communities of the past, sometimes just because the celebration of earlier great writers tends to secrete a chastened feeling of having fallen from such heights. As a confidential report on the series commissioned by Penguin in 1977 put it, the contributors 'tend to fall into rather routine lamentations against the modern world'.[26] The appearance of this knowing weariness in a reader's report in the later 1970s indicated just how decisively the heyday of such declinist literary-cultural history had, by that date, passed.

The Pelican Guide was by no means representative of English studies as a whole at the time, but one can see some of the same dynamics around a literary interpretation of cultural history at work in other minor subdisciplinary developments in the 1940s and 1950s, though without the same overarching cultural pessimism. For example, the beginnings of what came to be called 'Victorian Studies' can be traced to scholarship emanating from English departments, both in Britain and in the USA. It drew particularly on a series of influential works by John Holloway, Walter Houghton, Jerome Buckley, and Basil Willey concentrating on the intellectual life of Victorian Britain, though even here there could be a form of nostalgia at work. As Basil Willey, the most conservative of these writers, put it in 1949: 'In our own unpleasant century we are mostly displaced persons, and many feel tempted to take flight into the nineteenth as into a promised land.'[27] It may also be relevant to note that G. M. Young's sepia-tinted *Portrait of an Age* (1936) sold much better in the 1950s and 1960s than ever it had done in the first decade or more of its life, and in 1960 it was chosen to be one of the first of Oxford University Press's new paperbacks, going through seven paperback editions by 1973.[28] Looking back to the early years of the transformation of this interest into a thriving subdiscipline, Michael Wolff, who played something of a founding role in this development, recalled: 'The word "culture" was not then used as pervasively as it now is, though I had often spoken of what we were doing in Victorian studies as "cultural history".'[29] 'We', it should be noted, were overwhelmingly not historians. Much of the empirical groundwork for the new field was done by literary scholars interested in the history of periodicals and of reading more generally, such as Houghton or Richard Altick. As a later assessment put it: 'While literary studies has been the dominant partner within the Victorian studies project, cultural history has been its preferred methodology.'[30] Cultural history thus conceived was later to have its closest affinities with cultural studies, not with other branches of history.

A more prominent and more contested instance can be cited to underline the general point. It may seem that there is nothing further to be said about the notorious 'Two Cultures' controversy of the late 1950s and early 1960s. But even this overworked episode can be illuminated by recovering the clash between the imperial claims of a certain style of literary history and the sense of proprietorial entitlement among professional historians. Leavis had always been uncompromisingly clear about the value of the contributions to understanding to be expected from these quarters. 'It is the great novelists above all who give us our social history; compared with what is done in *their* work—their creative work—the histories of the professional social historian seem empty and unenlightening.'[31] This is the most high-toned, or even high-handed, version of the case, not helped by the fact that one is bound to wonder how much work by professional social historians since Trevelyan Leavis had actually read. After Leavis's notorious attack on Snow in 1962—which included the charge that 'He knows nothing of history'—the social and economic historians saw an opportunity to strike back.[32] Snow's close friend J. H. Plumb led the charge in confronting Leavis's account of the past, especially of the Industrial Revolution, with the findings of current historical scholarship, and the correspondence between Plumb and Snow reveals their concerted campaign to bring the artillery of professional historical scholarship to bear on Leavis's account of the past. In May 1962 Snow urged Plumb to give some radio talks 'about the historical findings on the Industrial Revolution' and asked for 'some information about the most up-to-date historical treatment'. Several weeks later, when Snow asked for more ammunition, Plumb quickly reassured him: 'We have a complete run of the *Economic History Review*.'[33]

As Snow insisted in his 'The Two Cultures: A Second Look', published in 1963: 'It is important for the pre-industrial believers to confront the social historians.'[34] Snow and Plumb agreed that the larger problem lay not just with Leavis but with the pernicious influence of the declinist view of history associated with literary critics more generally. As Plumb put it in a widely cited essay, antipathy to material progress had exercised a distorting power over literary and artistic representations of the past, adding pointedly: 'It runs like dry rot through literary criticism.'[35] Snow broadened the list of suspects to include E. P. Thompson, writing (in characteristic tones) to Plumb:

> I've no doubt that you've got your eye on E. P. Thompson. He is a lapsed (or dissident or Trotskyist) Marxist: I've never known anyone of that provenance have any judgement of any kind. But some of your chaps ought to cope with him. Things are going our way on this front, and when you've got your enemies down it is a good old English rule to kick them in the teeth.[36]

Those who voiced reservations about the benefits of economic progress tended to be stigmatized by Snow's supporters as 'happy peasants', longing for some organic society that never existed.[37] As a result of these and other episodes, any attempt to vindicate the claims of the organic was, as John Fraser put it, 'to lay oneself open to charges... of a major and reactionary misreading of cultural history'. And he went on, bearing out the comment by J. P. Cooper that I quoted in Chapter 1: 'And for a while in the Fifties and Sixties, it was hard to pick up one of the higher weeklies without coming across some sarcastic reference to the organic community or "the old wheelwright's shop".'[38] That counter-attack was largely successful: the next generation of literary scholars was less disposed to assert its dominion over the terrain of social and cultural history, while the more adventurous work of a new generation of professional historians in the 1960s and 1970s demonstrated their claims to sovereignty over it.

This episode also raises larger questions about the political affiliation of certain forms of history during this period. In so far as the literary critics after Eliot found congenial authorities among contemporary historians, it tended to be those figures whose focus on, or incorporation of, forms of social history involved a serious radical purpose or critical estimate, such as the Hammonds, Tawney, and, later, Thompson. And it also tended to be the case that it was left-wing historians who were most drawn to using literary sources at a time when that was unfashionable among their professional colleagues. In the 1940s and 1950s, probably no academic historian of the seventeenth century wrote more about literature than Christopher Hill. According to one later estimate:

> More than any other major historian of the seventeenth century, Hill values literature as an integral expression of English life. No-one else makes literary evidence so central to their interpretations; no one else so regularly reminds a generation fascinated with the inarticulate of those who read and wrote. Despite the modest nature of many of his texts, Hill is a historian of ideas and he has preserved intellectual history in a generation that has rejected more conventional intellectual historians.[39]

Similarly, Victor Kiernan and E. P. Thompson, both of whom studied English as undergraduates, wrote extensively on literary topics (Kiernan took a BA in English at Edinburgh; Thompson, taking advantage of the two-year degree available in wartime, took his BA in History and then spent his third year 'working on Elizabethan and Jacobean literature and history . . . his first love was probably always literature, especially poetry and drama').[40] It would be an exaggeration to see this as amounting to a paradox, but there is at first sight the minor puzzle that a form of commentary that in the hands of the most prominent literary critics tended to be declinist, and thus to nourish conservative attitudes towards the past, proved fertile soil for more progressive readings of history. In so far as there is anything genuinely puzzling here, it can be largely explained away by the hostility to industrial capitalism that united cultural critics of Right and Left. But it was also the case that those who wanted answers to some of the most pressing questions about the meaning of the human past found scant encouragement in the work of mainstream academic historians in the half century before the 1960s. Where Leavis or Knights may have seen an essential opposition between literature and Marxism (at least as represented by the English Marxism of the 1930s), some of their more radically minded historical colleagues of the next generation found a kind of common ground in the sympathetic recovery of those forms of experience excluded or occluded by official records.

III

The frequent conjoining of the names of Hoggart and Williams in mid-century discussions of cultural criticism is a reminder that literary-critical forms of cultural history found a favourable institutional location in adult education in the 1940s and 1950s. This was a setting that encouraged an emphasis on the centrality of the Industrial Revolution, an episode widely understood as initiating the distinctively modern form of the exploitation of the working class or, indeed, the very formation of that class. And, of course, it was from this milieu that E. P. Thompson wrote *The Making of the English Working Class*, the classic account of that formation. The publication of that book in 1963, and the great boost it gave to a radical kind of social history in the next two decades, takes us into a changed world beyond my chosen period, though it is relevant that, as already noted, Thompson read a good deal of English criticism at Cambridge in the 1940s and was later the editor of an admiring new edition of that staple of Leavisian reading lists, Sturt's *The Wheelwright's Shop*, where Thompson observed: 'It is worth remembering that we owe the recognition of the book as a classic to literary critics rather than social historians, and historians should be grateful to literary critics for their percipience.'[41] It would have to be said that the newly assertive social history of the 1960s and 1970s was not notable for its gratitude to literary critics of the previous two generations.[42]

The fact that Raymond Williams spent the formative years of his career as an adult-education tutor gave him a strong sense of audience and permanently marked his style. In later interviews and reflections he often spoke of trying to make ideas available to people who lacked much formal education, or of lending his authority to the task of liberating people from constraining or coercive ideas. Though at some level he also seemed to hanker after forms of academic recognition, his primary address was not to fellow-scholars, and this affected the initial reception of his work. As he wrote to his editor at Chatto, referring to the projected book that became *Culture and Society*: 'I fight shy of pushing out an idea through a university press.'[43] This applies particularly to *The Long Revolution*, published in 1961, which, although presented as a sequel to *Culture and Society*, was in reality a much more unorthodox book. Williams described it to his editor at Chatto as having 'three parts—theoretical, historical, and critical—on the development of English culture'. The book was 'not literary criticism, or only very partly so', but rather 'essays on the development of the reading public, the press, the educational system, and standard speech forms [taking]... certain key ideas—class, mobility, exile—in both literary and sociological terms, in what amounts to an attempt at a synoptic analysis of contemporary society'.[44] One thing that emerges clearly from this description is that for Williams the historical material is a contribution to the analysis of *contemporary* society.

The very conception of a 'long revolution' as something unfolding over time suggests that the project must be constitutively historical, and certainly the chapters in part two are potted histories. Yet the function of both parts one and two is essentially to dispose of obstructive or misconceived notions that might block or hamper a proper understanding of the present state of society, especially conservative arguments that claimed to see any form of democratic expansion as resulting in 'declining standards'.

If it seems difficult now to take the measure of *The Long Revolution* as a book, that is partly just because the three sections into which it is divided are so strikingly heterogeneous, both in matter and, still more, in level of treatment. Part one discusses, in remorselessly abstract terms, concepts of creativity, culture, society, and so on. These give off a very strong sense of the autodidact theorist at work, piecing together from wide-ranging but somewhat random reading a Heath Robinson conceptual assemblage that aimed to replace the 'outworn' antithesis of 'the individual and society'. Part two is made up of a series of empirical chapters on the history of several of the elements that compose what Williams saw as the third, cultural, prong of the 'long revolution' of his title—education, the 'reading public', the popular press, and so on. But to describe them as 'empirical', while it marks an obvious contrast with the chapters in part one, does not capture their curiously schematic quality. At one level, these chapters offer accounts of the history of their respective topics in the manner of a large-scale elementary textbook. Summaries of the development of, for example, education or the English language begin with a few brief remarks about the Middle Ages and then canter briskly down the centuries; the treatment is usually perfunctory until the nineteenth century is reached, and even then decades have to be skipped over or summed up in a phrase. But at another level the chapters have a strong argumentative drive that is somewhat at odds with their 'empirical' character: they are not so much condensed historical accounts as a series of rebuttals of an implicit counter-argument about 'cultural decline', a purpose that governs the selection and arrangement of what Williams liked to think of, in quasi-social-scientific terms, as 'the historical data'.[45] And then part three is quite different again, a polemic about some of the leading preoccupations of British culture at the beginning of the 1960s, emphasizing the obstacles to a properly socialist form of common culture. This part has some of the character of a free-standing pamphlet, including practical (though sometimes impracticable) policy proposals. Nor is the oddity of this part's relation to the first two confined to the generic disparity; there is also a certain tension in the tenor of the main arguments of each, with parts one and, especially, two emphasizing the steady 'advance' or 'growth' in cultural enfranchisement, while part three concentrates on the fallacies of a bien-pensant narrative of progress given the constituent class antagonisms of capitalism.

Much of the intellectual energy of *The Long Revolution* is devoted to relativizing some of the common assumptions of cultural debate in Britain at the end of the 1950s. But, while Williams still, as in earlier works, treats the Industrial Revolution as the central determinant of the character of English society thereafter, it is noticeable that he here often projects a much longer perspective, tracing his mini-histories from the Middle Ages onwards. Arguments about 'correct' pronunciation of English or complaints about the 'commercialization' of the reading public or alarm at the rise of a 'vulgar' press are all shown to have a long and recurring history, in the light of which the supposed developments of the last generation or so no longer appear persuasive or decisive. Implicitly, these chapters are rebutting some of the conservative conclusions drawn from the Leavisite analysis, a position from which Williams is more clearly distant than he had been in *Culture and Society*.

How well these historical chapters connect with the central argument about a 'long revolution' is very variable. Roughly speaking, those that deal with some form of cultural enfranchisement of the working class connect well enough; those that chart the 'sociology of a cultural form' (such as drama or even the realist novel) do so much less well. The chapter on the social background of English writers could, at a large stretch, be taken to show that the dominance of a certain narrowly educated class is relatively recent, but even then it allows no encouraging, let alone triumphalist, conclusions to be drawn. It is not easy to decide who are the implied readers of these chapters: perhaps people who share Williams's antipathy to conservative forms of the argument about 'declining standards' and who need to be supplied with brief digests of the relevant history? Yet the book seems to have made little impression on professional historians, in part, no doubt, because it was not easily legible as a work of history. Williams acknowledged, as we have seen, that he had 'risked an extension and variety of themes well beyond the limits of any kind of academic prudence', something that made many of the book's individual sections vulnerable to expert criticism. As he reflected, perhaps a little ruefully, three years after its publication: 'if the connexions I make and try to describe are not seen or not accepted, the book as a whole is bound to be difficult to bring into focus, and then its local difficulties are exaggerated.'[46]

The book quickly found a substantial readership. Following a relatively large first printing of 5,500 in 1961, Chatto had to rush out a further printing within a couple of months, and when it appeared in Pelican it soon sold over 50,000 copies.[47] But from reviewers it received a much less welcoming reception than its predecessor had done, and questions of disciplinary scope or identity came to the fore even more. According to Williams's later account: 'The degree of hostility was quite unforgettable. There was a full-scale attack of the most bitter kind in certain key organs. The *TLS* was particularly violent and *ad hominem*. But the reaction was very general.'[48] Reading those reviews (including the *TLS*) now, it is hard not to see Williams's description as a considerable exaggeration. Nonetheless, the chill wind of disciplinary as well as political disapproval could be felt blowing through some of the reviews. For example, to the unsympathetic eye of the conservative political historian Maurice Cowling, Williams was exceeding the bounds of any legitimate claim to intellectual authority.

> Merely because Lawrence saw intensely a small segment of English society and criticized it, it should not be imagined that it is the function of an English school to engage in 'social criticism' also. . . . The professional literary sensibility, in its professional field, has great authority; but in pretending to determine the course political action ought to take, it stretches itself beyond its limits.

This threatened what he called 'a new omnicompetence', and Cowling, ever alert to the attractions of killing two progressive birds with one conservative stone, mocked the overweening ambition of English scholars: 'There are no faculties in English universities (except the faculties of Political Science) where some dons are in greater danger of taking themselves too seriously.'[49] Cowling's essay appeared in the *Cambridge Review* in May 1961 shortly before Williams was due to take up his new appointment in the Cambridge English Faculty; it was clearly intended to be more of a warning shot than a welcoming embrace.

Such political animus was obviously not at issue with the much better-known two-part review of *The Long Revolution* by E. P. Thompson in *New Left Review*, also published in 1961, but for that very reason the review is particularly revealing of the reception of Williams's work among even well-disposed historians on the Left who had for some time been giving more sustained attention to questions of historical causality than the bulk of their mainstream professional colleagues. The main burden of Thompson's extended chastisement of Williams—for the piece was animated, as were so many of Thompson's spirited polemics, by a not wholly fraternal ardour—was that both *Culture and Society* and *The Long Revolution* risked representing the processes of change they described as altogether too eirenic or painless. What Williams saw as processes of 'growth', Thompson insisted had in fact been processes of conflict and struggle. But, along the way, Thompson also took issue with the genre of writing to which Williams's work belonged.

In *Culture and Society* Williams had focused on culture as 'a whole way of life', and in *The Long Revolution* he had expanded this remit to take in, as we have seen, what he now described as 'cultural history', defined as the study of 'relationships between elements in a whole way of life'. But, as Thompson pointedly commented: 'If Williams by "the whole way of life" really means the *whole* way of life he is making a claim, not for cultural history, but for history.' Thompson then went on: 'The fact that this claim can now be made, with some colour, against history by both critics and sociologists is a devastating comment upon the relegation of history to an inferior status in this country.' Thompson speculated briefly on the reasons for this condition. Perhaps Marxist historians had too much tended to ignore the kinds of cultural activity on which Williams focused; perhaps the lack in Britain of conceptual thinking about history, recently pointed to by E. H. Carr in his Trevelyan Lectures, was involved; perhaps, as Thompson put it, 'a further part lies in the eagerness with which academics in the empirical tradition have taken upon themselves the role of narrative drudges, making whole history schools into a kind of piece-meal baggage-train serving more ambitious departments'. Whatever the explanation, Thompson accepted that historians had not risen to a task that was properly theirs. 'I do not dispute, then, that Mr Williams may have been provoked into making his claim by the eagerness with which historians, under the chiding of Sir Lewis Namier and Professor Popper, have abandoned theirs. The place has been widely advertised as being "To Let".' What Thompson did dispute was that this space could be adequately occupied by a form of enquiry that focused on culture in the way that had been done by literary critics, in the wake of T. S. Eliot's conservative construal of that concept.[50]

For present purposes, there is no need to follow Thompson's critique into his valorization of a renewed form of the Marxist analysis of the relation between agency and determination in historical change. But it is worth pausing over his suggestion that critics, writing with what he called a 'kind of literary-sociological flair', had occupied a territory that professional historians had left vacant (he mentions Richard Hoggart alongside Williams as Eliot's leading contemporary heirs in this style). Whatever the truth of his general contentions about the place of history in Britain in the 1950s (a topic requiring more extended analysis), perhaps what was most striking about his challenge to Williams in the name of history is that it had to be made at all. For Thompson was surely right that both *Culture and Society* and *The Long Revolution* were historical works, and yet they were not presented or received as such. They had, after all, not been written by a historian and they scarcely ever referred to recent works of historical scholarship. To put the point in somewhat reductive guild terms, their world of reference was that of, say, *Essays in Criticism* rather than, say, the *English Historical Review*. The first of those journals carried long discussions of both of Williams's books, and, as we have seen, the earliest published adumbration of the argument of *Culture and Society* had appeared in its pages. The *EHR* noticed neither book.

In political terms, Thompson would presumably have taken this latter omission to constitute a badge of honour, but more generally his discussion was registering an unease about the disciplinary character of Williams's work and, especially, about some of the reasons for its current prominence. 'I am concerned', Thompson went on, 'at the fact that in the past few years so much stimulating writing has burgeoned in the field of criticism and literary-sociology: so little in the sciences and in traditional social studies; and so very little in the field of political theory'.[51] His was far from a narrowly academic concern with the relative standing of disciplines; he was expressing a passionate conviction that the kind of cultural critique that had been derived from literary criticism failed to grapple adequately with historical causation, and hence with all the questions about the primacy of class struggle that the Marxist tradition had focused on. His politics were, it hardly needs saying, at the opposite pole from Cowling's, but both of them were exercised by what they saw as the misplaced intellectual imperialism of literary criticism. In this respect, both were recognizing, as well as anticipating the end of, something that had been a significant feature of British culture since the 1920s.

Postscript

This book has argued, largely by means of detailed case studies, for the important place occupied by literary criticism in the broader intellectual history of mid-twentieth-century Britain. More specifically, it has suggested that such criticism functioned as an influential medium through which understandings of history, of various kinds, were negotiated and disseminated. Implicitly, the book has presumed that the category of 'literary criticism' is porous and unstable: reading, analysing, and responding to whatever is understood as 'literature' at any given moment will always draw on more than literature. Accordingly, the frontiers between forms of criticism, forms of literary history, and forms of general history are bound to be contested and shifting, with rival claims competing for dominion. Raymond Williams put one version of this case in its strong form when he wrote, in a sentence quoted earlier, that the use of language in literature 'is as much the record of the history of a people as political institutions and religions and philosophical modes'.[1] T. S. Eliot had been putting a similar case in more teasing terms when he wrote in that pregnant sentence from 1919 that serves as an epigraph to this book: 'The historian of literature must count with as shifting and as massive forces as the historian of politics.'[2] And it was Eliot who most frankly stated the consequences of this situation when he wrote of

> the dilemma which every honest literary critic, now and in the future, will have to face. On the one hand you cannot treat literary criticism as a subject isolated from every other subject of study; you must take account of general history, of philosophy, theology, economics, psychology, into all of which literary criticism merges. And on the other hand you cannot hope to embrace all of the various points of view implied by these various studies...[3]

In some respects, this hits a more modest or concessive note than many of the statements I have been discussing, but it also highlights some of the practical difficulties facing any attempt to write the history of literary criticism.

From the 1960s onwards, much of the debate in the Anglo-American academic world about the character and methods of intellectual history was conducted in relation either to the history of science or to the history of political thought. In both those fields there had been strong traditions of endogenous histories, principally dealing with a sequence of theoretical constructions and informed by the preoccupations of powerful modern disciplines, so they were fertile ground for a historicist counter-attack, though in both cases, especially the history of political thought, the continuing focus on a restricted number of canonical authors has limited the extent to which these fields have been fully subsumed into a wider intellectual history. The history of literary criticism has not, for the most part, been the scene of comparable revisionist campaigns; indeed, the field has received relatively little attention from intellectual historians more generally. Across the twentieth century there was no shortage of what, borrowing the term from the debates over the history of science, we may call 'internalist' histories, presenting a sequence of 'theories' and 'approaches'. Such accounts have their uses, but not only do they strip the story of much of its richness and often fail to do justice to the *practice* of literary criticism: they also tend to neglect what are potentially the most illuminating contexts for understanding individual critics' writings and omit what may be some of the most powerful explanations for the variety and impact of such criticism.

This book has touched on only one aspect of these wider relations—the commerce between literary criticism and a range of historical assumptions, frameworks, and claims—and it has confined itself to a few decades and to a single country. My canvas has, by design, been small. This is because, in addition to trying to illuminate a given topic, I have also hoped to illustrate a particular style of work. Such work involves a close and responsive attention to the verbal texture of the sources one is using, the kind of attention we may think to be characteristic of literary criticism itself—hence the reliance on extensive quotation. But it thereby involves, in addition, an intimate familiarity with a particular milieu or specific aspect of a culture. Writing history inevitably involves the use of both the telescope and the microscope. I have no inhibitions about deploying the former when appropriate—there is no shortage in this book of longer views and comparative judgements—but it will be evident that I am, temperamentally or as a matter of intellectual style, more drawn to the microscope and to the fine grain of discrimination that it enables.

Needless to say, such a limited topic can be shown, when subject to less sympathetic or more distanced scrutiny, to be parochial or to neglect matters that later generations have come to regard as mandatory. Indeed, it may be that such work is now in danger of falling into disrepute, scanted by those who believe that our times demand a focus on the transnational and damned by those promoting one or other form of direct engagement with contemporary concerns. I have to recognize that, in terms of who was thought to 'matter' in contemporary public debate or what aspects of the past were seen as 'significant' in that debate, the story told here risks being perceived, from a later perspective, as too indulgent towards the conventions of the period under scrutiny. Within the relatively narrow limits of the story I have tried to tell, I have not set out to challenge these characteristics or to unmask the significant exclusions they may entail, though I trust no reader will conclude that I thereby endorse them. There can, of course, be benefits in attempting to do what is now sometimes termed 'global intellectual history', which certainly avoids the parochial, but there are also costs. In any event, I have here attempted an appropriately bounded illustration of what can still be gained by working not just *on* an aspect of twentieth-century British culture where history and criticism intersected in telling ways, but also *in* a manner that attempts to combine elements of literary criticism and intellectual history.

In my view, the story told here is not one to which a later generation can feel superior, secure in the conviction that it has exposed and surpassed any inclination to indulge tendentious or nostalgic assumptions about the past by means of more rigorous and self-conscious critique. Each age imagines various pasts in response to changed circumstances and preoccupations in the present. The intellectual fashions that help to shape those imaginings may change, but such creative retrospection is not simply a phase that criticism, or even a whole culture, grows out of. Some future intellectual historian will be able to do for the historical assumptions underlying the dominant critical approaches of the decades since 1970 the equivalent of what I have attempted for the previous half-century. But it seems unlikely, given the range and depth of related social changes, that such an account could ever form as prominent a part of the history of that later period as the present discussion does for the years covered in this book. It also seems unlikely that any such study would confine itself to British (or, in practice, English) intellectual life in the way I have been able to do. Even in my chosen period, especially in the years after 1945, the academic culture of the United States is a presence increasingly to be reckoned with, while any tendency to insular monochromy needs to be streaked, in painting individual portraits, with such internationalizing elements as Eliot's cosmopolitanism and American roots, Empson's affiliations to the Far East, Williams's (in this period largely repressed) Welshness, and so on. The dimensions only touched on in these cases would call for more emphatic attention when examining later decades. Similarly, the cast of characters in the more recent period would not be so overwhelmingly male or so concentrated in the traditional centres of cultural power.

But, however much the limits of the present study might need to be challenged or extended when dealing with the more recent period, the theme itself will, I suggest, remain enduringly pertinent. To adapt a phrase from Frank Kermode—whom I have, in homage, already cited more than once—history is the imposition of a plot on time.[4] We live in time, but we understand the experience of life through form, and any structure manages our expectations, which easily fall into archetypal patterns, especially, as we have repeatedly seen, patterns of decline and fall. In making a selection from the infinite flux of what has been, we give it a shape, and all shapes suggest some primitive species of starting point and imply some vaguely adumbrated end. Making sense of our history, personal or collective, is, as I remarked in the Introduction, a constant struggle to find a way to master multifariousness without denying or violating it. If 'History has many cunning passages', as Eliot's familiar line declares, it should not surprise us that various forms of enquiry, literary criticism included, can find themselves being led through 'contrived corridors and issues' (Eliot again) as they try to assemble a usable past. I have attempted to track one sample of such traffic. Leslie Stephen acknowledged towards the end of the book that issued from his Ford Lectures that he was not providing a 'complete survey of the intellectual history of the time'.[5] In closing, I echo that caution, but nonetheless I offer this book as an illustration of what both intellectual historians and literary critics may have to gain by exploring their affinities, while at the same time suggesting that the results of such shared endeavours may also have their place in the field of 'British History' to which the Ford Lectures are dedicated.

Notes

INTRODUCTION

1. J. W. Burrow, *A Liberal Descent: Victorian Historians and the English Past* (Cambridge: Cambridge University Press, 1981), 65.

2. Stefan Collini, Donald Winch, and John Burrow, *That Noble Science of Politics: A Study in Nineteenth-Century Intellectual History* (Cambridge: Cambridge University Press, 1983), ch. 10.

3. Burrow, *Liberal Descent*, 240; see also James Kirby, *Historians and the Church of England: Religion and Historical Scholarship 1870–1920* (Oxford: Oxford University Press, 2016).

4. Ciaran Brady, *James Anthony Froude: The Intellectual Biography of a Victorian Prophet* (Oxford: Oxford University Press, 2013), esp. chs 7 and 10.

5. See Francis Turner Palgrave, *The Golden Treasury of the Best Songs and Lyrical Poems in the English Language* (1861), ed. Christopher Ricks (London: Penguin, 1991), 3, 432, 444. See also Michael J. Sullivan, 'Tennyson and The Golden Treasury', *Essays in Criticism*, 66 (2016), 431–43.

6. See, for illustration, Ted Underwood, *Why Literary Periods Mattered: Historical Contrast and the Prestige of Literary Studies* (Stanford: Stanford University Press, 2013), 118.

7. See the retrospect in René Wellek, 'Comparative Literature Today', *Comparative Literature*, 17 (1965), 325–37.

8. Stefan Collini, *Public Moralists: Political Thought and Intellectual Life in Britain 1850–1930* (Oxford: Oxford University Press, 1991), ch. 9.

9. E. de Sélincourt, *English Poets and the National Ideal* (London: Oxford University Press, 1915), 'Preface', 110, 116.

10. C. H. Firth, *The School of English Language and Literature: A Contribution to the History of Oxford Studies* (Oxford: Blackwell, 1909), 23; cf. D. J. Palmer, *The Rise of English Studies: An Account of the Study of English Language and Literature from its Origins to the Making of the Oxford English School* (London: Oxford University Press, 1965), 71.

11. C. H. Firth to H. J. C. Grierson, 23 July 1931; Grierson MSS 9332, National Library of Scotland.

12. John Kenyon, *The History Men: The Historical Profession in England since the Renaissance* (London: Weidenfeld & Nicolson, 1983), 271.

13. Peter Mandler, *History and National Life* (London: Profile, 2002), ch. 3; Michael Bentley, *Modernizing England's Past: English Historiography in the Age of Modernism 1870–1970* (Cambridge: Cambridge University Press, 2005), part II.

14. Mary O'Dowd, 'Popular Writers: Women Historians, the Academic Community, and National History Writing', in Ilaria Porciani and Jo Tollebeck (eds), *Setting the Standards: Institutions, Networks and Communities of National Historiography* (London: Palgrave, 2012), 365.

15. Mandler, *History and National Life*, 65, 86, 101.

16. Bentley, *Modernizing England's Past*, 208.

17. Christopher Parker, *The English Historical Tradition since 1850* (Edinburgh: John Donald, 1990), 10.

18. See David Cannadine, *G. M. Trevelyan: A Life in History* (London: HarperCollins, 1992). There is a large literature on most of these figures; two studies may particularly be mentioned: Victor Feske, *From Belloc to Churchill: Private Scholars, Public Culture, and the Crisis of British Liberalism, 1900–1939* (Chapel Hill, NC: University of North Carolina Press, 1996), and Julia Stapleton, *Sir Arthur Bryant: National History in Twentieth-Century Britain* (Lanham, MD: Lexington Books, 2005).

19. Parker, *The English Historical Tradition*, 127. Fisher's History 'continued to be reprinted or re-edited every year, bar 1939, until 1943, and again in 1949, 1952, and 1957' (p. 131).

20. Joseph Frank, 'Spatial Form in Modern Literature', *Sewanee Review*, 53 (1945), 221–40, as paraphrased in Chris Baldick, *Criticism and Literary Theory 1890 to the Present* (London: Longman, 1996), 69.

21. Edmund Wilson, *The Triple Thinkers: Twelve Essays on Literary Subjects* (2nd edn; Oxford: Oxford University Press, 1952 [1938]), 243 (Wilson was particularly referring to the criticism of T. S. Eliot); Frank Lentricchia, *After the New Criticism* (London: Methuen, 1983), p. xiii.

22. Quoted in J. P. Russo, *I. A. Richards: His Life and Work* (Baltimore: Johns Hopkins University Press, 1989), 35.

23. This view is most elegantly argued in David Perkins, *Is Literary History Possible?* (Baltimore: Johns Hopkins Press, 1992), a discussion to which I am indebted even when I depart from it.

24. Friedrich Nietzsche, 'On the Uses and Disadvantages of History for Life' (1974), *in Untimely Meditations*, trans. R. J. Hollingdale (Cambridge: Cambridge University Press, 1983), 59–123. The relevance of Nietzsche's essay is touched on from a different perspective in Perkins, *Literary History*, 175–86.

25. Nietzsche, 'On the Uses', 72.

26. Nietzsche, 'On the Uses', 76.

27. Matthew Arnold, 'The Study of Poetry' (1880), in *The Complete Prose Works of Matthew Arnold*, vol. ix, ed. R. H. Super (Ann Arbor: University of Michigan Press, 1973), 181.

28. Collini, *Public Moralists*, 355–6.

29. William C. Lubenow, 'Lytton Strachey's Eminent Victorians: The Rise and Fall of the Intellectual Aristocracy', in Miles Taylor and Michael Wolff (eds), *The Victorians since 1901: Histories, Representations, and Revisions* (Manchester: Manchester University Press, 2004), 24.

30. Ford Madox Ford, *Henry James* (1915), quoted in Michael Levenson, *A Genealogy of Modernism: A Study of English Literary Doctrine 1908–1922* (Cambridge: Cambridge University Press, 1984), 52.

31. T. E. Hulme, *Speculations: Essays on Humanism and the Philosophy of Art*, ed. Herbert Read (London: Routledge, 1924), esp. chs 1–3.

32. See R. F. Foster, *W. B. Yeats: A Life*, ii. *The Arch-Poet 1915–1939* (Oxford: Oxford University Press, 2003), 280–92.

33. W. B. Yeats (ed.), *The Oxford Book of Modern Verse 1892–1935* (Oxford: Oxford University Press, 1936), p. xxvii. See also Lucy McDiarmid, *Saving Civilization: Yeats, Eliot, and Auden between the Wars* (Cambridge: Cambridge University Press, 1984), 38.

34. T. S. Eliot (ed.), *The Literary Essays of Ezra Pound* (London: Faber, 1954), 12, 11.

35. David Nichol Smith, *The Functions of Criticism* (Oxford: Oxford University Press, 1909), 4, 15.

36. George Watson, *The Literary Critics: A Study of English Descriptive Criticism* (rev. edn; London: Chatto and Windus, 1986 [1962]), 201. Cf. Baldick's remark that no general history of criticism was written between Saintsbury and the mid-1950s; Baldick, *Criticism and Literary Theory*, 156.

37. T. S. Eliot, *The Sacred Wood: Essays on Poetry and Criticism* (London: Methuen, 1920); Raymond Williams, *The Long Revolution* (London: Chatto, 1961).

38. T. S. Eliot, *The Varieties of Metaphysical Poetry*, ed. Ronald Schuchard (London: Faber, 1993), 226.

CHAPTER I

1. J. P. Cooper (ed.), *The New Cambridge Modern History*, iv. *The Decline of Spain and the Thirty Years War, 1609–48* (Cambridge: Cambridge University Press, 1970), 8.

2. Valerie Eliot and John Haffenden (eds), *The Letters of T. S. Eliot*, iii. *1926–1927* (London: Faber, 2012), 141, 155–6, 155. This edition prints Geoffrey Faber's letter of 11 April 1926 to the Warden of All Souls in support of Eliot's application, Eliot's statement of his proposed research, and Faber's letter of 28 May 1926 to Eliot telling him of the failure of his candidacy.

3. T. S. Eliot, *The Varieties of Metaphysical Poetry*, ed. Ronald Schuchard (London: Faber, 1993), 74.

4. T. S. Eliot to Ezra Pound, 3 September 1923; to his mother, ['mid October'] 1923, in Valerie Eliot and Hugh Haughton (eds), *The Letters of T. S. Eliot*, ii. *1923–1925* (London: Faber, 2009), 208, 255. For Eliot's use of Robertson's Shakespeare criticism, see Steven Matthews, *T. S. Eliot and Early Modern Literature* (Oxford: Oxford University Press, 2013), esp. 54–8, 148–9.

5. T. S. Eliot to Sydney Schiff, 6 December 1920, in Valerie Eliot and Hugh Haughton (eds), *The Letters of T. S. Eliot*, i. *1898–1922* (rev. edn; London: Faber, 2009), 525.

6. 'T.S.E.', 'Humanist, Artist, and Scientist', *Athenaeum*, 10 October 1919, p. 1014. Eliot was here making a point principally about the history of philosophy.

7. See Stefan Collini, '"Vexing the Thoughtless": T. S. Eliot's Early Criticism', in Michael Hurley and Marcus Waithe (eds), *Thinking through Style: Non-Fiction Prose of the Long Nineteenth Century* (Oxford: Oxford University Press, 2018), 332–47.

8. See, e.g., Kenneth Asher, *Eliot and Ideology* (Cambridge: Cambridge University Press, 1995), 58.

9. I attempted to explore these views in Stefan Collini, 'The European Modernist as Anglican Moralist: The Later Social Criticism of T. S. Eliot', in Mark S. Micale and Robert L. Dietle (eds), *Enlightenment, Passion, Modernity: Historical Essays in European Thought and Culture* (Stanford: Stanford University Press, 2000), 207–29, 438–44.

10. T. S. Eliot, 'Commentary', *Criterion* (April 1924), 231.

11. T. S. Eliot, 'Reflections on Poetry', *Egoist* (November 1917), 151.

12. T. S. Eliot, 'The Function of Criticism' (1923), in Eliot, *Selected Essays* (3rd edn; London: Faber, 1951), 29.

13. T. S. Eliot to Bonamy Dobrée, 30 January 1931, in Valerie Eliot and John Haffenden (eds), *The Letters of T.S. Eliot*, v. *1930–31* (London: Faber, 2014), 476.

14. T. S. Eliot, 'Contemporary English Prose', *Vanity Fair*, 20 (July 1923), 15. This was the revised English text of 'Lettre d'Angleterre: Le Style dans la prose anglaise contemporaine', *Nouvelle revue française*, 19 (December 1922), 751–6.

15. T. S. Eliot, 'Poetical and Prosaic Use of Words', unpublished typescript, 1943. (Eliot's essay will appear in the relevant volume of the online edition of his complete prose; I am grateful to Dr Jason Harding for providing me with this reference.)

16. See Ronald Schuchard, 'T. S. Eliot as an Extension Lecturer 1916–1919', *Review of English Studies*, 25 (1974), 163–73, 292–304. 'The Reign of Elizabeth' was the subtitle given to the final six volumes of Froude's *History of England*, originally published in twelve volumes.

17. T. S. Eliot, review of Gooch, *Monthly Criterion*, 6 (November 1927), 471; see T. S. Eliot to Charles Whibley, 12 September 1927, in *Letters*, iii. 697. Gooch's book was first published in 1898.

18. Christopher Parker, *The English Historical Tradition since 1850* (Edinburgh: John Donald, 1990), 113–14.

19. Michael Bentley, *Modernizing England's Past: English Historiography in the Age of Modernism 1870–1970* (Cambridge: Cambridge University Press, 2005), 84.

20. C. Whibley to T. S. Eliot, 25 May 1927, quoted in *Letters*, iii. 538, n. 2.

21. The books reviewed were: William Trent et al., *A History of American Literature*, ii; George Saintsbury, *A History of the French Novel to the Close of the Nineteenth*

Century*; J. W Cunliffe, *English Literature during the Last Half-Century*; Frederick Pierce, *Currents and Eddies in the English Romantic Generation*; and Gregory Smith, *Scottish Literature: Character and Influence*.

22. 'T.S.E.', 'The Education of Taste', *Athenaeum*, 27 June 1919, p. 520.

23. 'T.S.E.', 'Was there a Scottish Literature?', *Athenaeum*, 1 August 1919, p. 681.

24. 'T.S.E.', 'Beyle and Balzac', *Athenaeum*, 30 May 1919, p. 392.

25. T. S. Eliot, 'A Neglected Aspect of Chapman' (unpublished lecture delivered at Cambridge November 1924), in Anthony Cuda and Ronald Schuchard (eds), *The Complete Prose of T. S. Eliot*, ii. *The Perfect Critic 1919–1926* (JHU and Faber 2014; Project Muse accessed 19 July 2016), 549, 554, 555.

26. *Letters*, ii. 531, 537.

27. Eliot, *Varieties of Metaphysical Poetry*, 53 (emphasis in original).

28. Eliot, *Varieties of Metaphysical Poetry*, 174–5.

29. Eliot, *Varieties of Metaphysical Poetry*, 158–9.

30. Eliot, *Varieties of Metaphysical Poetry*, 140.

31. Eliot, *Varieties of Metaphysical Poetry*, 224.

32. Eliot, *Varieties of Metaphysical Poetry*, 226.

33. Eliot, *Varieties of Metaphysical Poetry*, 227.

34. T. S. Eliot, 'Tradition and the Practice of Poetry', *Southern Review*, 21 (1985); quoted in Barry Spurr, *'Anglo-Catholic in Religion': T. S. Eliot and Christianity* (Cambridge: Lutterworth Press, 2010), 108.

35. Eliot, *Varieties of Metaphysical Poetry*, 41.

36. T. S. Eliot, *Homage to John Dryden: Three Essays on Poetry of the Seventeenth Century* (London: Hogarth Press, 1924), 9.

37. T. S. Eliot, *For Lancelot Andrewes: Essays on Style and Order* (London: Faber, 1970 [1st edn, 1928]), 7.

38. T. S. Eliot, *The Sacred Wood* (2nd edn; London: Methuen, 1928), p. viii.

39. T. S. Eliot, *The Use of Poetry and the Use of Criticism: Studies in the Relation of Criticism to Poetry in England* (London: Faber, 1933), 62.

40. T. S. Eliot, 'The Metaphysical Poets' [1921], in *Selected Essays* (London: Faber, 1932; rev. edn, 1951), 287–8.

41. Edwin Muir, review of 'Homage to Dryden' [*sic*], *Calendar of Modern Letters*, 1 (May 1925), 242.

42. T. S. Eliot, 'The Frontiers of Criticism' (1956), repr. in T. S. Eliot, *On Poetry and Poets* (London: Faber, 1957), 106.

43. Spurr, *'Anglo-Catholic in Religion'*, ch. 5, gives a cogent account of why it is not strictly accurate to speak of 'conversion', but he nonetheless concedes that this is the accepted description.

44. I have attempted to explore Eliot's deployment of the authority of 'the man of letters' in Stefan Collini, *Absent Minds: Intellectuals in Britain* (Oxford: Oxford University Press, 2006), ch. 13.

45. For fuller discussion of this point, see Collini, 'European Modernist as Anglican Moralist'.

46. Spurr, *'Anglo-Catholic in Religion'*, 84.

47. Spurr, *'Anglo-Catholic in Religion'*, ch. 4. For the uneven chronology of the larger religious decline, see S. J. D. Green, *The Passing of Protestant England* (Cambridge: Cambridge University Press, 2010).

48. T. S. Eliot, 'Lancelot Andrewes', *Times Literary Supplement*, 23 March 1926, pp. 621–2, repr. in Eliot, *For Lancelot Andrewes*, quotations at pp. 12, 15.

49. Eliot to E. G. Selwyn, 9 December 1926, in *Letters*, iii. 336–7. 'Archbishop Bramhall' appeared in *Theology*, 15 (July 1927), 11–17, repr. in Eliot, *For Lancelot Andrewes* as 'John Bramhall'.

50. Eliot, 'John Bramhall', 28–9.

51. T. S. Eliot, 'The English Tradition: Some Thoughts as a Preface to Study', *Christendom*, 10 (June 1940), 101–8; 'The English Tradition: Address to the School of Sociology', *Christendom*, 10 (December 1940), 228–37.

52. Eliot, 'The English Tradition: Address to the School of Sociology', 226, 233, 228.

53. For this genealogy, see Willard Wolfe, *From Radicalism to Socialism: Men and Ideas in the Formation of Fabian Socialist Doctrines, 1881–1889* (New Haven: Yale University Press, 1975), esp. part I.

54. Eliot, 'The English Tradition: Address to the School of Sociology', 233, 237.

55. For its canonical status, see F. W. Bateson, 'Contributions to a Dictionary of Critical Terms, II: Dissociation of Sensibility', *Essays in Criticism*, 1 (1951), 302–12. For an example of the influence of Eliot's notion in the quite different field of architecture, see Anthony Geraghty, 'The "Dissociation of Sensibility" and the "Tyranny of the Intellect": T. S. Eliot, John Summerson, and Christopher Wren', in Frank Salmon (ed.), *The Persistence of the Classical: Essays on Architecture Presented to David Watkin* (London: Philip Wilson, 2008) (I am grateful to Prof. William Whyte for this reference).

56. T. S. Eliot, 'Milton II', *Proceedings of the British Academy* (1947), repr. in T. S. Eliot, *On Poetry and Poets* (London: Faber, 1957), 148, 153.

57. Quoted in Alexander Hutton, '"Culture and Society" in Conceptions of the Industrial Revolution in Britain, 1930–1965', Ph.D. dissertation, Cambridge, 2014, pp. 283–4 (I am grateful to Dr Hutton for permission to quote this passage).

58. Frank Kermode, *Romantic Image* (London: Routledge, 1957), 140.

59. Kermode, *Romantic Image*, 140, 141, 139.

60. Kermode, *Romantic Image*, 166.

CHAPTER 2

1. F. R. Leavis and Denys Thompson, *Culture and Environment: The Training of Critical Awareness* (London: Chatto, 1933), 93.

2. As early as 1979 Francis Mulhern could, justifiably, observe: 'The meaning that *Scrutiny* discerned in the social history of modern England is by now a legend' (Francis Mulhern, *The Moment of 'Scrutiny'* (London: New Left Books, 1979), 57).

3. See F. R. Leavis, *Letters in Criticism*, ed. John Tasker (London: Chatto, 1974), 58; Denys Thompson, 'Teacher and Friend', in Denys Thompson (ed.), *The Leavises: Recollections and Impressions* (Cambridge: Cambridge University Press, 1984), 48; Christopher Hilliard, *English as a Vocation: The 'Scrutiny' Movement* (Oxford: Oxford University Press, 2012), 47–9.

4. Hilliard, *English as a Vocation*, 50.

5. F. R. Leavis, *Education and the University: A Sketch for an 'English School'* (London: Chatto, 1943), 48.

6. Richard Storer, '*Education and the University*: Structure and Sources', in Ian MacKillop and Richard Storer (eds), *F. R. Leavis: Essays and Documents* (Sheffield: Sheffield Academic Press, 1995), 137.

7. David Gervais, *Literary Englands: Versions of 'Englishness' in Modern Writing* (Cambridge: Cambridge University Press, 1993), 139, 143.

8. F. R. Leavis, 'T. S. Eliot as Critic' [1958], repr. in F. R. Leavis, *'Anna Karenina' and Other Essays* (London: Chatto, 1967), 177–8. Cf. the different emphasis in F. R. Leavis, 'Approaches to T. S. Eliot' [1949], repr in F. R. Leavis, *The Common Pursuit* (London: Chatto, 1952), 280.

9. See Stefan Collini, 'Vexing the Thoughtless: T. S. Eliot's Early Criticism', in Michael Hurley and Marcus Waithe (eds), *Thinking through Style: Non-Fiction Prose of the Long Nineteenth Century* (Oxford: Oxford University Press, 2018), 332–47.

10. Here I differ slightly from Leavis's biographer, Ian MacKillop, who, in the only substantial scholarly reference to Leavis's thesis, emphasizes adumbrations of later Leavisian themes: Ian MacKillop, *F. R. Leavis: A Life in Criticism* (London: Allen Lane, 1995), 73–4.

11. F. R. Leavis, 'The Relationship of Journalism to Literature: Studied in the Rise and Earlier Development of the Press in England', Ph.D. dissertation, Cambridge, 1924, pp. 291–2.

12. Leavis, 'Relationship of Journalism', 329.

13. Leavis, 'Relationship of Journalism', 336, 338, quoting Irving Babbitt, *The Masters of Modern French Criticism* (London: Constable, 1913), 100.

14. Habermas's *Habilitationsschrift* was submitted in 1959 and published in 1962 as *Strukturwandel der Öffentlichkeit*; it appeared in English as *The Structural Transformation of the Public Sphere: An Inquiry into a Category of Bourgeois Society*, trans. Thomas Burger and Frederick Lawrence (Cambridge, MA: MIT Press, 1989). See esp. sect. II, 'Social Structures of the Public Sphere', for the use of Stephen, Trevelyan, and other English authorities.

15. W. J. Courthope, *Life in Poetry, Law in Taste* (London: Macmillan, 1901), 29, quoted in Chris Baldick, *Criticism and Literary Theory 1890 to the Present* (London: Longman, 1996), 37–8.

16. Baldick, *Criticism and Literary Theory*, 37.

17. David Cannadine, *G. M. Trevelyan: A Life in History* (London: Harper Collins, 1992), 99.

18. Alexandre Beljame, *Men of Letters and the English Public in the Eighteenth Century: 1660–1744, Dryden, Addison, Pope*, ed. Bonamy Dobrée and trans. Emily Overend Lorimer (London: Routledge and Kegan Paul, 1948 [first published in French 1881; 2nd edn, 1897]), pp. ix–x, 385–6.

19. 'F. R. Leavis', Board of Graduate Study files, 1, 1920–37, file 992; University Archives, Cambridge University Library. I am grateful to the Archivist, Ms Jacqueline Cox, for help in locating this source.

20. MacKillop says the internal examiner was Leavis's supervisor, Sir Arthur Quiller-Couch, but, while that seems to have been the usual practice in Cambridge at the time, the file shows that it was clearly not followed in this case; MacKillop, *F. R. Leavis*, 73–4.

21. F. R. Leavis, 'Sociology and Literature', *Scrutiny*, 13 (1945), 74–81; Leavis, *Common Pursuit*, 195–203.

22. The version of the essay published in *The Common Pursuit* omits this, since by that date the translation had appeared.

23. Leavis, 'Sociology and Literature', 77; *Common Pursuit*, 198.

24. A. S. Collins, *The Profession of Letters 1780–1832: Authorship in the Age of Johnson* (London: Routledge, 1928), 5, 9.

25. Leavis, 'Sociology and Literature', 77n.; *Common Pursuit*, 198n.

26. For the first remark, see Q. D. Leavis to David Craig, 24 May 1955, archives of Girton College, Cambridge; I am grateful to Christopher Hilliard for this reference. For the second, Q. D. Leavis, 'A Glance Backward, 1965', in Q. D. Leavis, *Collected Essays*, i. *The Englishness of the English Novel*, ed. G. Singh (Cambridge: Cambridge University Press, 1983), 13, 11. It would be pleasing to think that such immortality might be enjoyed by all books based on Ford Lectures.

27. Bonamy Dobrée, 'Introduction', in Beljame, *Men of Letters*; for his reservations about Eliot's claim, see Bonamy Dobrée, 'The Claims of Sensibility', *Humanitas* (Autumn 1946), 55–8, at 57.

28. Leavis, 'Sociology and Literature', 79; *Common Pursuit*, 201.

29. It was reprinted both in F. R. Leavis, *For Continuity* (Cambridge: Minority Press, 1933), and in the 1948 edition of *Education and the University*.

30. F. R. Leavis, *How to Teach Reading: A Primer for Ezra Pound* (1932), repr. in the expanded edition of F. R. Leavis, *Education and the University* (Cambridge: Cambridge University Press, 1979), 106.

31. F. R. Leavis, 'What's Wrong with Criticism?', *Scrutiny*, 1 (1932–3), 145.

32. J. A. Smith, '*Scrutiny*'s Eighteenth Century', *Essays in Criticism*, 64 (2014), 318–40.

33. F. R. Leavis, 'William Empson: Intelligence and Sensibility', *Cambridge Review*, 16 January 1931, pp. 186–7, repr. in F. R. Leavis, *Valuation in Criticism and Other Essays*, ed. G. Singh (Cambridge: Cambridge University Press, 1986), 28.

34. Leavis and Thompson, *Culture and Environment*, 93.

35. Leavis and Thompson, *Culture and Environment*, 2.

36. Having already drafted but not published this phrase, I had understandably mixed feelings when I read in Hilliard's excellent *English as a Vocation*: 'The

capital of the modernity that troubled *Scrutiny*'s core contributors was not Victorian Manchester but interwar Muncie, Indiana' (pp. 55–6).

37. Leavis and Thompson, *Culture and Environment*, 53.

38. Leavis and Thompson, *Culture and Environment*, 4–5.

39. Leavis and Thompson, *Culture and Environment*, 6.

40. I am grateful to the late David Pocock for furnishing me with details of the backgrounds and careers of his fellow-migrants from English to Anthropology; Pocock's account of his own relationship with Leavis is included in the collection of Leavis materials he deposited in the library of Emmanuel College, Cambridge.

41. His pedagogical scheme was developed in most detail in a series of articles in *Scrutiny*: 'Education and the University (I): Sketch for an English School', 9 (1940), 98–120; 'Education and the University (II): Criticism and Comment', 9 (1940), 259–70; 'Education and the University (III): Literary Studies', 9 (1941), 306–22; 'Education and the University (IV): Considerations at a Critical Time', 11 (1943), 162–7; the book version, *Education and the University: A Sketch for an 'English School'*, was published by Chatto in 1943. For *Mill on Bentham and Coleridge*, see n. 58.

42. F. R. Leavis, 'English Poetry in the Seventeenth Century', *Scrutiny*, 4 (1935), 252. This review essay then formed the first chapter of F. R. Leavis, *Revaluation: Tradition and Development in English Poetry* (London: Chatto, 1936), quotation at p. 34.

43. Cf. from a student's notes in the late 1950s: 'Dissociation of Sensibility: Eliot recorded a fact of the first importance about the seventeenth century, but there is no satisfactory account or interpretation of it', in MacKillop and Storer (eds), *F. R. Leavis, Essays and Documents*, 72.

44. L. C. Knights, 'Tradition and Ben Jonson', *Scrutiny*, 4 (1935), 151n. See also Denys Thompson, 'The Robber Barons', *Scrutiny*, 5 (1936), 8, 11.

45. See Stefan Collini, 'Where did it All Go Wrong?: Cultural Critics and "Modernity" in Inter-War Britain', in E. H. H. Green and D. M. Tanner (eds), *The Strange Survival of Liberal England: Political Leaders, Moral Values, and the Reception of Economic Debate* (Cambridge: Cambridge University Press, 2007), 247–74.

46. Leavis, *Education and the University*, 49.

47. W. W. Robson, 'The Teaching of English Literature, I: The Future of English Studies', *Times Literary Supplement*, 25 July 1968, p. 773, col. 5.

48. Leavis, *Education and the University*, 54.

49. F. R. Leavis, 'Education and the University: Criticism and Comment', *Scrutiny*, 9 (1940–1), 266.

50. Leavis, *Education and the University*, 53–4.

51. David Hopkins, 'Dr Leavis's Seventeenth Century', *Essays in Criticism*, 64 (2014), 293–317.

52. F. R. Leavis, *English Literature in our Time and the University* (London: Chatto, 1969), 94–5.

53. See Michael Bentley, *Modernizing England's Past: English Historiography in the Age of Modernism 1870–1970* (Cambridge: Cambridge University Press, 2005), esp. part II.

54. F. R. Leavis, 'Education and the University: Sketch for an English School', *Scrutiny*, 9 (1940–1), 114–15; *Education and the University*, 58–9.

55. The symbolism, and the misrepresentations, are well discussed in Donald Winch, 'Mr Gradgrind and Jerusalem', in Stefan Collini, Richard Whatmore, and Brian Young (eds), *Economy, Polity, and Society: British Intellectual History 1750–1950* (Cambridge: Cambridge University Press, 2000), 243–66.

56. Michael Oakeshott, 'The New Bentham', *Scrutiny*, 1 (1932–3), 114–31, quotation at p. 130.

57. D. W. Harding, 'Evaluations (1): I. A. Richards', *Scrutiny*, 1 (1932–3), 327–38; F. R. Leavis, 'Dr Richards, Bentham and Coleridge', *Scrutiny*, 3 (1934–5), 382–402, quotation at p. 385.

58. F. R. Leavis, 'Mill, Beatrice Webb and the "English School": Preface to an Unprinted Volume', *Scrutiny*, 16 (1949), 104–26; this is largely reproduced as the introduction (pp. 1–38) in F. R. Leavis (ed.), *Mill on Bentham and Coleridge* (London: Chatto, 1950); page references will hereafter be given to the *Scrutiny* version.

59. F. R. Leavis to R. G. Cox, 19 June 1946; Leavis Papers, DCPP/Cox/1, Downing College Archives, Cambridge; a copy of the typed guidance on reading is attached to this letter.

60. Leavis, 'Mill, Beatrice Webb, and the "English School"', 110–11. As a further small indication of Leavis's reliance upon Leslie Stephen, he here cites the latter's 'English Men of Letters' volume on George Eliot as important for understanding 'her intellectual and religious background', a work now to be supplemented by Trilling on Matthew Arnold (p. 112, n. 6).

61. Leavis, 'Mill, Beatrice Webb, and the "English School"', 114, 116, 119.

62. Leavis, 'Mill, Beatrice Webb, and the "English School"', 120, 123, 121.

63. Leavis, 'Mill, Beatrice Webb, and the "English School"', 124, 122, 124.

64. Winch, 'Mr Gradgrind and Jerusalem', 245–6.

65. F. R. Leavis, *The Great Tradition: George Eliot, Henry James, Joseph Conrad* (London: Chatto, 1948; Pelican, 1972), 269.

66. Leavis, 'Mill, Beatrice Webb, and the "English School"', 123–4.

67. Leavis, 'Mill, Beatrice Webb, and the "English School"', 124, 125, 126.

68. Leavis recommended both these books to successive generations of Downing English students; see, e.g., MacKillop and Storer (eds), *F. R. Leavis*, 64.

69. From the introduction to *British History in the Nineteenth Century*, quoted in Cannadine, *Trevelyan*, 109.

70. Quoted in Cannadine, *Trevelyan*, 108–9.

71. 'What more is needed concerning Mill's development will be found very accessible in Leslie Stephen's *The English Utilitarians, Vol III: John Stuart Mill*' (Leavis, 'Mill, Beatrice Webb, and the "English School"', 121n.).

72. R. G. Cox, 'The Great Reviews (II)', *Scrutiny*, 6 (1937–8), 175.

CHAPTER 3

1. L. J. Potts, 'The Seventeenth Century' [review of *The Seventeenth-Century Background*], *Cambridge Review*, 4 May 1934, pp. 365–7.

2. Potts, 'Seventeenth Century', 365–6.

3. H. J. C. Grierson, 'What Is Truth?' [review of *The Seventeenth-Century Background*], *Scrutiny*, 3 (December 1934), 299, 297, 302–3. Grierson added, somewhat opaquely: 'A greater change in human thinking, Professor Stout has said, took place in the later years of the seventeenth century than has ever occurred since men began to think' (p. 296).

4. Basil Willey, *The Seventeenth-Century Background: Studies in the Thought of the Age in Relation to Poetry and Religion* (London: Chatto, 1934; Peregrine Books edn 1962), 45.

5. Willey, *Seventeenth-Century Background*, 47.

6. Willey, *Seventeenth-Century Background*, 83–4.

7. Basil Willey, *Cambridge and Other Memories* (London: Chatto, 1968), 60.

8. A. N. Whitehead, *Science and the Modern World* (Cambridge: Cambridge University Press, 1926), 71, 72.

9. Whitehead, *Science and the Modern World*, 132–3, 122.

10. Whitehead, *Science and the Modern World*, 284.

11. Whitehead, *Science and the Modern World*, 14, 225. Neither citation was very substantial: the first supported a claim about the medieval inheritance of Roman law, and the second provided an example of the topographical beliefs of a sixth-century monk.

12. James Johnston Auchmuty, *Lecky: A Biographical and Critical Essay* (London: Longman, 1945), 66, 130.

13. Willey, *Seventeenth-Century Background*, 26.

14. Willey, *Seventeenth-Century Background*, 16, 18.

15. Willey, *Seventeenth-Century Background*, 27, 28.

16. Willey, *Seventeenth-Century Background*, 176–7.

17. Willey, *Seventeenth-Century Background*, 53.

18. Willey, *Seventeenth-Century Background*, 264, 277.

19. Willey, *Seventeenth-Century Background*, 60.

20. John Beer, 'Basil Willey 1897–1978', *Proceedings of the British Academy*, 66 (1980), 473–93, quotations at pp. 473, 486.

21. There had been one indirect allusion in his first book, where Locke is referred to as the father of 'laissez-faire economics' (Willey, *Seventeenth-Century Background*, 240).

22. Basil Willey, *The Eighteenth-Century Background: Studies on the Idea of Nature in the Thought of the Period* (London: Chatto, 1940), 291.

23. Willey, *Eighteenth-Century Background*, 291–2.

24. M. M. Mahood, 'Review of S. L. Bethell, *The Cultural Revolution of the Seventeenth Century*', *Review of English Studies*, 4 (1953), 76.

25. Willey, *Cambridge and Other Memories*, 31.

26. Basil Willey, *Spots of Time: A Retrospect of the Years 1897–1920* (London: Chatto, 1965), 101.

27. Willey, *Nineteenth Century Studies*, 69.

28. [H. J. Laski], 'Review of *Nineteenth-Century Studies*', *Times Literary Supplement*, 2 December 1949, p. 790.

29. Graham Hough, 'The Nineteenth Century', *Cambridge Review*, 11 February 1950, pp. 316–17.

30. J. C. Maxwell, 'Review of *Nineteenth-Century Studies*', *Universities Quarterly* (February 1950), 204–6.

31. Stefan Collini, '"The Chatto List": Publishing Literary Criticism in Mid-Twentieth-Century Britain', *Review of English Studies*, 63 (2012), 634–63, esp. 644–7.

32. An earlier version of parts of the following account appeared in Stefan Collini, 'Where did it All Go Wrong? Cultural Critics and "Modernity" in Interwar Britain', in E. H. H. Green and Duncan Tanner (eds), *The Strange Survival of Liberal England* (Cambridge: Cambridge University Press, 2007), 247–74.

33. Denys Thompson, 'The Machine Unchained', *Scrutiny*, 2/2 (September 1933), 188; Donald F. Kitching, 'Will Economics Follow the Robbins Road?', and H. E. Batson, 'Mr Kitching on the Insignificance of Economics', *Scrutiny*, 1/2 (September 1933), 165–74, 175–81; H. E. Batson, 'Amateurism and Professionalism in Economics', *Scrutiny*, 3/1 (June 1934), 37–43; L. C. Knights, 'Shakespeare and Profit Inflations: Notes for the Historian of Culture', *Scrutiny*, 5/1 (June 1936), 48–60; this was to form the first chapter of *Drama and Society in the Age of Jonson*, published the following year.

34. Leavis, *For Continuity*, 21.

35. Denys Thompson, 'England and the Octopus', *Scrutiny*, 3/2 (September 1934), 175.

36. F. R. Leavis, 'Under which King, Bezonian?', in Leavis, *For Continuity*, 162.

37. L. C. Knights, *Drama and Society in the Age of Jonson* (Harmondsworth: Penguin, 1962 [1st edn, Chatto, 1937).

38. Raymond Williams, *Politics and Letters: Interviews with* New Left Review (London: New Left Books, 1979), 92; E. P. Thompson, '*Left Review*' (1971), repr. in Raymond Thompson, *Persons and Polemics* (London: Merlin, 1994), 234.

39. F. W. Bateson, *English Poetry: A Critical Introduction* (London: Longmans, 1950), 97.

40. Elizabeth Bowen, 'Ben Jonson', *New Statesman*, 9 May 1937, p. 775; Guy Burgess, 'The Seventeenth-Century Synthesis', *Spectator*, 23 March 1934, p. 466.

41. L. C. Knights, 'Middleman', 118–19; this is a typescript autobiography now held in the Cambridge University Library; I am grateful to Prof. Ben Knights for furnishing me with a copy.

42. Knights, *Drama and Society*, 30.

43. Knights, *Drama and Society*, 34, 37.

44. C. T. McIntire, *Herbert Butterfield: Historian as Dissenter* (New Haven: Yale University Press, 2004), ch. 5; Michael Bentley, *The Life and Thought of Herbert*

Butterfield: History, Science and God (Cambridge: Cambridge University Press, 2011), 216, 263.

45. Knights, *Drama and Society*, 34.

46. This was, in fact, a slight misquotation: 'The point might be enforced by saying (there is no need to elaborate) that Shakespeare did not invent the language he used...' (Leavis, *For Continuity*, 164).

47. Knights, *Drama and Society*, 20–1.

48. Knights evidently took Yeats's historical reflections seriously: see his 1941 essay for a sympathetic discussion of Yeats's assertions about the loss of 'unity of being' in the modern world: 'Poetry and Social Criticism: The Work of W. B. Yeats' [originally published in the *Southern Review* in 1941], repr. in L. C. Knights, *Explorations: Essays in Criticism Mainly on the Literature of the Seventeenth Century* (Harmondsworth: Penguin, 1964 [1st edn, Chatto, 1946]), 176–90.

49. Knights, *Drama and Society*, 149.

50. Knights, *Drama and Society*, 25.

51. Knights, *Drama and Society*, 29, 34.

52. Knights, *Drama and Society*, 17, 259.

53. Knights, *Drama and Society*, 183.

54. Knights, 'Middleman', 191.

55. Knights, *Drama and Society*, 21.

56. Knights, *Drama and Society*, 149–50.

57. Knights, *Drama and Society*, 149.

58. H. M. Robertson, *Aspects of the Rise of Economic Individualism: A Criticism of Max Weber and his School* (Cambridge: Cambridge University Press, 1933).

59. Talcott Parsons, 'H. M. Robertson on Max Weber and his School', *Journal of Political Economy*, 43 (1935), 688–96.

60. Peter Ghosh, *Max Weber and 'The Protestant Ethic': Twin Histories* (Oxford: Oxford University Press, 2014).

61. L. C. Knights, 'Bacon and the Seventeenth-Century Dissociation of Sensibility', *Scrutiny*, 11/3 (Summer 1943), repr. in Knights, *Explorations*, quotation at p. 101.

62. Knights, *Explorations*, 101–2.

63. Knights, *Explorations*, 117–19.

64. Harold Wendell Smith, '"Reason" and the Restoration Ethos', 18/2 (Autumn 1951), 118–36; '"The Dissociation of Sensibility"', 18/3 (Winter 1951–2), 175–88; 'Nature, Correctness, and Decorum', 18/4 (June 1952), 287–314; 'Cowley, Marvell, and the Second Temple', 19/3 (Spring 1953), 184–205.

65. Smith, 'Dissociation of Sensibility', 187–8.

66. Marjorie Cox, 'Correspondence', *Scrutiny*, 18 (1951–2), 189.

67. Durkheim made this case as part of his criticism of Herbert Spencer's individualism in *De la division du travail social* (Paris: Alcan, 1893); see the discussion in Steven Lukes, *Emile Durkheim, his Life and Work: A Historical and Critical Study* (London: Allen Lane, 1973), ch. 7.

CHAPTER 4

1. Roger Sale, 'The Achievement of William Empson', *Hudson Review*, 19 (1966), 369–90, repr. in Roger Sale, *Modern Heroism: Essays on D. H. Lawrence, William Empson, and J. R. R. Tolkien* (Berkeley and Los Angeles: University of California Press, 1973), quotation at p. 138.

2. William Empson, *Seven Types of Ambiguity* (London: Chatto, 1953 [1st edn, 1930]). Empson made numerous significant revisions of the 1930 text for the second edition in 1947, but they do not affect my argument. The third edition of 1953, which essentially reproduces the 1947 text, was thereafter frequently reprinted and is the form in which the book has been most widely read.

3. Empson, *Seven Types*, 2–3. In the first edition, the phrase in parentheses read: '("for oh, the hobby-horse is forgot" and the Puritans have cut down the Maypoles)'.

4. Empson, 'Note for the Third Edition' (1953), p. xvi; and see the exchange with F. W. Bateson, 'Bare Ruined Choirs', *Essays in Criticism*, 3 (1953), 357–62.

5. Empson, *Seven Types*, 20.

6. Oscar Wilde, 'The Critic as Artist', in *Intentions* (1891); quotation in Richard Ellmann (ed.), *The Artist as Critic: Critical Writings of Oscar Wilde* (New York: Random House, 1969), 346.

7. Empson, *Seven Types*, 103.

8. Empson, *Seven Types*, 187.

9. Empson, *Seven Types*, 236.

10. Empson, *Seven Types*, 237.

11. See Ch. 2, n. 33.

12. Empson, *Seven Types*, 242. Later in his career he elaborated this conviction in a series of detailed studies: see William Empson, *Using Biography* (London: Chatto, 1984).

13. Empson, *Seven Types*, 243.

14. Empson, *Seven Types*, 244–5. The first edition has 'he may indeed have created' for 'indeed he may create'.

15. Empson, *Seven Types*, 255.

16. Empson, *Seven Types*, 256.

17. Sale, 'Achievement of William Empson', 162.

18. William Empson, *Some Versions of Pastoral* (London: Chatto, 1935; Peregrine edn, 1966), 17.

19. Empson, *Some Versions*, 17.

20. Empson, *Some Versions*, 18.

21. Empson, *Some Versions*, 19.

22. Empson, *Some Versions*, 23.

23. Arthur Mizener, 'The Truest Poetrie', *Partisan Review*, 5 (June 1938), 57.

24. William Empson, *The Structure of Complex Words* (London: Chatto, 1951), 44.

25. Quoted in John Haffenden, *William Empson*, ii. *Against the Christians* (Oxford: Oxford University Press, 2006), 275.

26. Quoted in Haffenden, *Against the Christians*, 274.

27. Empson, *Complex Words*, 202.

28. William Empson, 'The Verbal Analysis', *Kenyon Review* (1950), 594–601, repr. in William Empson, *Argufying: Essays on Literature and Culture*, ed. John Haffenden (London: Chatto, 1987), 107.

29. Empson, *Complex Words*, 174. This is reproduced almost verbatim from his earlier article on 'The English Dog (Part II)', *Life and Letters*, 18 (Spring 1938), 42.

30. Empson, *Complex Words*, 158.

31. Empson, *Complex Words*, 158–9.

32. Empson, *Complex Words*, 163.

33. William Empson, 'Reply to Roger Sale', *Hudson Review*, 20 (1967–8), 535–6.

34. William Empson, *Milton's God* (London: Chatto, 1961), 253–4.

35. See Empson, *Argufying*, 437, 616–17, 630.

36. Empson, *Milton's God*, 258, 276–7.

37. Empson, 'Reply to Roger Sale', 535.

38. This case is argued with particular vigour in Chris Baldick, *The Social Mission of English Criticism 1848–1932* (Oxford: Oxford University Press, 1983).

39. William Empson, 'The Style of the Master', in Richard Marsh and Tambimuttu (eds), *T. S. Eliot: A Symposium* (London: Editions Poetry London, 1948), 35.

40. Empson to Roger Sale, n.d. [1973], in John Haffenden (ed.), *Selected Letters of William Empson* (Oxford: Oxford University Press, 2006), 546.

CHAPTER 5

1. Q. D. Leavis, *Fiction and the Reading Public* (London: Chatto, 1932).

2. F. R. Leavis, *Mass Civilization and Minority Culture* (Cambridge: Gordon Fraser, 1930), 13.

3. She had applied to work on the topic 'The Novel: Its Function and the Development of its Technique'; in the course of her first term of research she defined her topic as 'The Sociological Value of Popular Fiction'; when she submitted it, the title was 'Fiction and the Reading Public: A Study in Social Anthropology'. Board of Graduate Study files, 1, 1920–1937, file 993, Q. D. Leavis; University Archives, Cambridge University Library.

4. According to MacKillop: 'In the introduction to *Fiction and the Reading Public*, she [sc. QDL] specified a large debt to the sociology of Robert S. and Helen M. Lynd's *Middletown*' (Ian MacKillop, *F. R. Leavis: A Life in Criticism* (London: Allen Lane, 1995), 145). This must refer to the thesis rather than the book, since there is no mention of the Lynds in the introduction or anywhere else in the book, though their title looks to have been an awkward addition to the bibliography.

5. QDL, 'A Glance Backward' (1965), in Q. D. Leavis, *Collected Essays*, i. *The Englishness of the English Novel*, ed. G. Singh (Cambridge: Cambridge University Press, 1983), 15.

6. QDL, *Fiction and the Reading Public*, 117.
7. QDL, *Fiction and the Reading Public*, 100.
8. QDL, *Fiction and the Reading Public*, 123, 132, 146.
9. QDL, *Fiction and the Reading Public*, 129–30.
10. QDL, *Fiction and the Reading Public*, 156, 268.
11. QDL, *Fiction and the Reading Public*, 172, 169, 231.
12. QDL, 'A Glance Backward', 16, 17.
13. I. A. Richards, *Coleridge on Imagination* (London: Kegan Paul, 1934), 193, 195.
14. QDL, *Fiction and the Reading Public*, 39.
15. QDL, *Fiction and the Reading Public*, 21, 279.
16. QDL, *Fiction and the Reading Public*, 271–2.
17. Quoted in Christopher Hilliard, *English as a Vocation: The 'Scrutiny' Movement* (Oxford: Oxford University Press, 2012), 181. Holbrook had been a student at Downing during the Second World War and became a prolific writer on education.
18. I. A. Richards's examiner's report, Board of Graduate Study files, 1920–1937, file 993, Q. D. Leavis; University Archives, Cambridge University Library. In his report, the other examiner, E. M. Forster, observed rather sadly: 'She is better qualified to examine books than to appreciate them. Her capacity for enjoyment seems small.'
19. John Hayward, 'Intelligent Orientation', *London Mercury*, 35 (1936), 70–1.
20. F. R. Leavis, *Revaluation: Tradition and Development in English Poetry* (London: Chatto, 1936), 36.
21. Leavis, *Revaluation*, 10.
22. F. R. Leavis, 'Literary Studies—A Reply' (1956), in F. R. Leavis, *Valuation in Criticism and Other Essays*, ed. G. Singh (Cambridge: Cambridge University Press, 1986), 214.
23. In this instance I take the phrase from F. R. Leavis, 'Elites, Oligarchies and an Educated Public' (1971), in F. R. Leavis, *Nor Shall My Sword: Discourses on Pluralism, Compassion and Social Hope* (Chatto, 1972), 217–18, though it repeated a point he had been making in similar terms over several decades.
24. I develop this analysis at greater length in Stefan Collini, *Absent Minds: Intellectuals in Britain* (Oxford: Oxford University Press, 2006), esp. part V.
25. See the figures given in Stefan Collini, '"The Chatto list": Publishing Literary Criticism in Mid-Twentieth-Century Britain', *Review of English Studies*, 63 (2012), 634–63.
26. F. R. Leavis, 'The Orthodoxy of Enlightenment' (1961), in F. R. Leavis, *'Anna Karenina' and Other Essays* (London: Chatto, 1967), 235–41, at 241.
27. Richard Hoggart, *The Uses of Literacy: Aspects of Working-Class Life with Special Reference to Publications and Entertainments* (London: Chatto, 1957; page references are to the 1992 Penguin edition, which includes an interview with Hoggart conducted by John Corner).
28. An earlier version of parts of the following account appeared in Stefan Collini, 'Richard Hoggart: Literary Criticism and Cultural Decline in Twentieth-Century

Britain', in Sue Owen (ed.), *Richard Hoggart and Cultural Studies* (Basingstoke: Palgrave, 2008), 33–56.

29. Richard Hoggart, *Speaking to Each Other*, i. *About Society* (London: Chatto, 1970; Penguin edn, 1973), 63.

30. Richard Hoggart, *An Imagined Life: Life and Times 1959–1991* (Oxford: Oxford University Press, 1993 [1st edn, Chatto, 1992]), 94.

31. Richard Hoggart, *A Sort of Clowning: Life and Times 1940–1959* (Oxford: Oxford University Press, 1991 [1st edn, Chatto, 1990]), 134–5.

32. Hoggart, *A Sort of Clowning*, 134.

33. Hoggart, *Uses of Literacy*, 360.

34. Hoggart, *Uses of Literacy*, 382–3.

35. Hoggart to F. R. Leavis, 4 May 1953; Hoggart papers. I consulted these papers when they were still in Richard Hoggart's possession and uncatalogued; they have since been deposited in the University of Sheffield Library.

36. Raymond Williams, quoted in John McIlroy, 'Teacher, Critic, Explorer', in W. John Morgan and Peter Preston (eds), *Raymond Williams: Politics, Education, Letters* (Basingstoke: Macmillan, 1993), 23–4, 30.

37. Richard Hoggart, *Auden: An Introductory Essay* (London: Chatto, 1951), 9.

38. R. G. Cox, 'Auden as Critic and Poet', *Scrutiny*, 18 (1951), 158–61.

39. For early pieces by Hoggart, see *Highway*, 38 (July 1947), 198; 40 (November 1948), 17–20; 40 (June 1949), 194–5; *Adult Education*, 20 (June 1948), 187–94, and Williams's response, 21 (1948), 96–8. For Williams's involvement with *Essays in Criticism*, see Raymond Williams, *Politics and Letters: Interviews with* New Left Review (London: New Left Books, 1979), 84.

40. Richard Hoggart, *Speaking to Each Other*, ii. *About Literature* (London: Chatto, 1971), 12–13.

41. F. R. Leavis, *Education and the University* (Cambridge: Cambridge University Press, 1979 [1st edn, Chatto, 1943]), 34.

42. Hoggart, *Speaking*, ii. 16.

43. F. R. Leavis, *The Great Tradition* (Harmondsworth: Penguin, 1972 [1st edn, Chatto, 1948]), 23.

44. Hoggart, *An Imagined Life*, 93.

45. See, e.g., Hoggart, *Uses of Literacy*, 6, 348, 352, 353; see also Michael Bailey, Ben Clarke, and John K. Walton, *Understanding Richard Hoggart: A Pedagogy of Hope* (London: Wiley-Blackwell, 2011i), esp. 59–64, 99–133.

46. Hoggart, *Uses of Literacy*, 25, 77, 139, 318–19.

47. e.g. Ross McKibbin, *Classes and Cultures: England 1918–1951* (Oxford: Oxford University Press, 1998), 109.

48. See Stefan Collini, 'The Literary Critic and the Village Labourer: "Culture" in Twentieth-Century Britain', *Transactions of the Royal Historical Society*, 6th ser., 14 (2004), 93–116. Presumably it was partly on account of this structural similarity that Graham Hough, in the passage discussed in that article, included Hoggart among the 'happy peasants' who, by implication, were yearning for this state of pre-industrial simplicity.

49. Hoggart, *Uses of Literacy*, 171, 173–4.

50. Hoggart, *Uses of Literacy*, 193, 213, 216, 244, 289, 323, 327, 325.

51. Hoggart, *Uses of Literacy*, 329–30, 189, 283–4.

52. George Orwell, *The Lion and the Unicorn: Socialism and the English Genius* (1941), in Peter Davison (ed.), *George Orwell: The Complete Works*, xii (London: Secker and Warburg, 1998), 408.

53. Hoggart, *Uses of Literacy*, 286–7.

54. Hoggart, *Uses of Literacy*, 316.

55. Hoggart, *Uses of Literacy*, 247–8.

56. Hoggart, *Uses of Literacy*, 338–9.

57. Hoggart, *Uses of Literacy*, 234, 338.

58. Hoggart, *Uses of Literacy*, 141.

59. Hoggart, *Uses of Literacy*, 343.

60. Hoggart, *Uses of Literacy*, 250.

61. Matthew Arnold, *Friendship's Garland* (1871), in R. H. Super (ed.), *The Complete Prose Works of Matthew Arnold* (11 vols; Ann Arbor: University of Michigan Press, 1960–77), v. 21–2.

62. T. S. Eliot, 'The Function of Criticism' (1923), in T. S. Eliot, *Selected Essays* (London: Faber, 1932; rev. edn 1951), 27.

63. F. R. Leavis, *For Continuity* (Cambridge: Minority Press, 1933), 75; 'Two Cultures? The Significance of C. P. Snow' (1962), in F. R. Leavis, *Two Cultures? The Significance of C. P. Snow*, ed. Stefan Collini (Cambridge: Cambridge University Press, 2013), 54, 59.

64. See, e.g., the section on 'Placing the Centre in its Context' in the fifth *Annual Report* of Centre for Contemporary Cultural Studies, which is based on a lecture given by Hall in 1967.

65. See n. 48.

CHAPTER 6

1. Raymond Williams, *Keywords: A Vocabulary of Culture and Society* (London: Fontana, 1976), 11.

2. Raymond Williams, *Culture and Society, 1780–1950* (London: Chatto, 1958), p. vii (emphasis added). Since both the Chatto and the 1961 Penguin editions of this book are so widely used, I shall give page references to both (Penguin edn, 11).

3. This suggestion, I should acknowledge, is partly addressed to my former self. In the late 1990s I left unpublished a paper entitled 'The Origins of Cultural Criticism: The Culture-and-Society Tradition Re-Visited' because of a sense of its inadequacy; I briefly returned to the theme from another angle in my Prothero Lecture 'The Literary Critic and the Village Labourer: "Culture" in Twentieth-Century Britain', *Transactions of the Royal Historical Society*, 14 (2004), 93–116, esp. 107–12.

4. Raymond Williams, 'The Idea of Culture', *Essays in Criticism*, 1 (1953), 243.

5. Williams, 'Idea of Culture', 243.

6. The entry in the current (online) edition of the dictionary modifies the definitions and provides some further illustrations.

7. Williams, *Culture and Society*, 3 (Penguin edn, 23).

8. Williams, 'Idea of Culture', 247–8.

9. Williams, *Culture and Society*, 33–4 (Penguin edn, 51–2). The Wordsworth quotation and part of the accompanying commentary appear in 'Idea of Culture', 260–1.

10. Williams, *Culture and Society*, 110 (Penguin edn, 120).

11. Williams, 'Idea of Culture', 247; cf. *Culture and Society*, 110 (Penguin edn, 120).

12. Williams, *Culture and Society*, 114 (Penguin edn, 124).

13. Raymond Williams, *Politics and Letters: Interviews with* New Left Review (London: New Left Books, 1979), 28, 152.

14. See Dai Smith, *Raymond Williams: A Warrior's Tale* (Cardigan: Parthian, 2008), 244–8; John McIlroy and Sallie Westwood (eds), *Border Country: Raymond Williams in Adult Education* (Leicester: NIACE, 1993), 51, 53.

15. See McIlroy and Westwood (eds), *Border Country*, 35, 37.

16. McIlroy and Westwood (eds), *Border Country*, 53.

17. 'Effect of the Machine on the Countryman's Work, Life, and Community', Box 5, no. 10 (2007/24), Raymond Williams papers, University of Swansea; see also the discussion in Smith, *Raymond Williams*, 253–5.

18. Timothy Boon, 'Industrialisation and Catastrophe: The Victorian Economy in British Film Documentary, 1930–50', in Miles Taylor and Michael Wolff (eds), *The Victorians since 1901: Histories, Representations, and Revisions* (Manchester: Manchester University Press, 2004), 113, 117, 118.

19. The opening sentences of this draft reappear, in somewhat revised form, in Williams, 'Idea of Culture', 244.

20. '(1) The Isolation of Culture', Box 5, no. 10 (2007/24), Raymond Williams papers, University of Swansea.

21. Raymond Williams, *Drama from Ibsen to Eliot* (London: Chatto, 1952), 26, 27, 28; cf. 30–2.

22. Williams, *Politics and Letters*, 194.

23. I am indebted to my former research student Alexander Hutton for these details from the archives of the Oxford Extra-Mural Delegacy; see his forthcoming book *Teaching Industrial England*.

24. Cf. McIlroy and Westwood (eds), *Border Country*, 290.

25. Quoted in Smith, *Raymond Williams*, 333.

26. Williams, *Politics and Letters*, 97.

27. I am grateful to Prof. Angus Hawkins for drawing my attention to the likely edition of the Halévy volume Williams referred to.

28. A passing comment in a letter in the Chatto Archives alerted me to its possible existence: 'I have just had Empson's new book to review for *English* and find it fascinating' (Williams to Ian Parsons, 30 October 1951; Chatto Archives, University of Reading).

29. Raymond Williams, 'Review of *The Structure of Complex Words*', *English*, 9 (1952), 27. The last phrase is from his report on the 1950 summer school held in Hertford College, Oxford, discussed in Chapter 7.

30. Raymond Williams, 'Second Thoughts: I. T. S. Eliot on Culture', *Essays in Criticism*, 6 (1956), 302–18.

31. Williams, *Culture and Society*, 233 (Penguin edn, 229–30).

32. Williams, *Culture and Society*, 48 (Penguin edn, 64).

33. Quoted in Williams, *Culture and Society*, 61 (Penguin edn, 76).

34. Wiliams, *Culture and Society*, 51 (Penguin edn, 67).

35. Williams, *Culture and Society*, 112 (Penguin edn, 121).

36. Lowe made the remark in his speech in the House of Commons on 15 July 1867; A. P. Martin, *Life and Letters of Rt Hon. Robert Lowe, Viscount Sherbrooke* (2 vols; London: Longmans, 1893).

37. Williams seems never to have acknowledged or retracted this error, and, as far as I know, none of the commentators on his work has remarked on it.

38. The new introduction was written for the 1982 Hogarth Press edition, repr. Columbia University Press, 1983; quotation at p. x.

39. Williams, *Culture and Society*, 325, 327 (Penguin edn, 312, 314).

40. Williams, *Culture and Society*, 328 (Penguin edn, 314).

41. Williams, *Politics and Letters*, 99.

42. Williams, *Politics and Letters*, 116.

43. Dieter Pevsner, Memo on *Culture and Society* (21 April 1959), DM1107/A520; Penguin Archives, University of Bristol.

44. V. G. Kiernan, 'Culture and Society', *New Reasoner*, 9 (Summer 1959), 76–7, 78.

45. Kiernan, 'Culture and Society', 75–6.

46. Richard Johnson, 'Culture and the Historians', in Jon Clarke, Chas Critchley, and Richard Johnson (eds), *Working-Class Culture: Studies in History and Theory*, (London: Hutchinson, 1979), 59.

CHAPTER 7

1. Raymond Williams, *The Long Revolution* (Harmondsworth: Penguin, 1965 [1st edn, Chatto, 1961]), 10.

2. See Ch. 2, n. 39.

3. See Ch. 2, n. 42.

4. See Ch. 3, n. 33.

5. L. C. Knights, 'The University Teaching of English and History: A Plea for Correlation', *Southern Review* (1939), repr. in L. C. Knights, *Explorations: Essays in Criticism mainly on the Literature of the Seventeenth Century* (Harmondsworth: Penguin, 1964 [1st edn, Chatto 1946]), 196, 198, 200–1.

6. See Ch. 4, n. 28.

7. Raymond Williams, 'Literature in Relation to History', *Rewley House Papers*, 3/1 (1949–50), esp. 306–7; see also the discussion in Dai Smith, *Raymond Williams:*

A Warrior's Tale (Cardigan: Parthian, 2008), 307–9. (Smith gives the phrase 'the record of the history of a people' as 'the record of a history of a people'.)

8. Jose Harris, 'The Arts and Social Sciences, 1939–1970', in Brian Harrison (ed.), *The History of the University of Oxford*, viii. *The Twentieth Century* (Oxford: Oxford University Press, 1994), 235–6.

9. H. B. Parkes, 'The Historian's Task', *Scrutiny*, 7 (March 1939), 434–5. See the discussion in the Introduction, pp. 8–10.

10. F. R. Leavis to R. G. Cox, 11 February 1951; Leavis Papers, DCPP/Cox/1/36; Downing College, Cambridge.

11. R. G. Cox, 'History and Criticism in the Home University', *Scrutiny*, 18 (June 1951), 56, 59.

12. Christopher Hill, *Puritanism and Revolution* (London: Secker, 1958), 6. The Penguin volume was Maurice Ashley, *England in the Seventeenth Century* (Harmondsworth: Penguin, 1952).

13. Quoted in Michael Bentley, *Modernizing England's Past: English Historiography in the Age of Modernism 1870–1970* (Cambridge: Cambridge University Press, 2005), 112.

14. See Geoffrey Parker, 'George Norman Clark 1890–1979', *Proceedings of the British Academy*, 66 (1980), 414–17.

15. Boris Ford, 'Round and About the *Pelican Guide to English Literature*', in Denys Thompson (ed.), *The Leavises: Recollections and Impressions* (Cambridge: Cambridge University Press, 1984), 106.

16. See Ford, 'Round and About', in Thompson (ed.), *The Leavises*, 103–12; for Williams's role more generally, see J. E. Morpurgo, *Allen Lane: King Penguin* (London: Hutchinson, 1979).

17. Boris Ford, Memo, 'The Penguin [*sic*] Guide to English Literature', DM1107/A465; Penguin Archives, University of Bristol.

18. Boris Ford, 'The Concise *C.H.E.L.*', *Scrutiny*, 10 (1941–2), 205.

19. Ford, 'Concise *C.H.E.L.*', 205.

20. Boris Ford, 'General Introduction', in Boris Ford (ed.), *The Pelican Guide to English Literature*, i. *The Age of Chaucer* (Harmondsworth: Penguin, 1954), 9. The original version of Ford's introduction can be found in all the early volumes of the *Pelican Guide*; it was considerably pruned for later editions.

21. Ford, 'General Introduction', 9–10.

22. Ford, 'General Introduction', 7.

23. G. H. Bantock, 'The Social and Intellectual Background', in Boris Ford (ed.), *The Pelican Guide to English Literature*, vii. *The Modern Age* (Harmondsworth: Penguin, 1961), 38, 41, 42, 44, 48.

24. 'Sales Figures, 1935–85', DM/1294/4/2/7; 'The Pelican Guide', DM1107/A465; Donald Brown to Charles Clark, 5 February 1965, DM1107/A465; Penguin Archives, University of Bristol.

25. Christopher Hilliard, *English as a Vocation: The 'Scrutiny' Movement* (Oxford: Oxford University Press, 2012), 213–14.

26. 'Report on *The Pelican Guide to English Literature*' by A. A. H. Inglis, 14 September 1977, DM1952, Box 613; Penguin Archives, University of Bristol.

27. Basil Willey, *Nineteenth-Century Studies: Coleridge to Matthew Arnold* (London: Chatto, 1949), 52.

28. See Miles Taylor and Michael Wolff (eds), *The Victorians since 1901: Histories, Representations, and Revisions* (Manchester: Manchester University Press, 2004), 76.

29. Michael Wolff, in Taylor and Wolff (eds), *Victorians Since 1901*, p. xiv.

30. Helen Rogers, 'Victorian Studies in the UK', in Taylor and Wolff (eds), *Victorians since 1901*, 246.

31. F. R. Leavis, *Two Cultures? The Significance of C. P. Snow*, ed. Stefan Collini (Cambridge: Cambridge University Press, 2013), 93.

32. Leavis, *Two Cultures?*, ed. Collini, 61.

33. Snow to Plumb, 24 May 1962; Plumb to Snow, 1 July 1962; C. P. Snow Papers, Harry Ransom Humanities Center, Austin, Texas.

34. C. P. Snow, 'A Second Look', in Snow, *The Two Cultures*, ed. Stefan Collini (Cambridge: Cambridge University Press, 1993), 83–4.

35. J. H. Plumb (ed.), *Crisis in the Humanities* (Harmondsworth: Penguin, 1963), 42.

36. Snow to Plumb, 24 December 1963; Folder 'CPS and Pam: Seventies', Plumb Papers, Cambridge University Library. These papers were uncatalogued when I used them; I am grateful for the assistance of their curator, Bill Noblett.

37. Graham Hough, Plumb's colleague and ally, so referred to Leavis, Hoggart, Holbrook, and Williams; see the discussion in Stefan Collini, 'The Literary Critic and the Village Labourer: "Culture" in Twentieth-Century Britain', *Transactions of the Royal Historical Society*, 6th ser., 14 (2004), 94–5, 114–15.

38. John Fraser, 'Reflections on the Organic Community', *Human World*, 15–16 (1974), 60; cf. Leavis's exasperated reference to 'that business of "the old wheelwright's shop"' in 'Luddites? Or There is Only One Culture' (1966), in Leavis, *Two Cultures?*, ed. Collini, 96.

39. Cynthia Herrup, 'Christopher Hill and the People of Stuart England', in Walter L. Arnstein (ed.), *Recent Historians of Great Britain: Essays on the Post-1945 Generation* (Ames, IA: Iowa State University Press, 1990), 69.

40. Dorothy Thompson, quoted in Christos Efstathiou, *E. P. Thompson: A Twentieth-Century Romantic* (London: Merlin Press, 2015), 17.

41. E. P. Thompson, 'Foreword', in George Sturt, *The Wheelwright's Shop* (Cambridge: Cambridge University Press, 1993), p. viii.

42. See, e.g., the account of this development in Miles Taylor, 'The Beginnings of Modern British Social History?', *History Workshop Journal*, 43 (1997), 155–76.

43. Williams to Ian Parsons, 30 August 1953; Chatto Archives, University of Reading.

44. Williams to Norah Smallwood, 5 April 1959; Chatto Archives, University of Reading.

45. Williams, *Long Revolution*, 9–10.

46. Williams, 'Foreword to the Pelican Edition', in Williams, *Long Revolution*, 8.

47. Raymond Williams, *Politics and Letters: Interviews with* New Left Review (London: New Left Books, 1979), 7. Surveying the development of both literary and historical accounts of the Victorian period, Martin Hewitt calls *Culture and Society* and *The Long Revolution* 'two immensely influential books' (Taylor and Wolff (eds), *Victorians since 1901*, 91).

48. Williams, *Politics and Letters*, 133.

49. Maurice Cowling, 'Mr Raymond Williams', *Cambridge Review*, 27 May 1961, pp. 548–9.

50. E. P. Thompson, 'The Long Revolution', *New Left Review*, 9 (May–June 1961), 24–33; 10 (July–August 1961), 34–9.

51. Thompson, 'Long Revolution', 38.

POSTSCRIPT

1. Raymond Williams, 'Literature in Relation to History', *Rewley House Papers*, 3 (1949–50), 307.

2. 'T. S. E.', 'Was there a Scottish literature?', *Athenaeum*, 1 August 1919, p. 681.

3. T. S. Eliot, *The Varieties of Metaphysical Poetry*, ed. Ronald Schuchard (London: Faber, 1993), 226.

4. Frank Kermode, *The Sense of an Ending: Studies in the Theory of Fiction* (Oxford: Oxford University Press, 1967), 17, 44–5.

5. Leslie Stephen, *English Literature and Society in the Eighteenth Century* (London: Duckworth, 1904), 185.

Index

Printed and bound by CPI Group (UK) Ltd, Croydon, CR0 4YY